Garfield
Gets His Just Desserts

BY JIM DAVIS

Ballantine Books • New York

A Ballantine Books Trade Paperback Original

Published in the United States by Ballantine Books, an imprint of The Random House Publishing Group,
a division of Random House, Inc., New York.

BALLANTINE and colophon are registered trademarks of Random House, Inc.

ISBN 978-0-345-91387-6

Printed in the United States of America

www.ballantinebooks.com

9 8 7 6 5 4 3 2

GARFIELD'S FOOD FOR THOUGHT

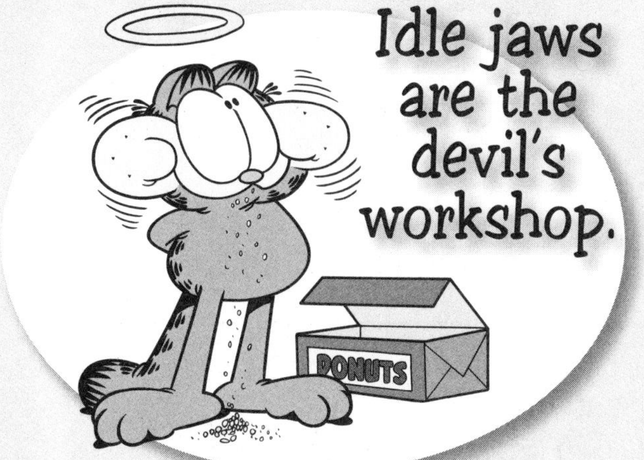
Idle jaws are the devil's workshop.
DONUTS

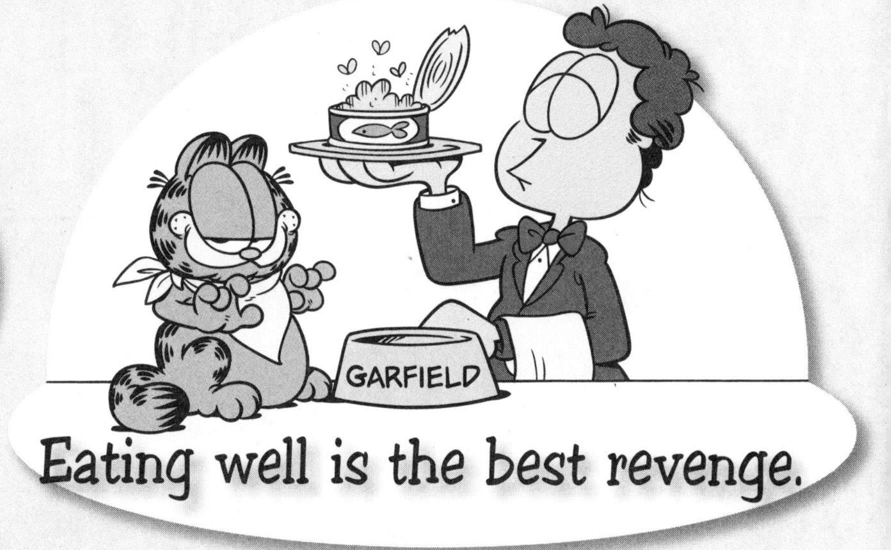
GARFIELD
Eating well is the best revenge.

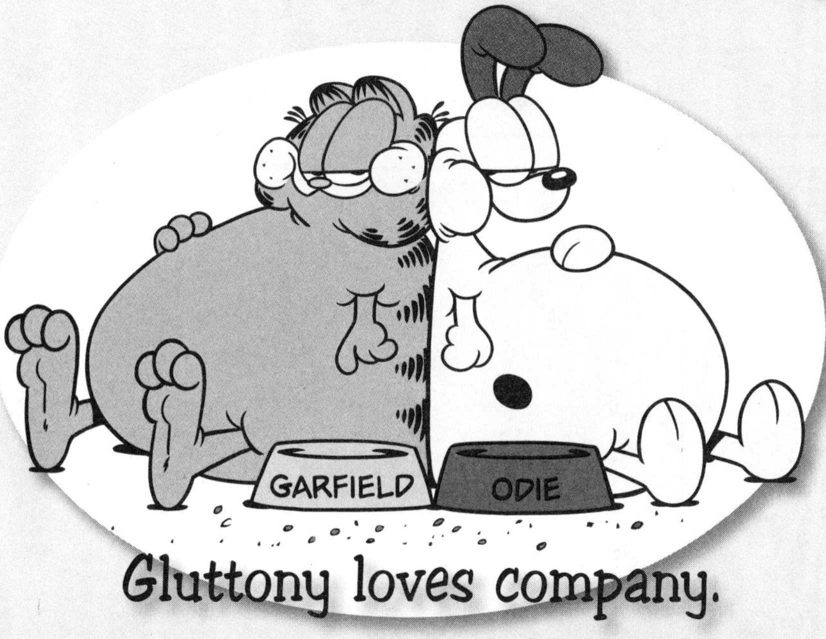
GARFIELD
ODIE
Gluttony loves company.

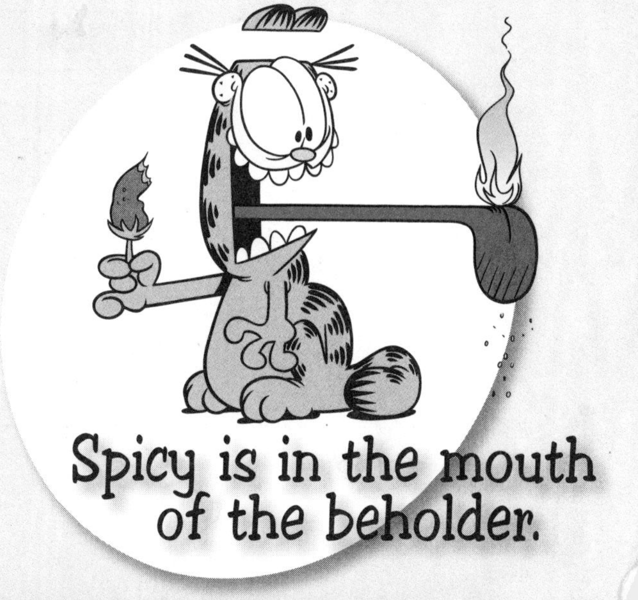
Spicy is in the mouth of the beholder.

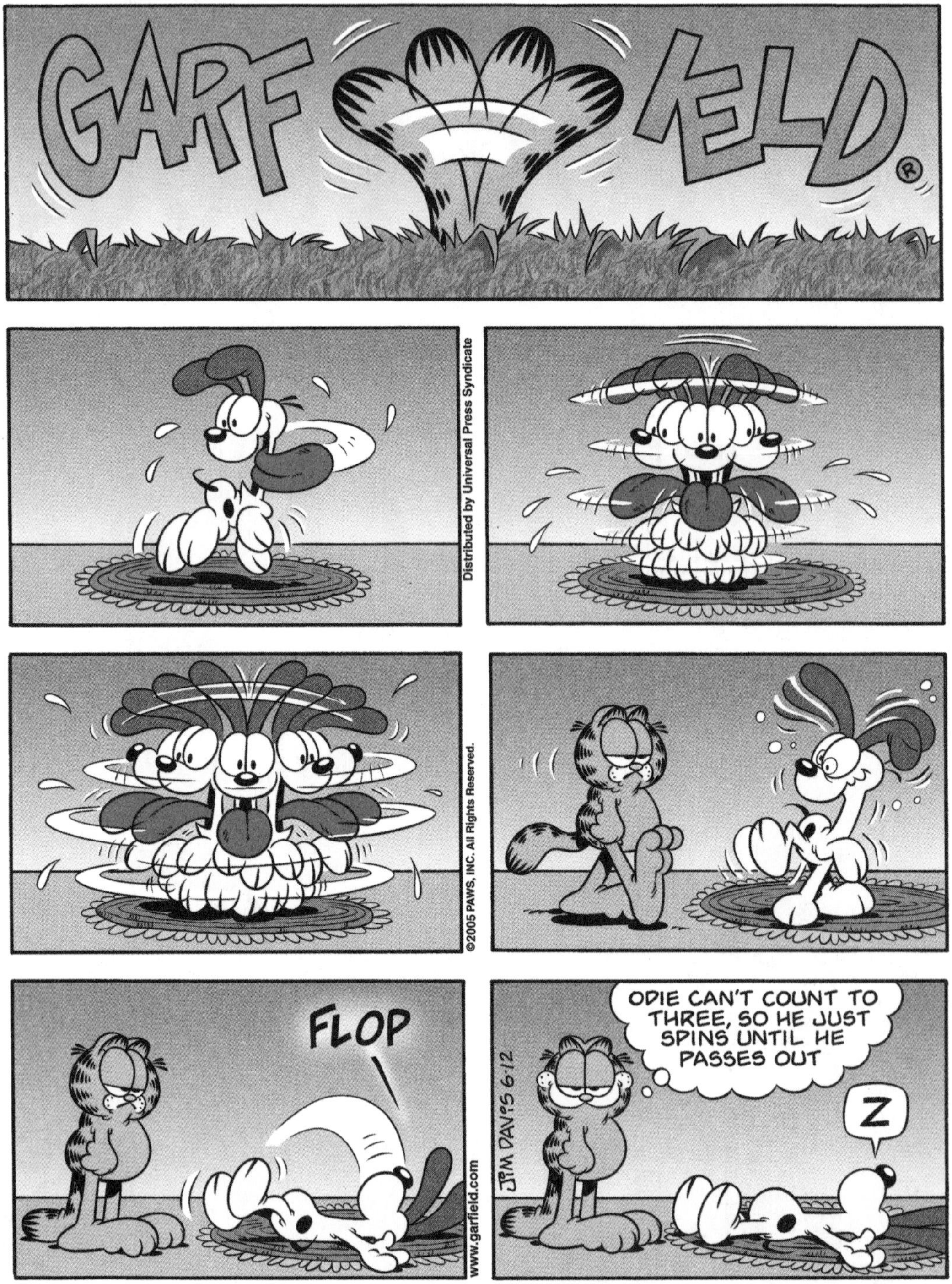
GARFIELD®
Distributed by Universal Press Syndicate
©2005 PAWS, INC. All Rights Reserved.
FLOP
www.garfield.com
JIM DAVIS 6-12
ODIE CAN'T COUNT TO THREE, SO HE JUST SPINS UNTIL HE PASSES OUT
Z

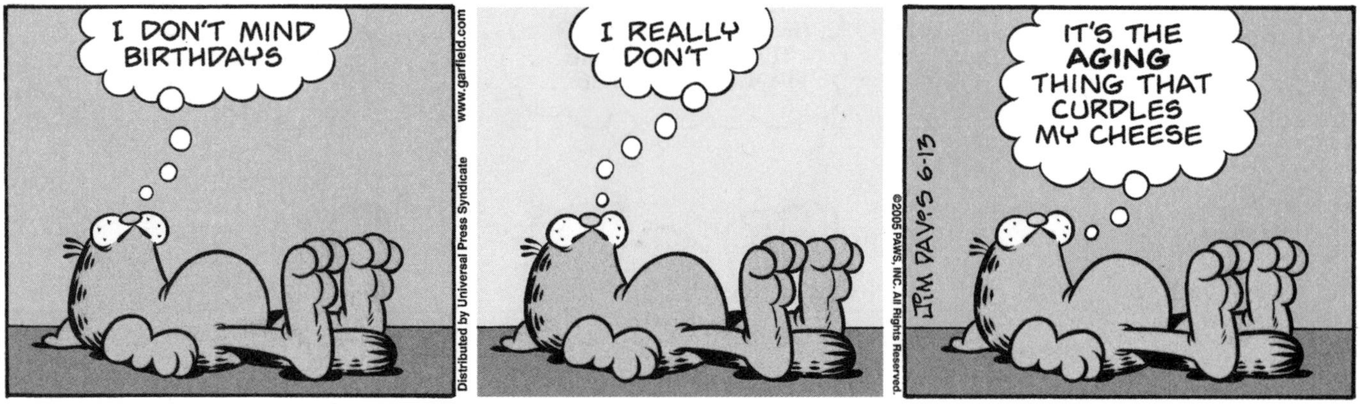
I DON'T MIND BIRTHDAYS
I REALLY DON'T
IT'S THE **AGING** THING THAT CURDLES MY CHEESE
www.garfield.com
Distributed by Universal Press Syndicate
©2005 PAWS, INC. All Rights Reserved.
JIM DAVIS 6-13

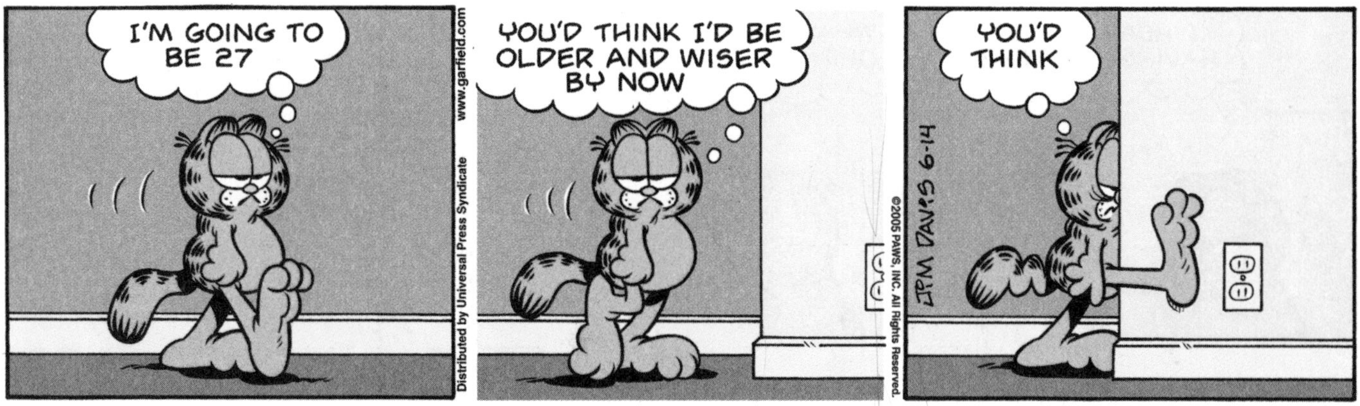
I'M GOING TO BE 27
YOU'D THINK I'D BE OLDER AND WISER BY NOW
YOU'D THINK
www.garfield.com
Distributed by Universal Press Syndicate
©2005 PAWS, INC. All Rights Reserved.
JIM DAVIS 6-14

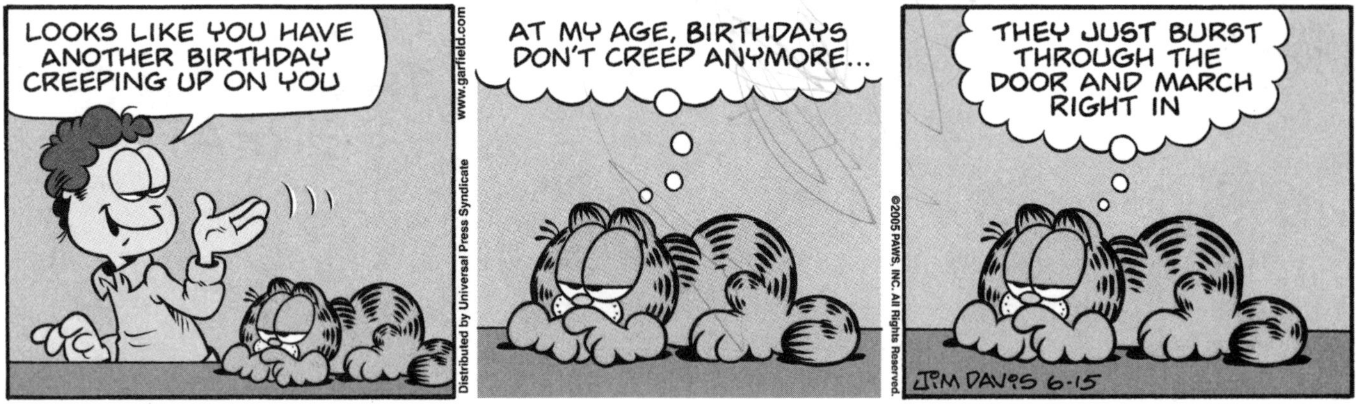
LOOKS LIKE YOU HAVE ANOTHER BIRTHDAY CREEPING UP ON YOU
AT MY AGE, BIRTHDAYS DON'T CREEP ANYMORE...
THEY JUST BURST THROUGH THE DOOR AND MARCH RIGHT IN
www.garfield.com
Distributed by Universal Press Syndicate
©2005 PAWS, INC. All Rights Reserved.
JIM DAVIS 6-15

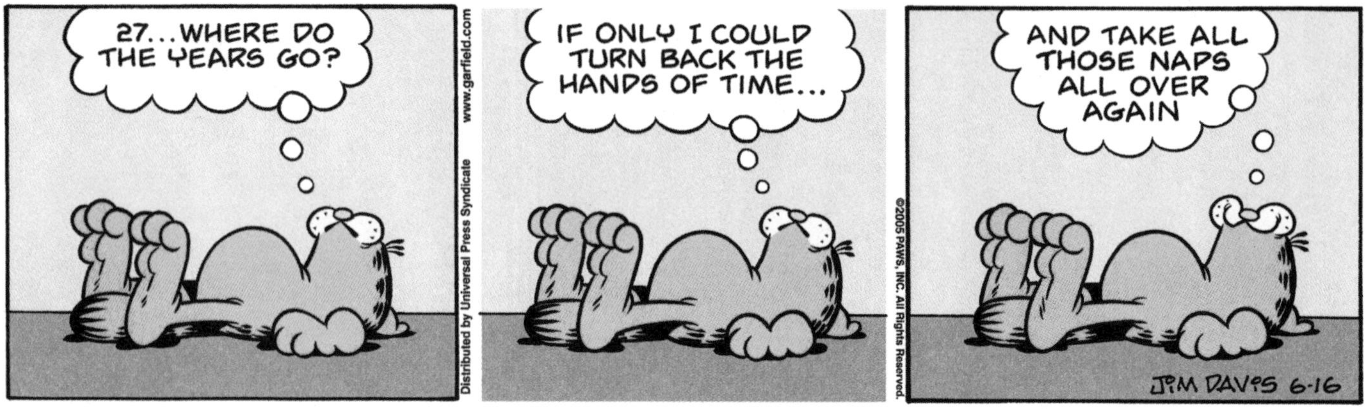
27...WHERE DO THE YEARS GO?
IF ONLY I COULD TURN BACK THE HANDS OF TIME...
AND TAKE ALL THOSE NAPS ALL OVER AGAIN
JIM DAVIS 6-16
www.garfield.com
Distributed by Universal Press Syndicate
©2005 PAWS, INC. All Rights Reserved.

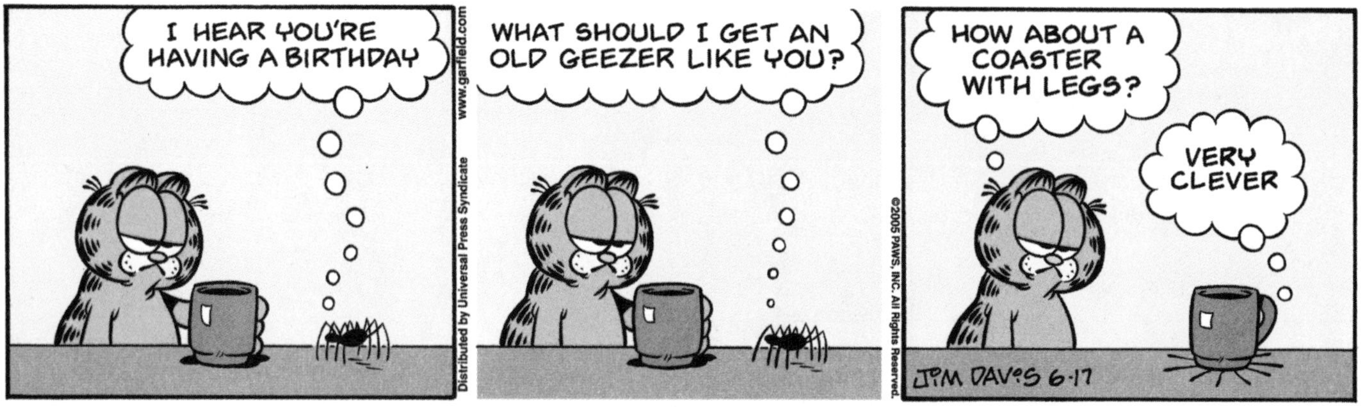
I HEAR YOU'RE HAVING A BIRTHDAY
WHAT SHOULD I GET AN OLD GEEZER LIKE YOU?
HOW ABOUT A COASTER WITH LEGS?
VERY CLEVER
JIM DAVIS 6-17
www.garfield.com
Distributed by Universal Press Syndicate
©2005 PAWS, INC. All Rights Reserved.

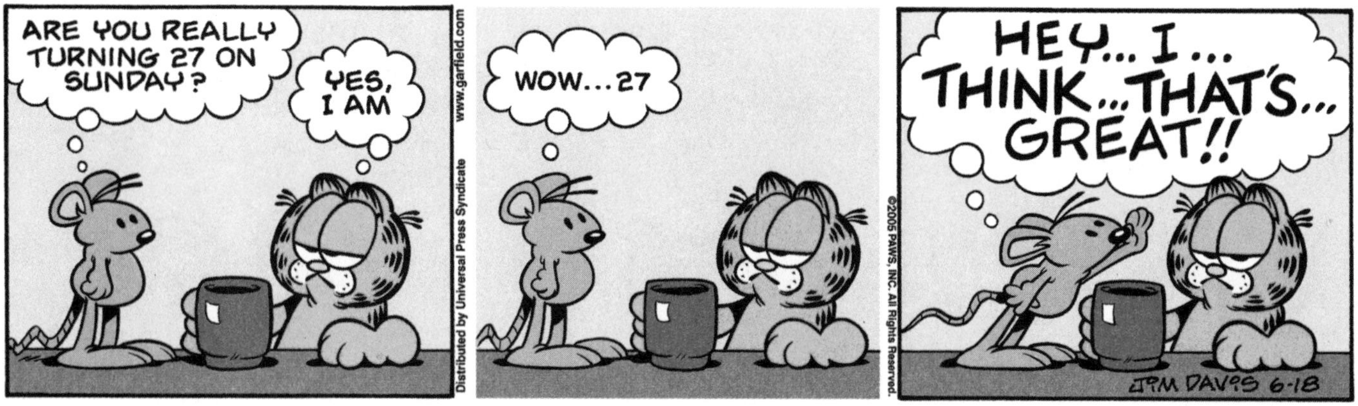
ARE YOU REALLY TURNING 27 ON SUNDAY?
YES, I AM
WOW...27
HEY... I... THINK...THAT'S... GREAT!!
JIM DAVIS 6-18
www.garfield.com
Distributed by Universal Press Syndicate
©2005 PAWS, INC. All Rights Reserved.

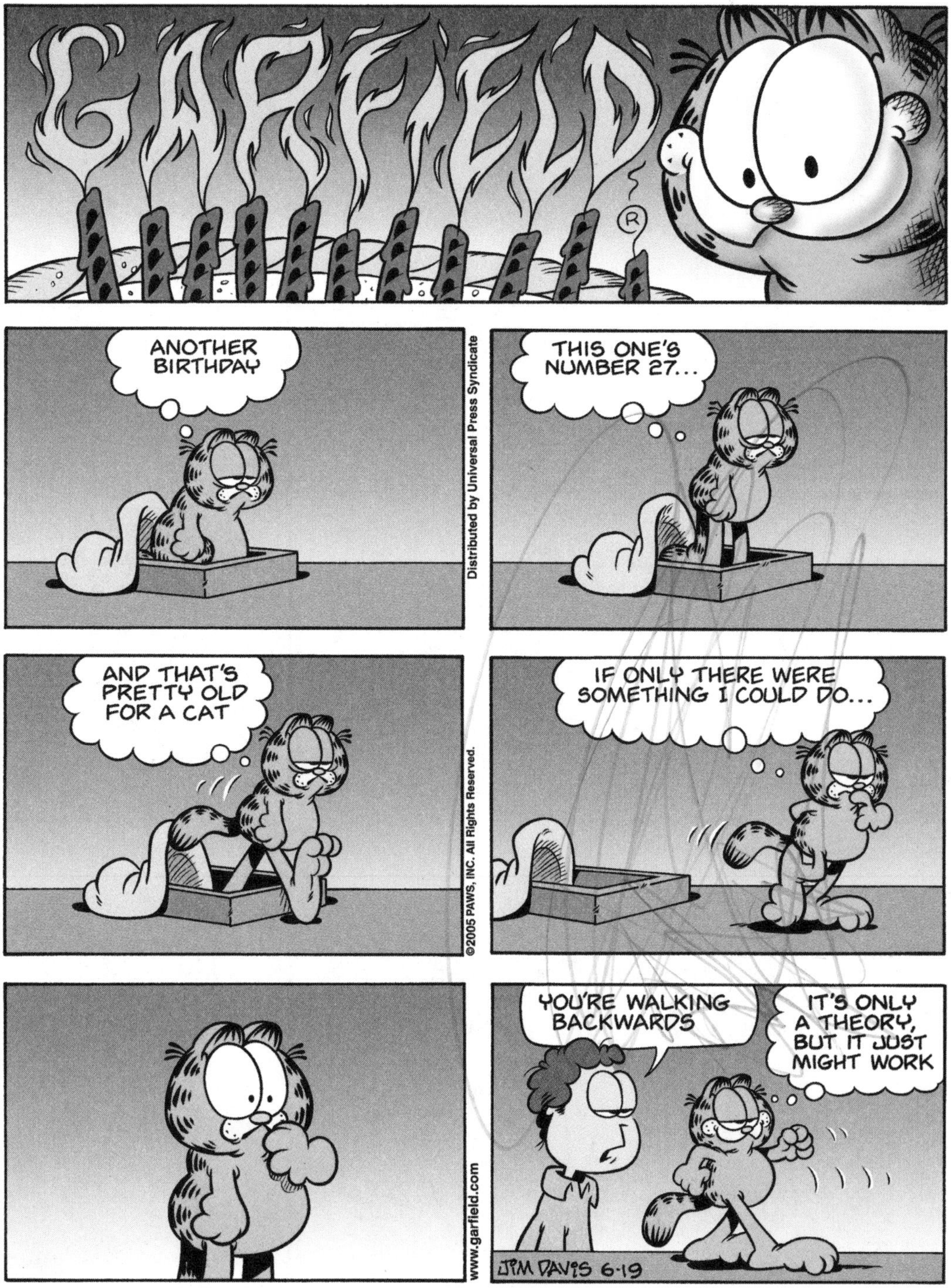
GARFIELD
ANOTHER BIRTHDAY
THIS ONE'S NUMBER 27...
AND THAT'S PRETTY OLD FOR A CAT
IF ONLY THERE WERE SOMETHING I COULD DO...
YOU'RE WALKING BACKWARDS
IT'S ONLY A THEORY, BUT IT JUST MIGHT WORK
JIM DAVIS 6·19
Distributed by Universal Press Syndicate
©2005 PAWS, INC. All Rights Reserved.
www.garfield.com

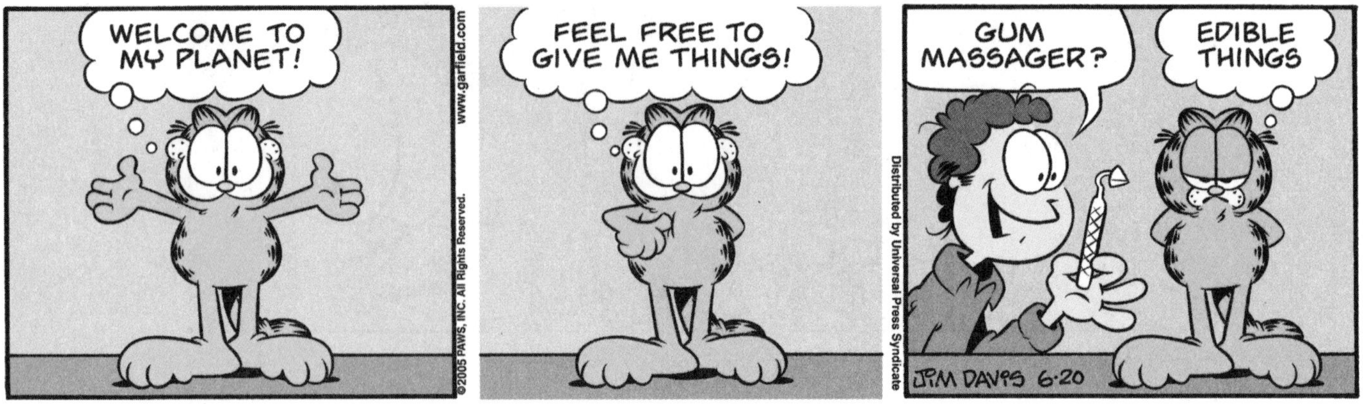
WELCOME TO MY PLANET!
©2005 PAWS, INC. All Rights Reserved. www.garfield.com
FEEL FREE TO GIVE ME THINGS!
Distributed by Universal Press Syndicate
GUM MASSAGER?
EDIBLE THINGS
JIM DAVIS 6·20

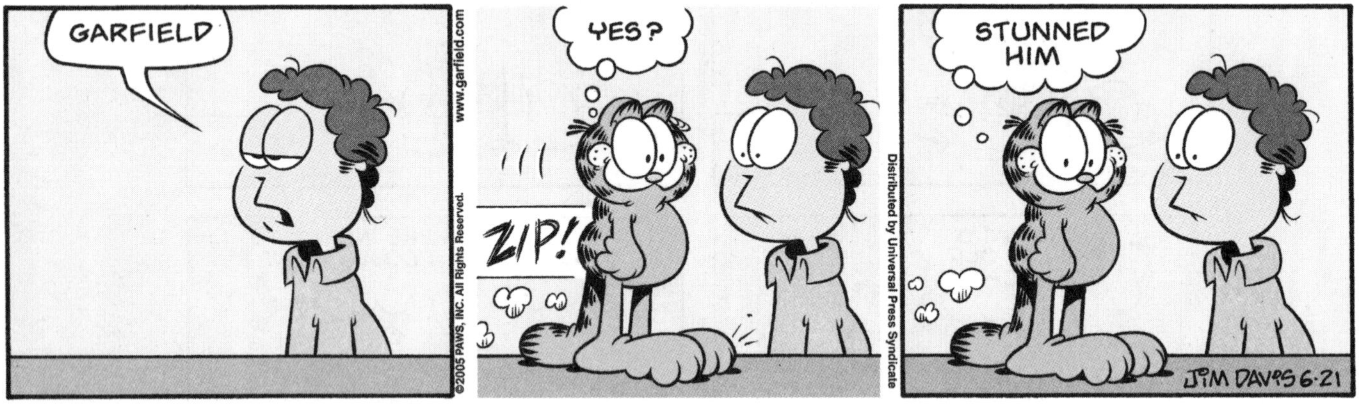
GARFIELD
©2005 PAWS, INC. All Rights Reserved. www.garfield.com
YES?
ZIP!
Distributed by Universal Press Syndicate
STUNNED HIM
JIM DAVIS 6·21

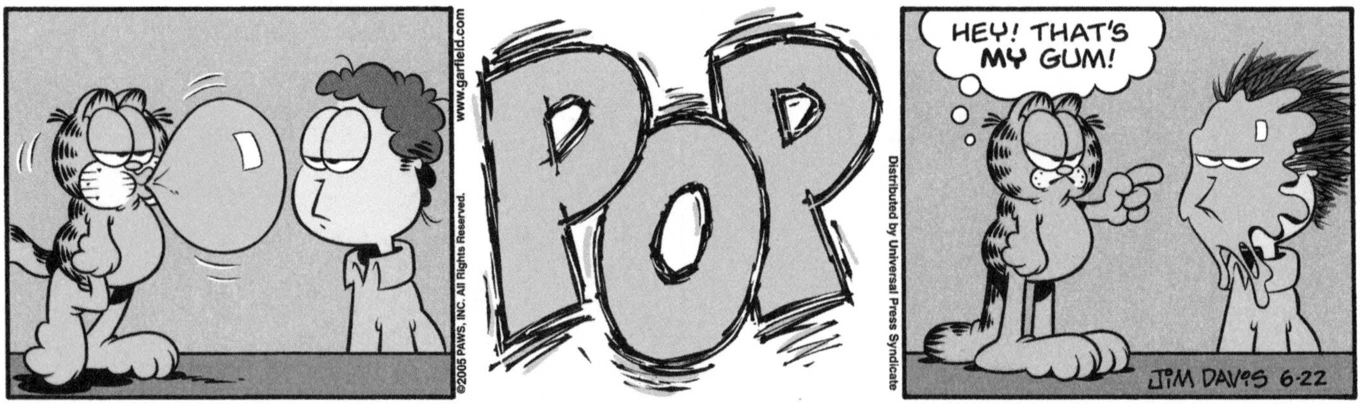
©2005 PAWS, INC. All Rights Reserved. www.garfield.com
POP
Distributed by Universal Press Syndicate
HEY! THAT'S MY GUM!
JIM DAVIS 6·22

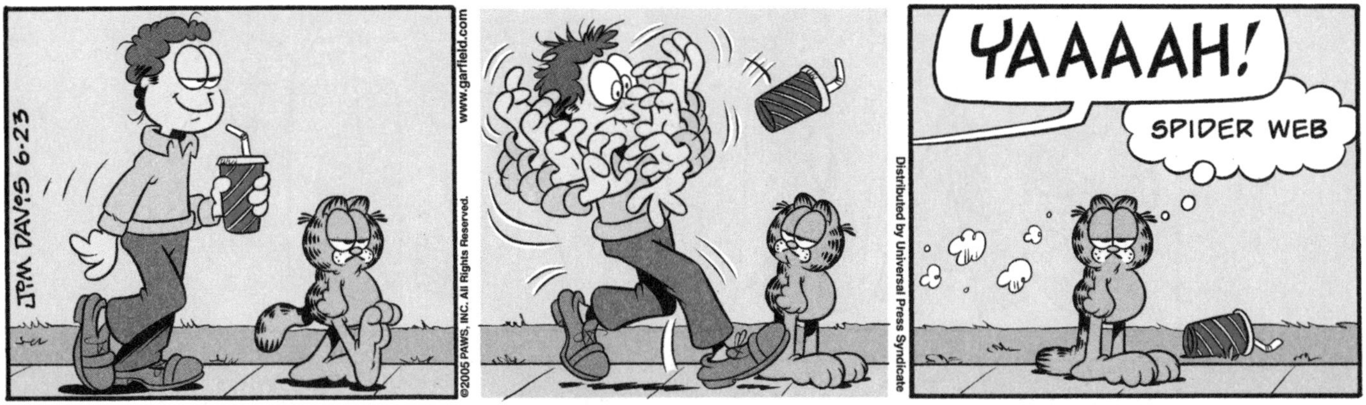
JIM DAVIS 6-23
YAAAAH!
SPIDER WEB

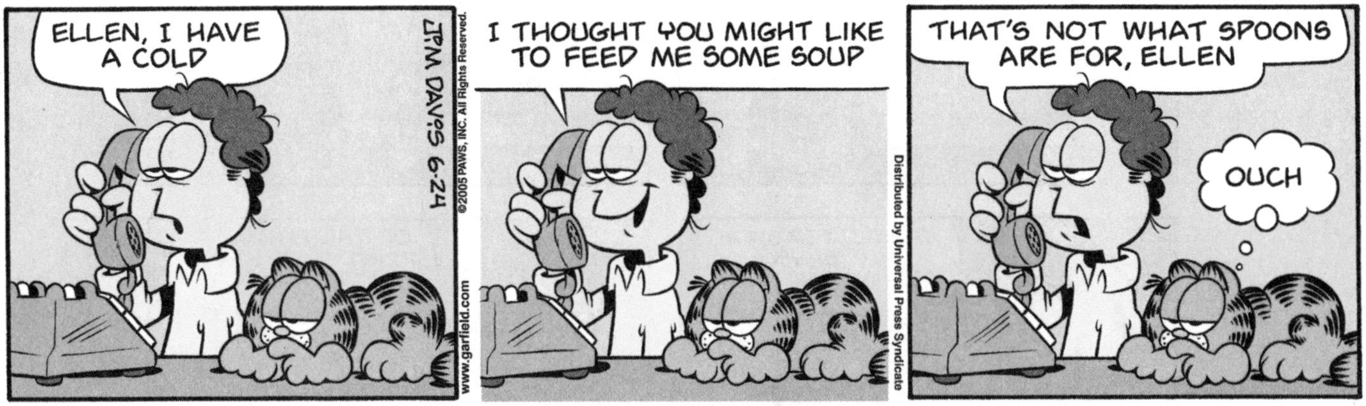
JIM DAVIS 6-24
ELLEN, I HAVE A COLD
I THOUGHT YOU MIGHT LIKE TO FEED ME SOME SOUP
THAT'S NOT WHAT SPOONS ARE FOR, ELLEN
OUCH

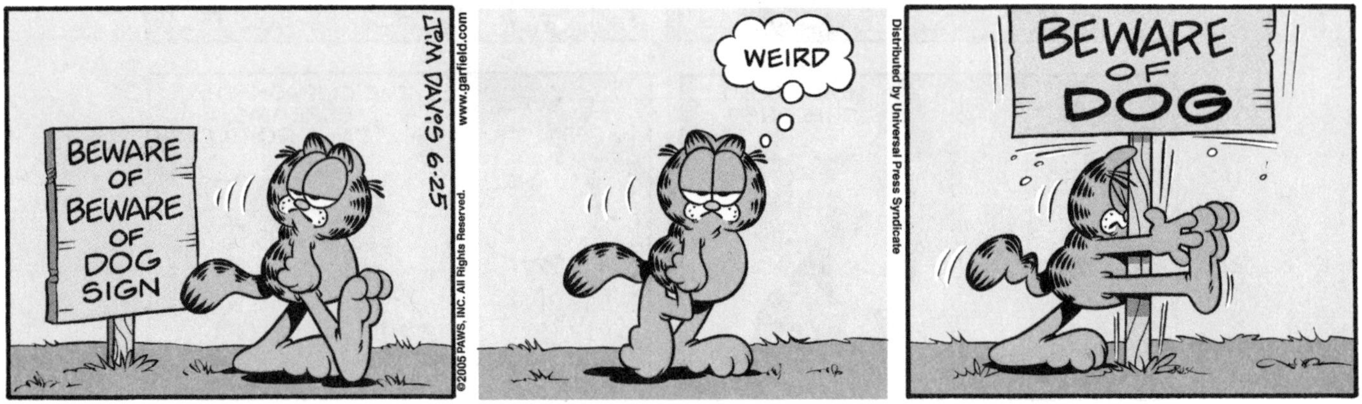
JIM DAVIS 6-25
BEWARE OF BEWARE OF DOG SIGN
WEIRD
BEWARE OF DOG

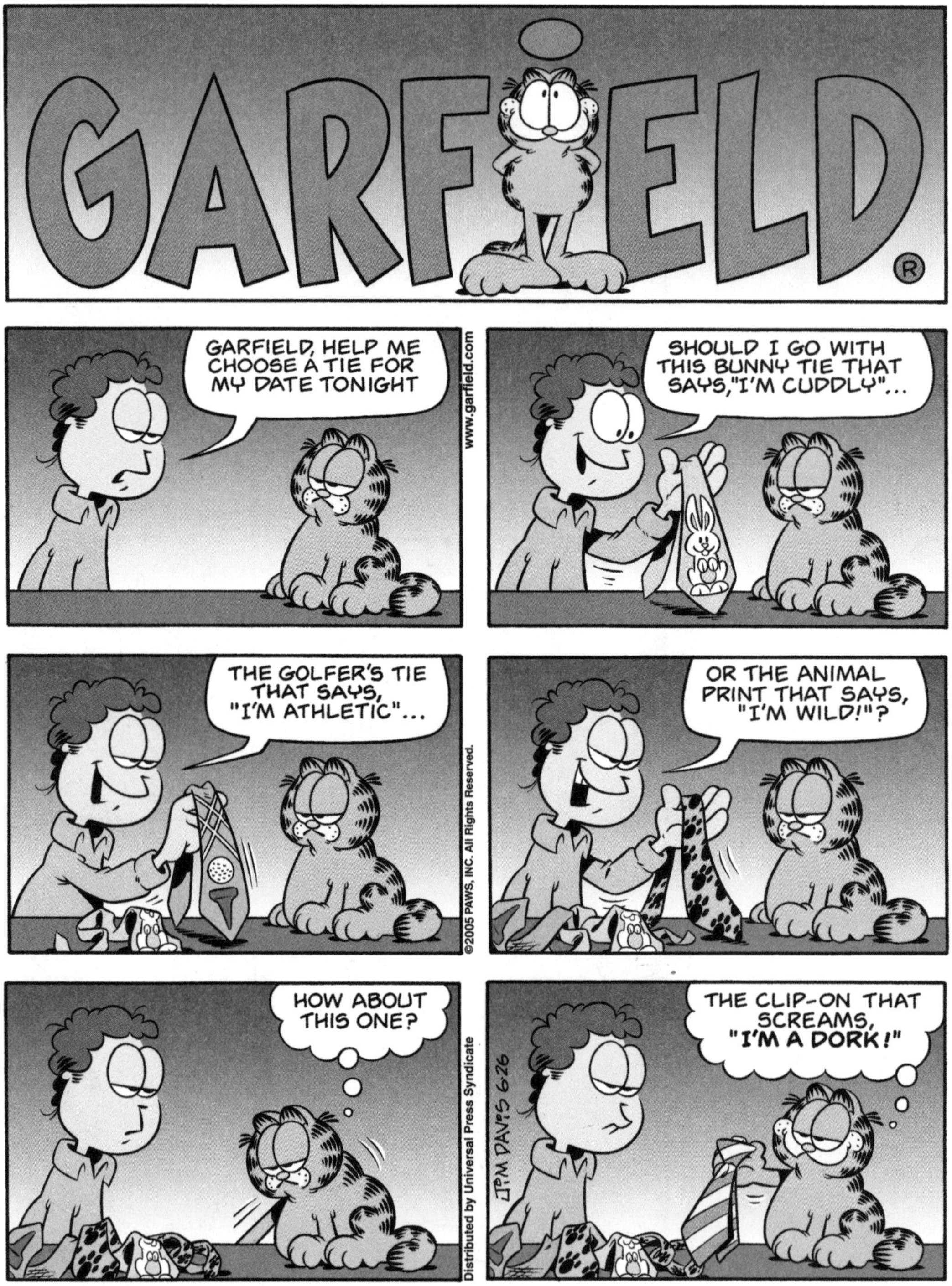
GARFIELD
GARFIELD, HELP ME CHOOSE A TIE FOR MY DATE TONIGHT
www.garfield.com
SHOULD I GO WITH THIS BUNNY TIE THAT SAYS, "I'M CUDDLY"...
THE GOLFER'S TIE THAT SAYS, "I'M ATHLETIC"...
©2005 PAWS, INC. All Rights Reserved.
OR THE ANIMAL PRINT THAT SAYS, "I'M WILD!"?
HOW ABOUT THIS ONE?
Distributed by Universal Press Syndicate
JIM DAVIS 6-26
THE CLIP-ON THAT SCREAMS, "I'M A DORK!"

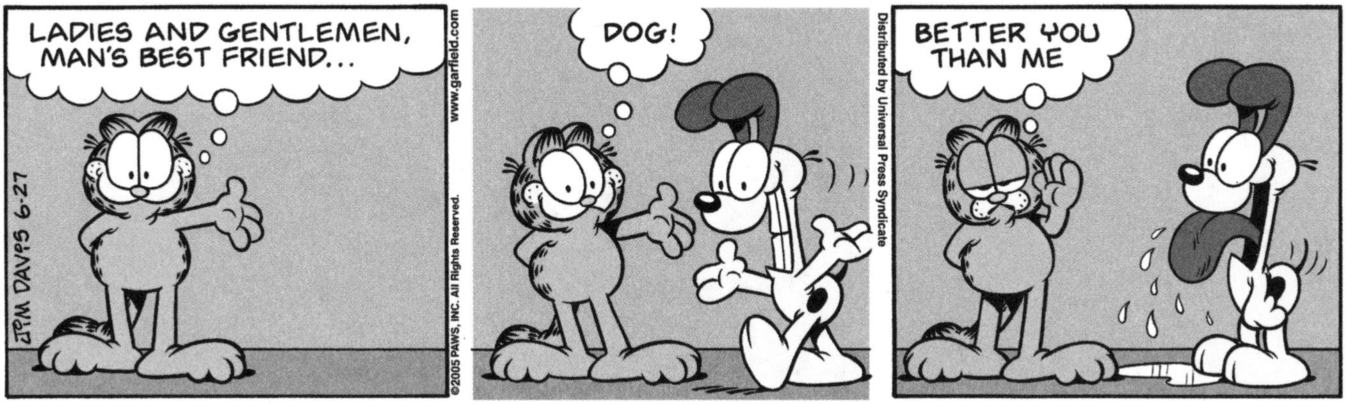
LADIES AND GENTLEMEN, MAN'S BEST FRIEND...
JIM DAVIS 6-27
DOG!
BETTER YOU THAN ME
www.garfield.com
©2005 PAWS, INC. All Rights Reserved.
Distributed by Universal Press Syndicate

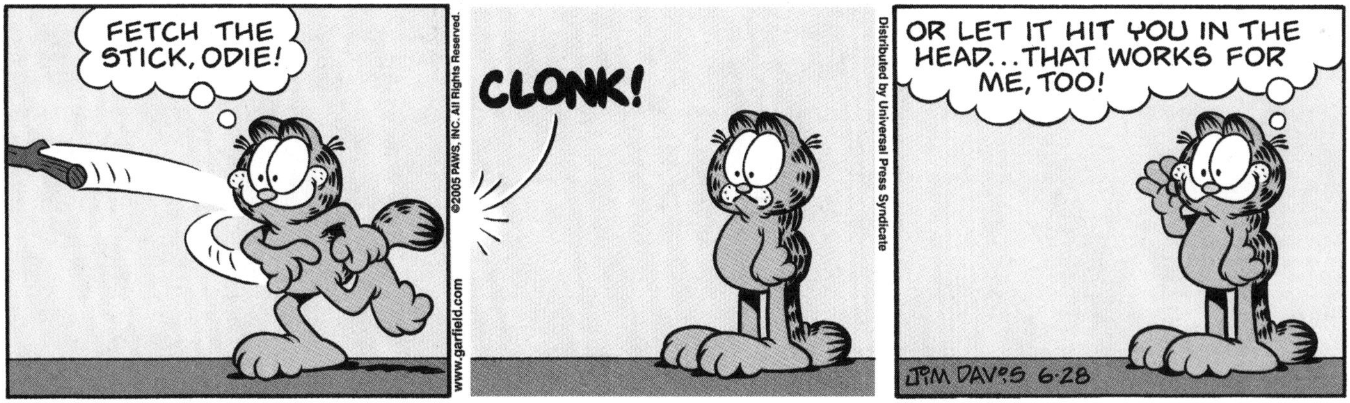
FETCH THE STICK, ODIE!
CLONK!
OR LET IT HIT YOU IN THE HEAD...THAT WORKS FOR ME, TOO!
JIM DAVIS 6-28
www.garfield.com
©2005 PAWS, INC. All Rights Reserved.
Distributed by Universal Press Syndicate

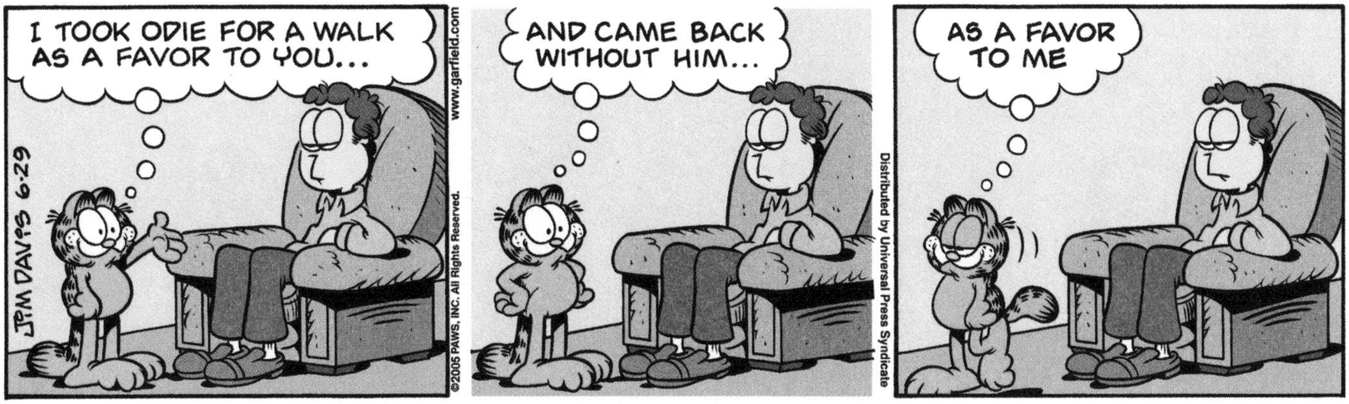
I TOOK ODIE FOR A WALK AS A FAVOR TO YOU...
JIM DAVIS 6-29
AND CAME BACK WITHOUT HIM...
AS A FAVOR TO ME
www.garfield.com
©2005 PAWS, INC. All Rights Reserved.
Distributed by Universal Press Syndicate

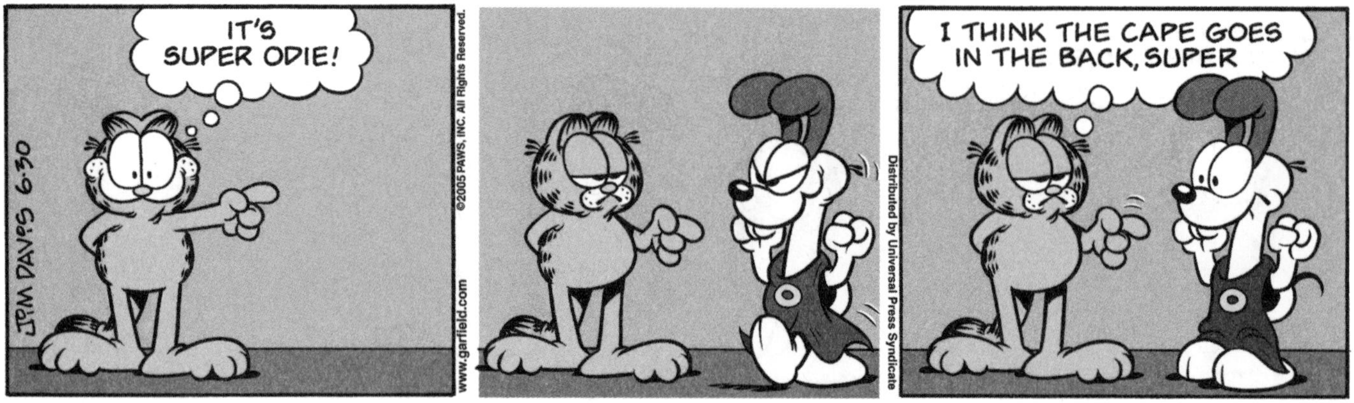
IT'S SUPER ODIE!
JIM DAVIS 6-30
©2005 PAWS, INC. All Rights Reserved.
www.garfield.com
Distributed by Universal Press Syndicate
I THINK THE CAPE GOES IN THE BACK, SUPER

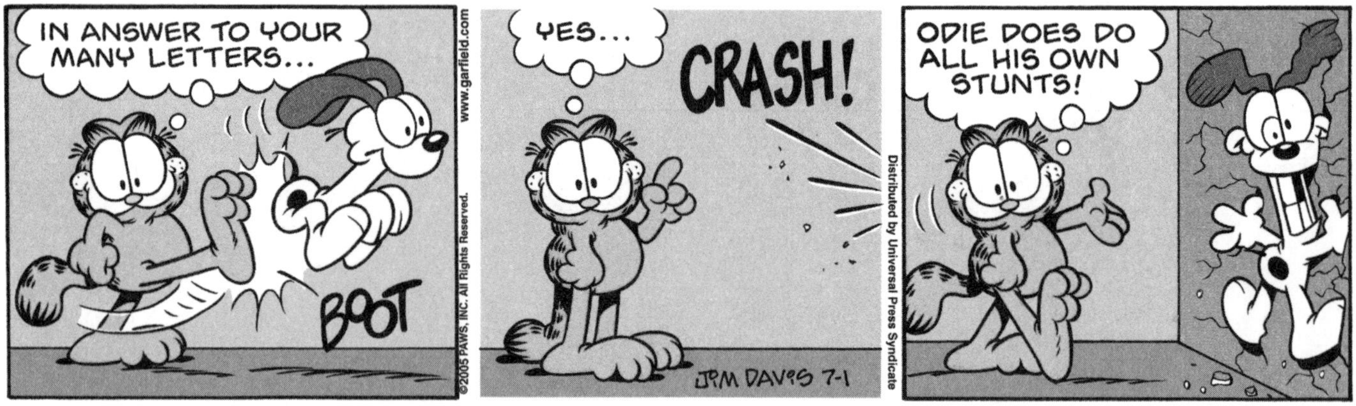
IN ANSWER TO YOUR MANY LETTERS...
BOOT
©2005 PAWS, INC. All Rights Reserved.
www.garfield.com
YES...
CRASH!
JIM DAVIS 7-1
Distributed by Universal Press Syndicate
ODIE DOES DO ALL HIS OWN STUNTS!

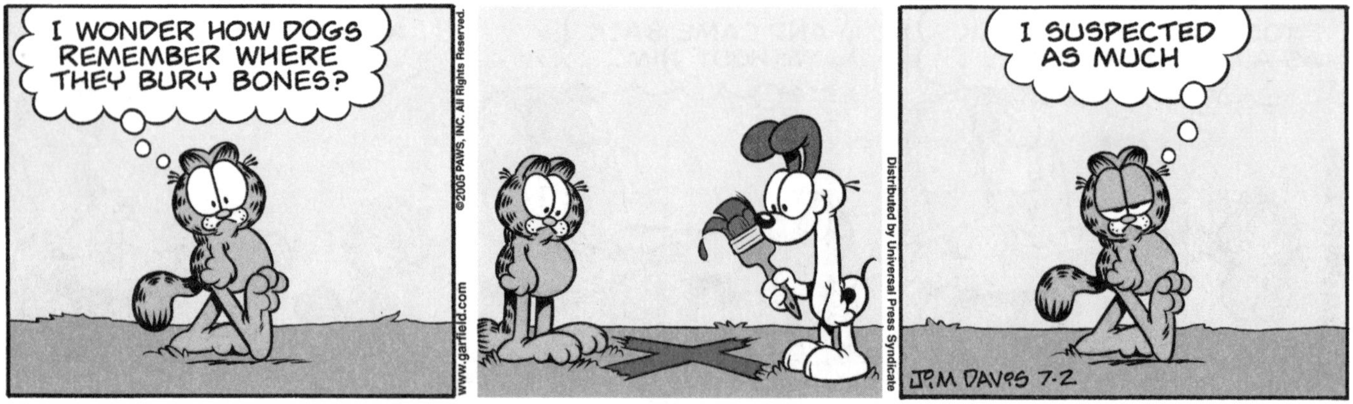
I WONDER HOW DOGS REMEMBER WHERE THEY BURY BONES?
©2005 PAWS, INC. All Rights Reserved.
www.garfield.com
Distributed by Universal Press Syndicate
I SUSPECTED AS MUCH
JIM DAVIS 7-2

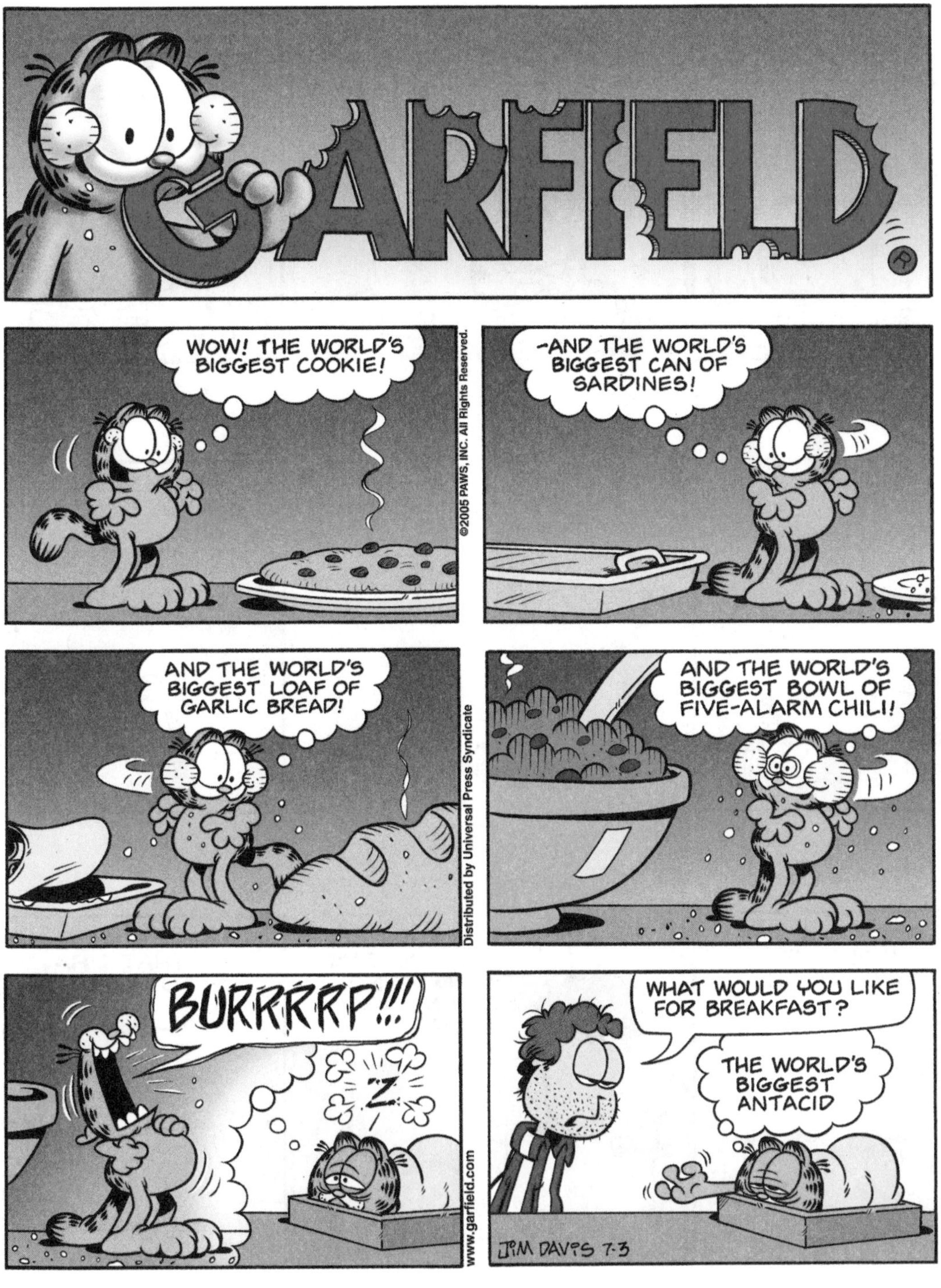

GARFIELD ®
WOW! THE WORLD'S BIGGEST COOKIE!
©2005 PAWS, INC. All Rights Reserved.
–AND THE WORLD'S BIGGEST CAN OF SARDINES!
AND THE WORLD'S BIGGEST LOAF OF GARLIC BREAD!
Distributed by Universal Press Syndicate
AND THE WORLD'S BIGGEST BOWL OF FIVE-ALARM CHILI!
BURRRRP!!!
Z
www.garfield.com
WHAT WOULD YOU LIKE FOR BREAKFAST?
THE WORLD'S BIGGEST ANTACID
JIM DAVIS 7-3

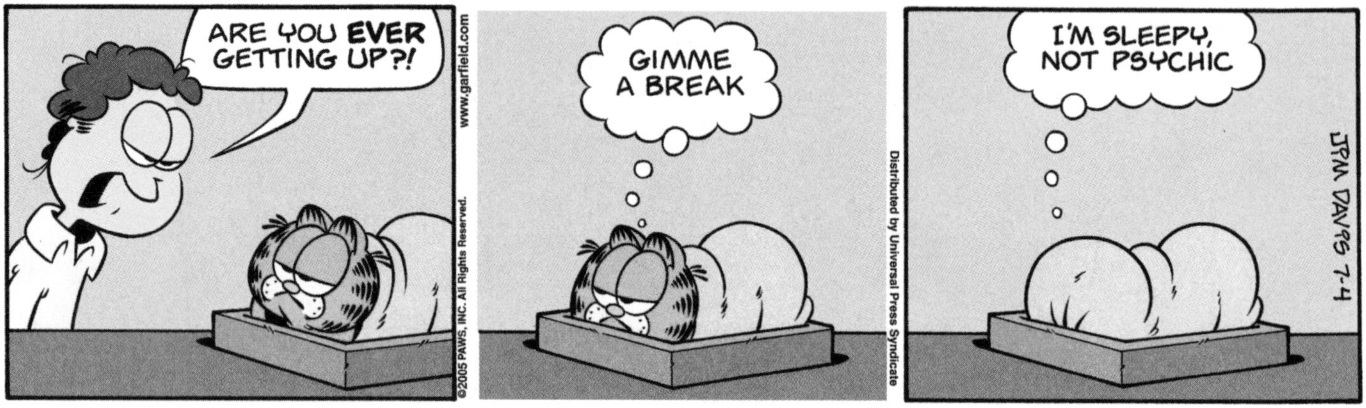
ARE YOU **EVER** GETTING UP?!
GIMME A BREAK
I'M SLEEPY, NOT PSYCHIC
©2005 PAWS, INC. All Rights Reserved.
www.garfield.com
Distributed by Universal Press Syndicate
JIM DAVIS 7-4

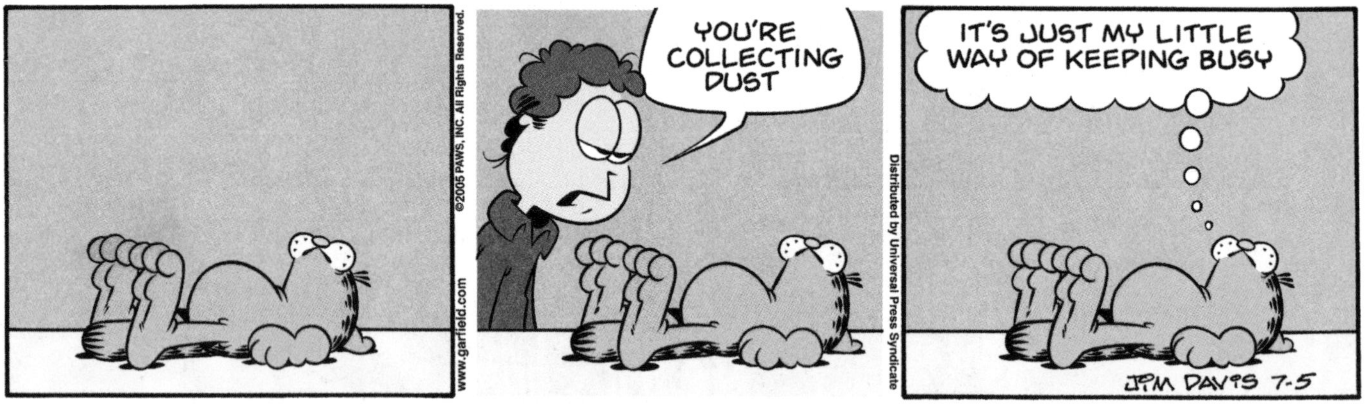
YOU'RE COLLECTING DUST
IT'S JUST MY LITTLE WAY OF KEEPING BUSY
©2005 PAWS, INC. All Rights Reserved.
www.garfield.com
Distributed by Universal Press Syndicate
JIM DAVIS 7-5

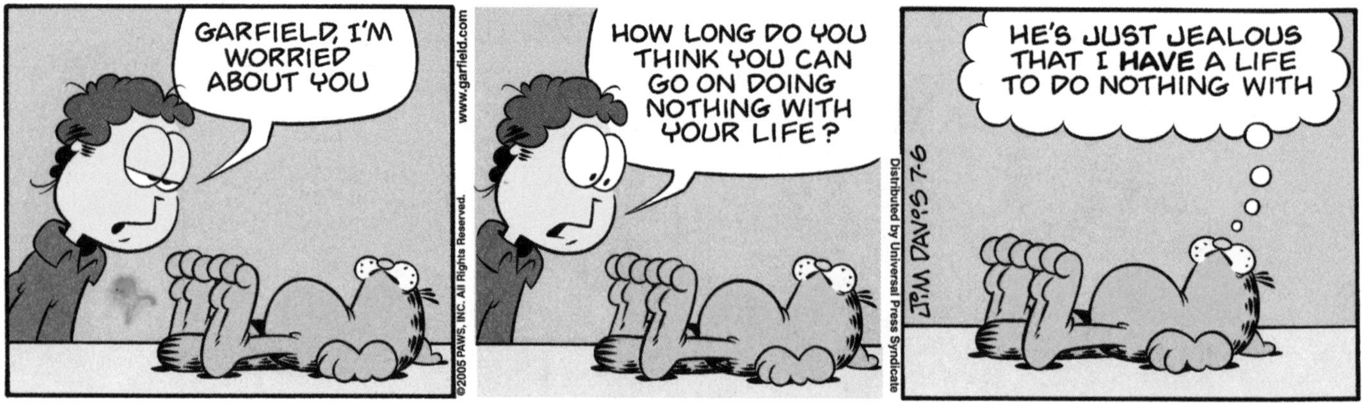
GARFIELD, I'M WORRIED ABOUT YOU
HOW LONG DO YOU THINK YOU CAN GO ON DOING NOTHING WITH YOUR LIFE?
HE'S JUST JEALOUS THAT I **HAVE** A LIFE TO DO NOTHING WITH
©2005 PAWS, INC. All Rights Reserved.
www.garfield.com
Distributed by Universal Press Syndicate
JIM DAVIS 7-6

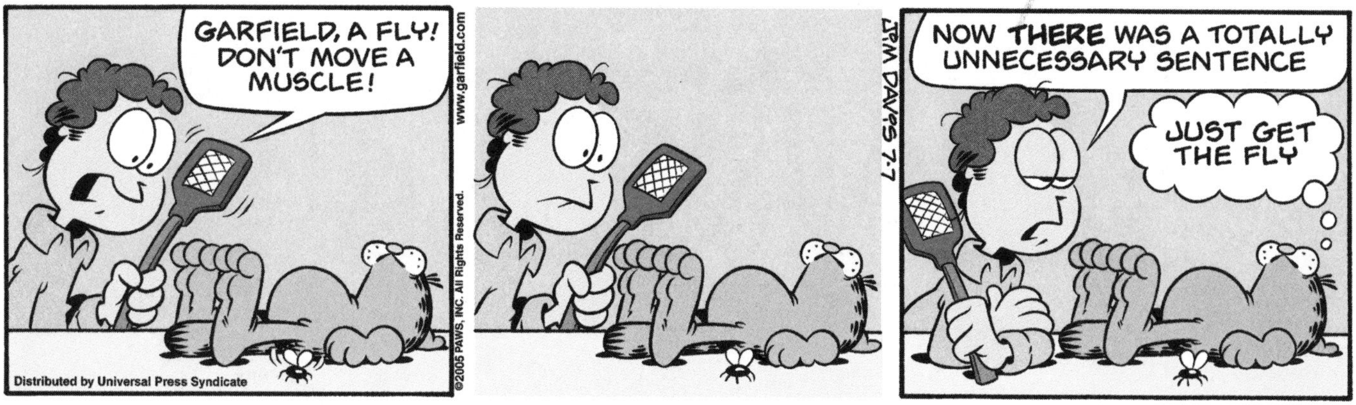
GARFIELD, A FLY! DON'T MOVE A MUSCLE!
NOW THERE WAS A TOTALLY UNNECESSARY SENTENCE
JUST GET THE FLY
JIM DAVIS 7-7
Distributed by Universal Press Syndicate
©2005 PAWS, INC. All Rights Reserved.
www.garfield.com

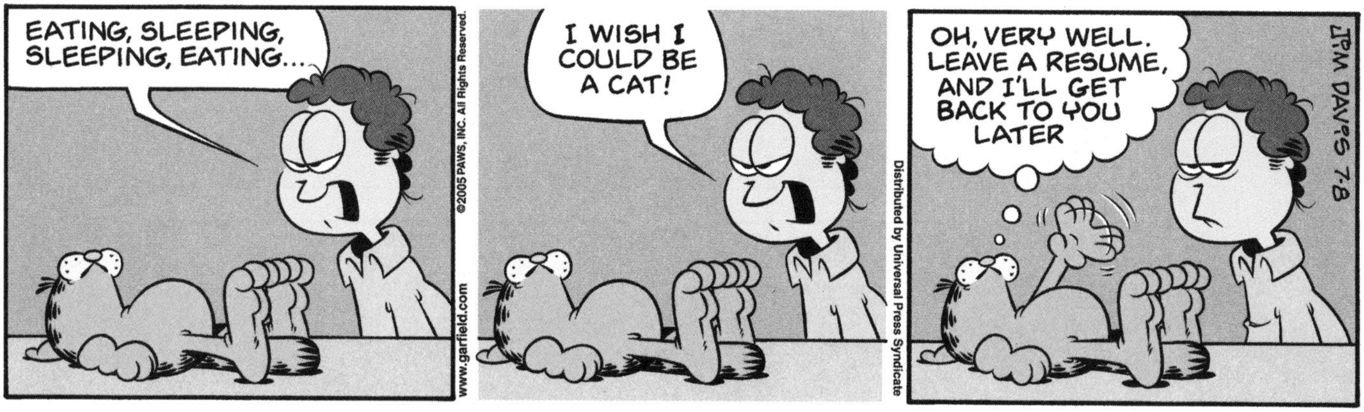
EATING, SLEEPING, SLEEPING, EATING...
I WISH I COULD BE A CAT!
OH, VERY WELL. LEAVE A RESUME, AND I'LL GET BACK TO YOU LATER
JIM DAVIS 7-8
©2005 PAWS, INC. All Rights Reserved.
www.garfield.com
Distributed by Universal Press Syndicate

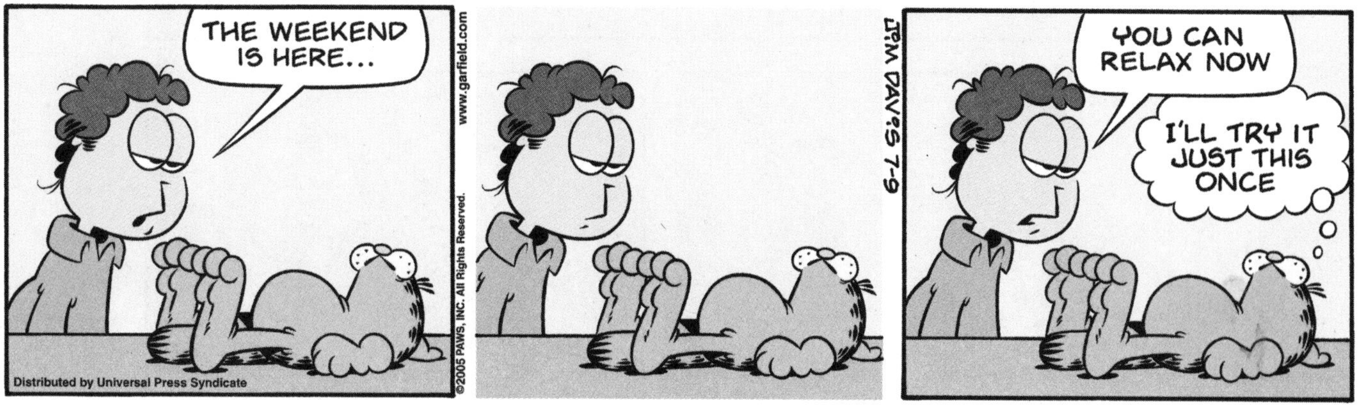
THE WEEKEND IS HERE...
YOU CAN RELAX NOW
I'LL TRY IT JUST THIS ONCE
JIM DAVIS 7-9
Distributed by Universal Press Syndicate
©2005 PAWS, INC. All Rights Reserved.
www.garfield.com

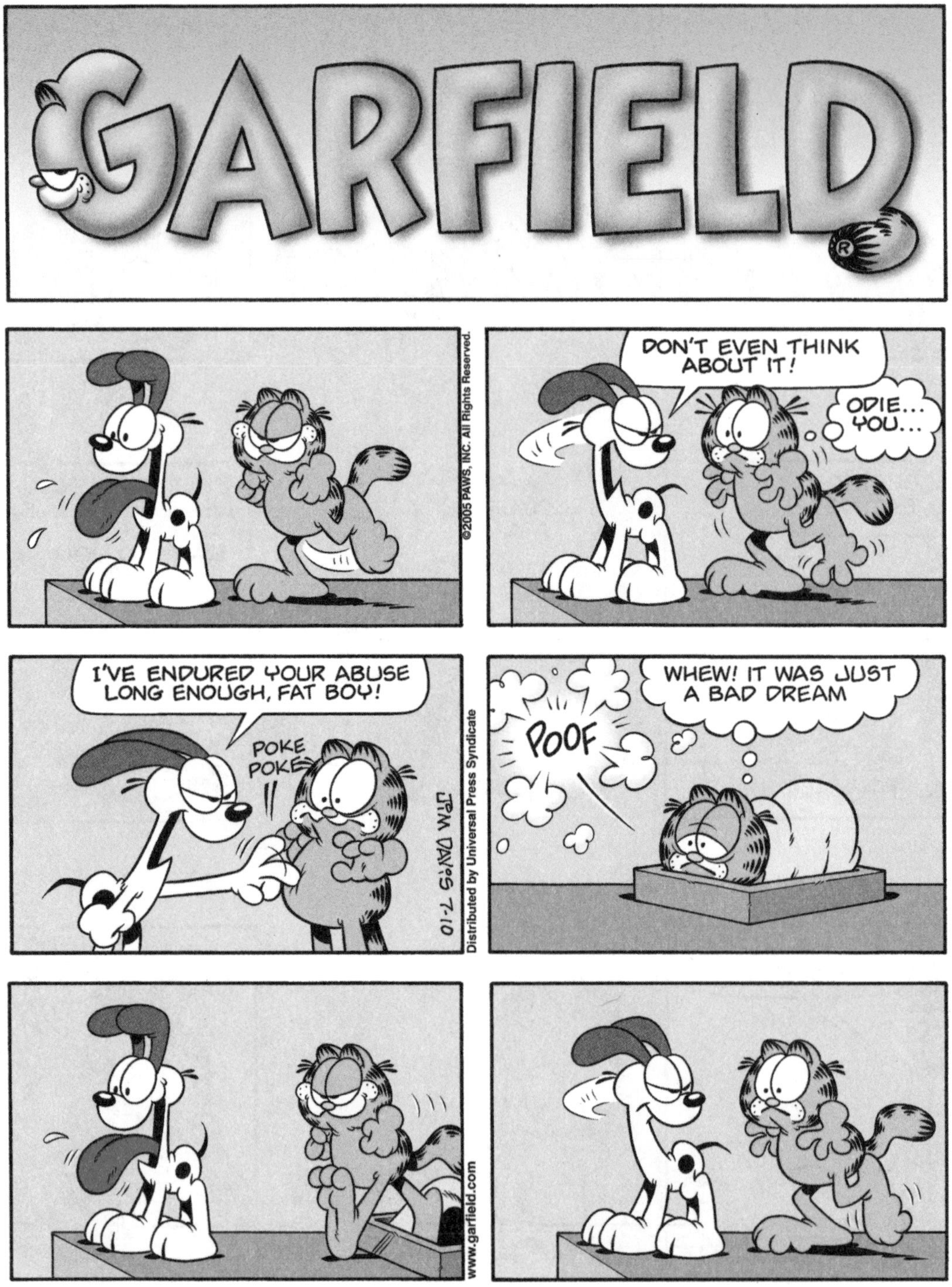
GARFIELD
©2005 PAWS, INC. All Rights Reserved.
DON'T EVEN THINK ABOUT IT!
ODIE... YOU...
I'VE ENDURED YOUR ABUSE LONG ENOUGH, FAT BOY!
POKE POKE
JIM DAVIS 7-10
Distributed by Universal Press Syndicate
POOF
WHEW! IT WAS JUST A BAD DREAM
www.garfield.com

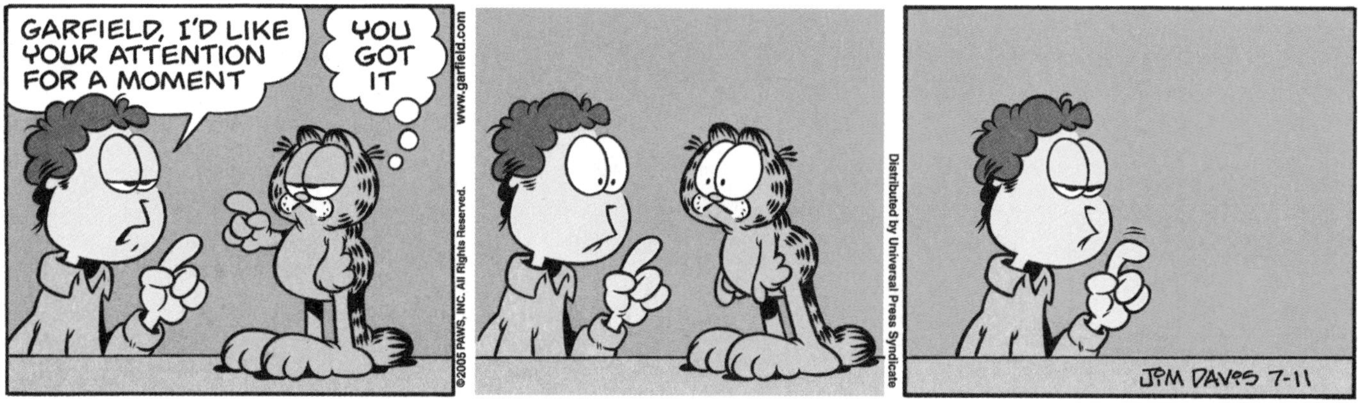
GARFIELD, I'D LIKE YOUR ATTENTION FOR A MOMENT
YOU GOT IT
JIM DAVIS 7-11
©2005 PAWS, INC. All Rights Reserved.
www.garfield.com
Distributed by Universal Press Syndicate

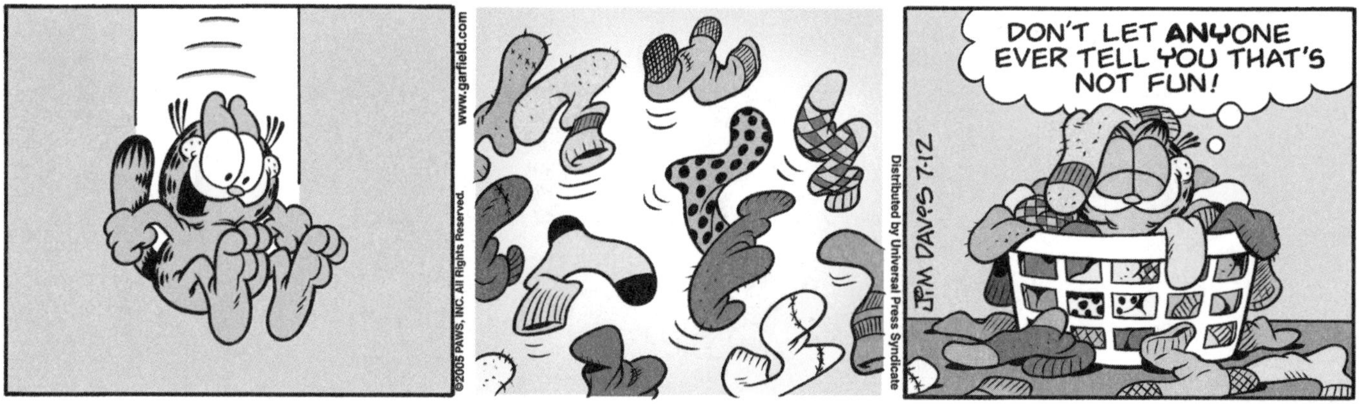
DON'T LET **ANY**ONE EVER TELL **YOU** THAT'S NOT FUN!
JIM DAVIS 7-12
©2005 PAWS, INC. All Rights Reserved.
www.garfield.com
Distributed by Universal Press Syndicate

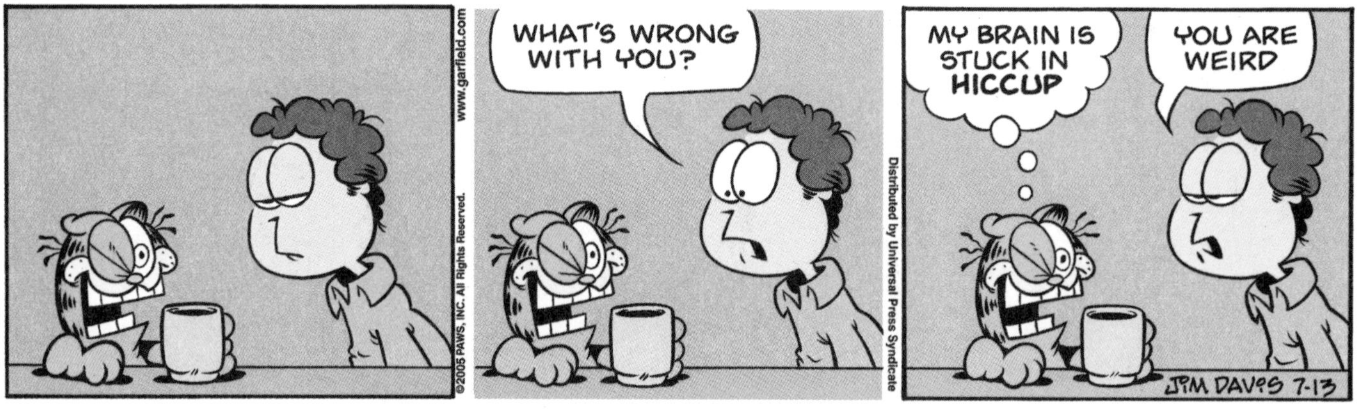
WHAT'S WRONG WITH YOU?
MY BRAIN IS STUCK IN **HICCUP**
YOU ARE WEIRD
JIM DAVIS 7-13
©2005 PAWS, INC. All Rights Reserved.
www.garfield.com
Distributed by Universal Press Syndicate

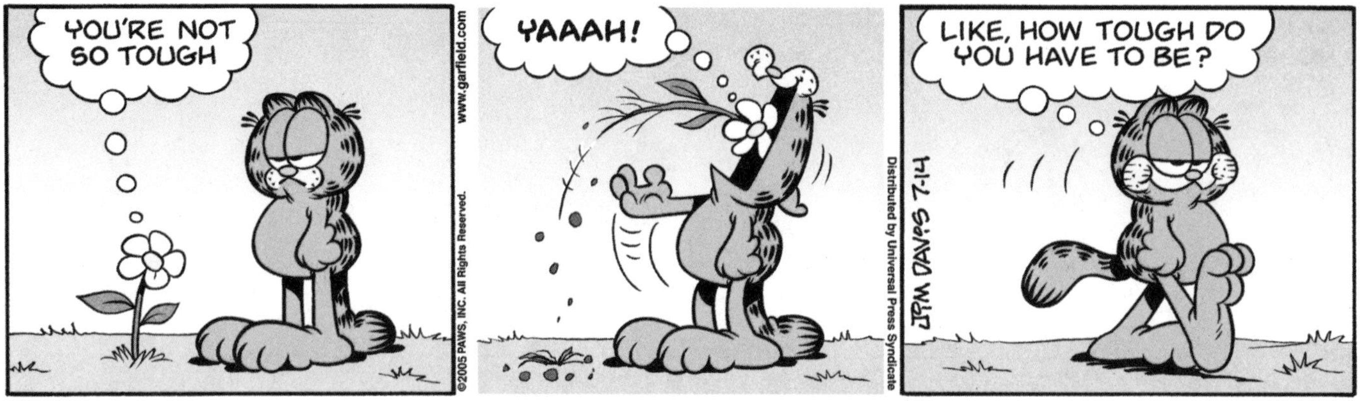
YOU'RE NOT SO TOUGH
YAAAH!
LIKE, HOW TOUGH DO YOU HAVE TO BE?
JIM DAVIS 7-14

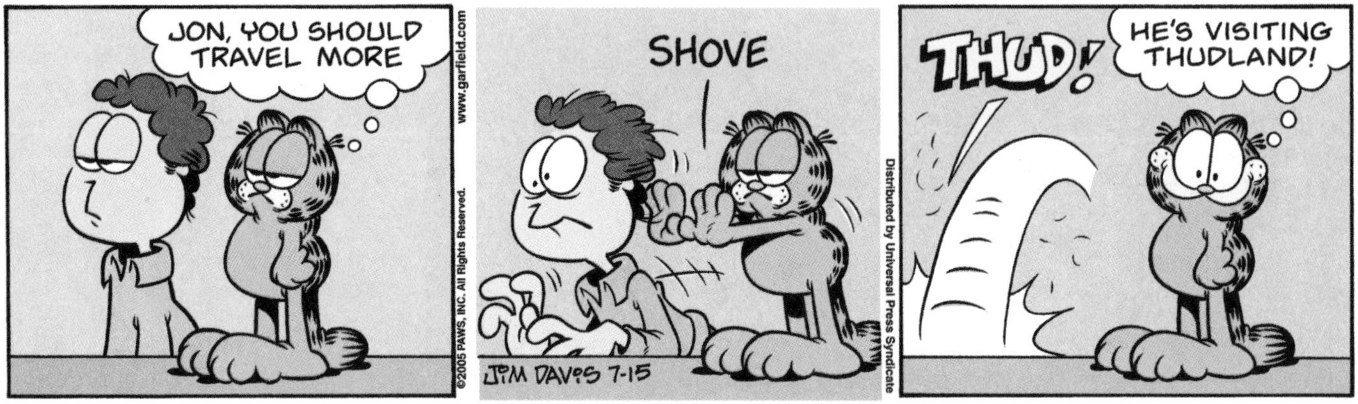
JON, YOU SHOULD TRAVEL MORE
SHOVE
JIM DAVIS 7-15
THUD!
HE'S VISITING THUDLAND!

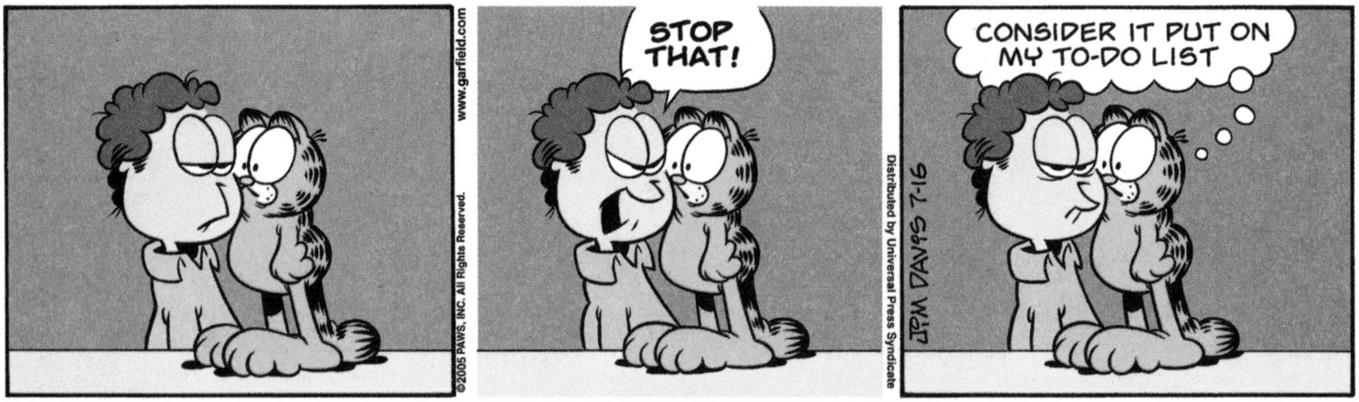
STOP THAT!
JIM DAVIS 7-16
CONSIDER IT PUT ON MY TO-DO LIST

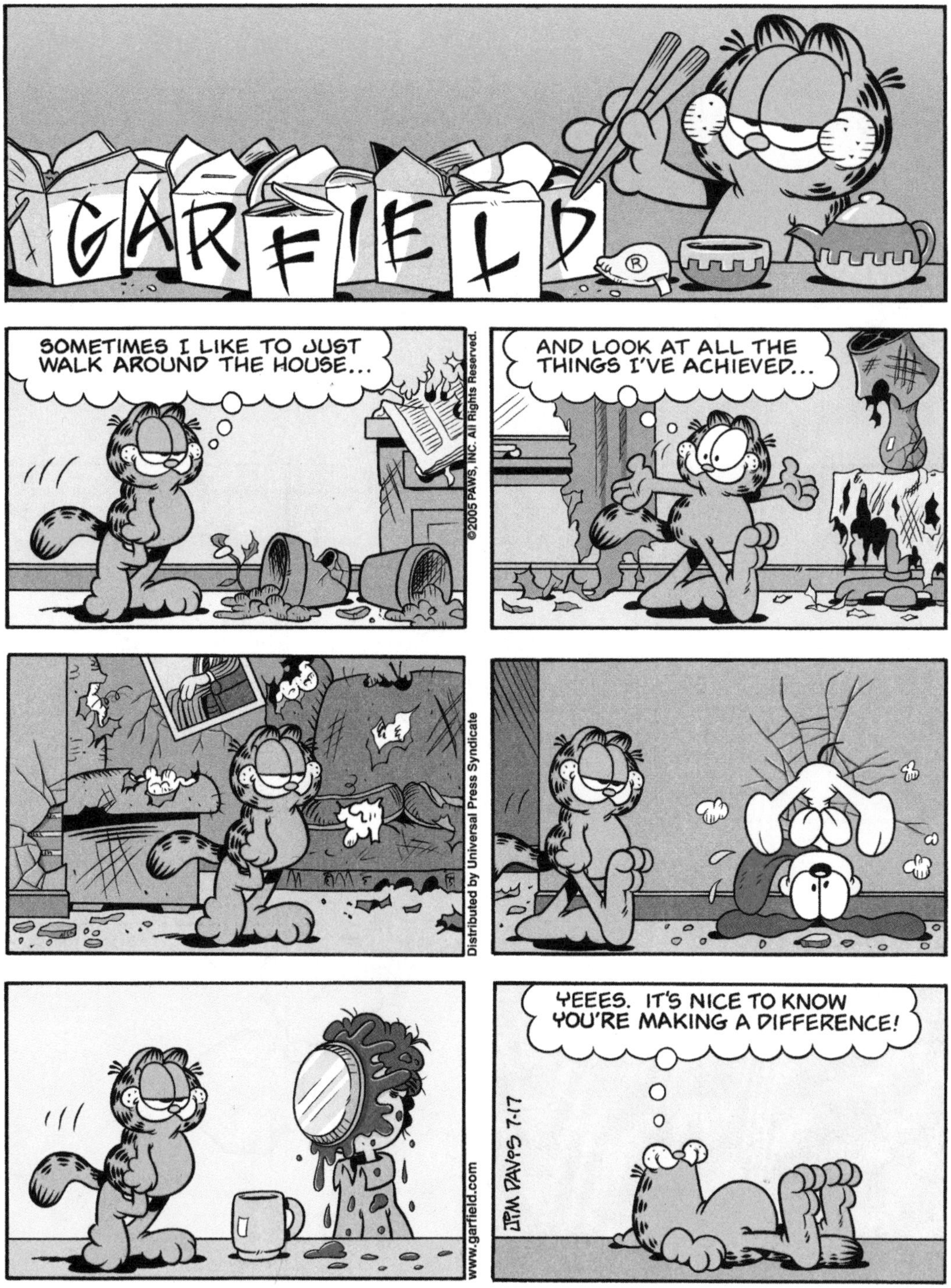
GARFIELD
SOMETIMES I LIKE TO JUST WALK AROUND THE HOUSE...
©2005 PAWS, INC. All Rights Reserved.
AND LOOK AT ALL THE THINGS I'VE ACHIEVED...
Distributed by Universal Press Syndicate
www.garfield.com
JPM DAVPS 7-17
YEEES. IT'S NICE TO KNOW YOU'RE MAKING A DIFFERENCE!

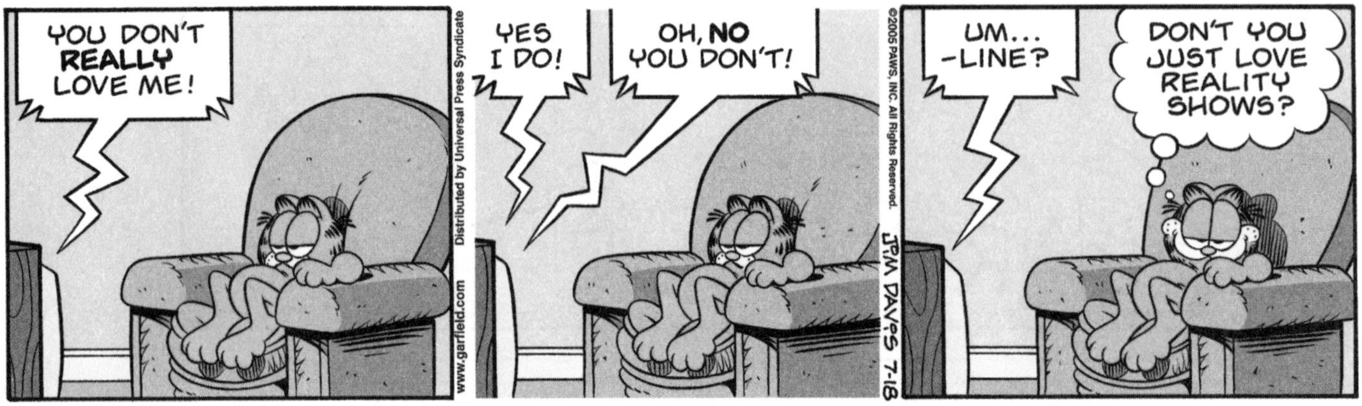
YOU DON'T REALLY LOVE ME!
Distributed by Universal Press Syndicate
www.garfield.com
YES I DO!
OH, NO YOU DON'T!
©2005 PAWS, INC. All Rights Reserved.
JIM DAVIS 7-18
UM... -LINE?
DON'T YOU JUST LOVE REALITY SHOWS?

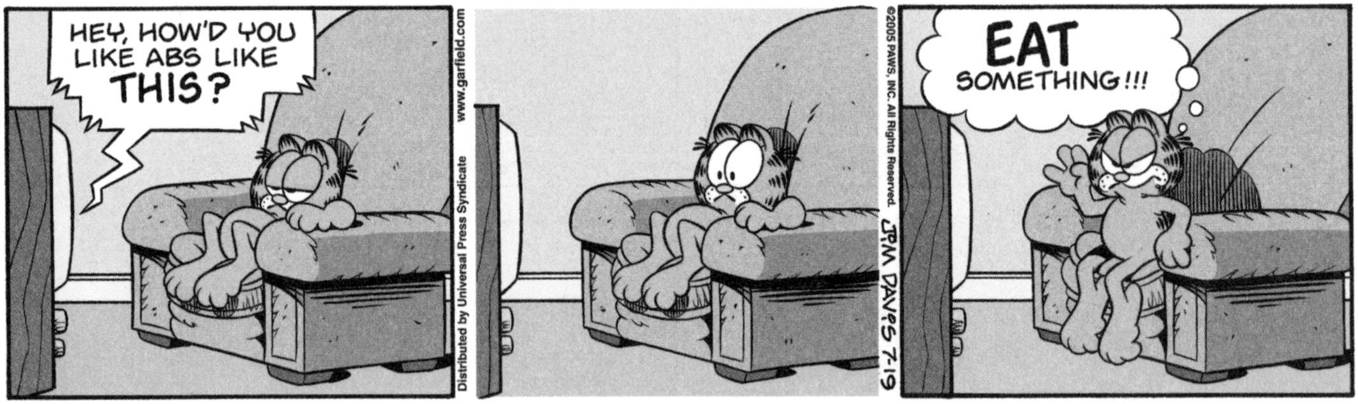
HEY, HOW'D YOU LIKE ABS LIKE THIS?
www.garfield.com
Distributed by Universal Press Syndicate
©2005 PAWS, INC. All Rights Reserved.
JIM DAVIS 7-19
EAT SOMETHING!!!

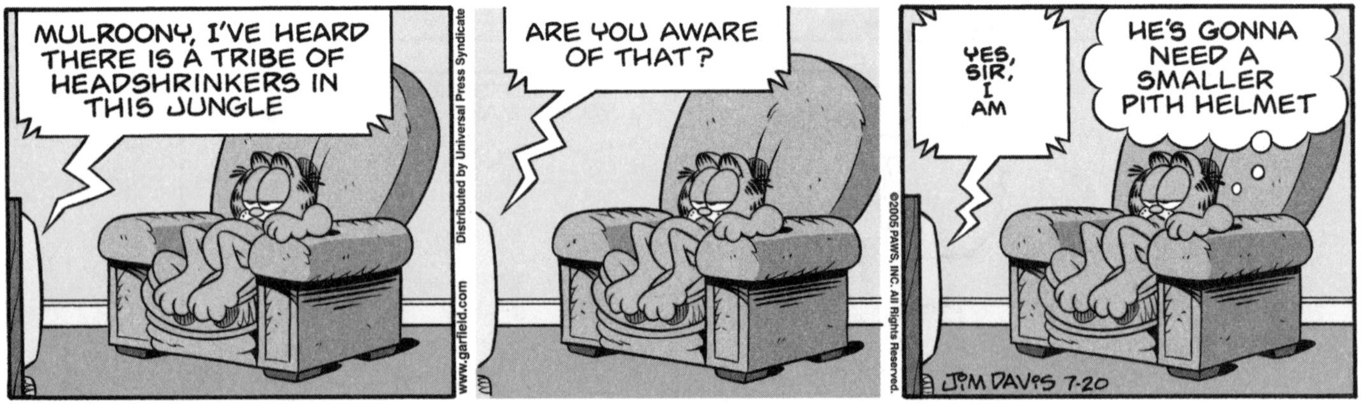
MULROONY, I'VE HEARD THERE IS A TRIBE OF HEADSHRINKERS IN THIS JUNGLE
Distributed by Universal Press Syndicate
www.garfield.com
ARE YOU AWARE OF THAT?
©2005 PAWS, INC. All Rights Reserved.
YES, SIR, I AM
HE'S GONNA NEED A SMALLER PITH HELMET
JIM DAVIS 7-20

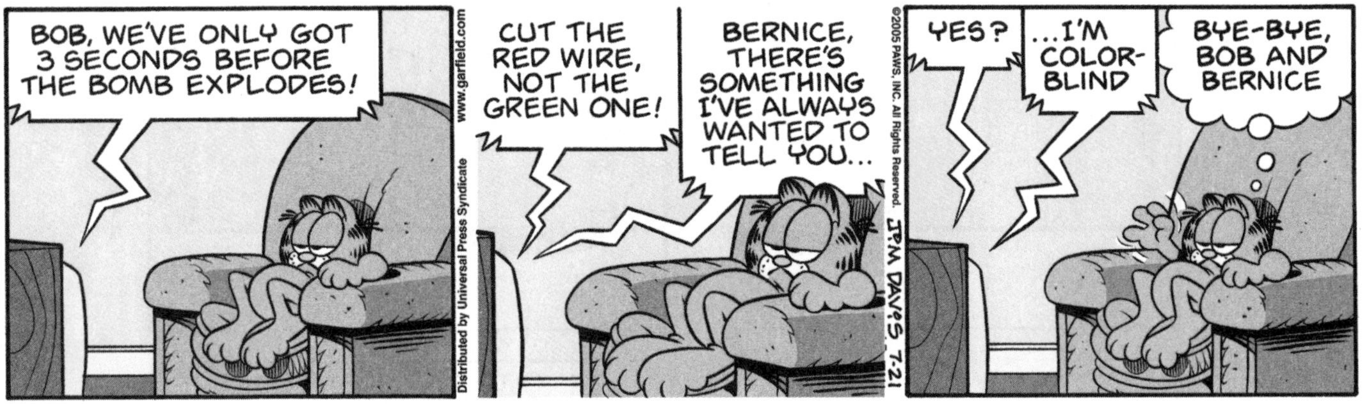
BOB, WE'VE ONLY GOT 3 SECONDS BEFORE THE BOMB EXPLODES!
CUT THE RED WIRE, NOT THE GREEN ONE!
BERNICE, THERE'S SOMETHING I'VE ALWAYS WANTED TO TELL YOU...
YES?
...I'M COLOR-BLIND
BYE-BYE, BOB AND BERNICE
www.garfield.com Distributed by Universal Press Syndicate
©2005 PAWS, INC. All Rights Reserved.
JPM DAVIS 7-21

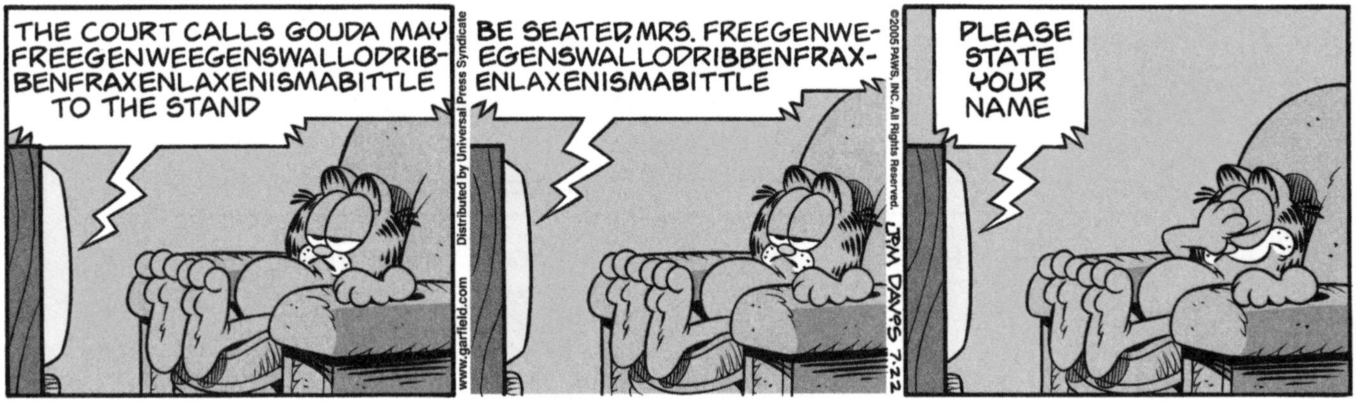
THE COURT CALLS GOUDA MAY FREEGENWEEGENSWALLODRIB-BENFRAXENLAXENISMABITTLE TO THE STAND
BE SEATED, MRS. FREEGENWE-EGENSWALLODRIBBENFRAX-ENLAXENISMABITTLE
PLEASE STATE YOUR NAME
Distributed by Universal Press Syndicate www.garfield.com
©2005 PAWS, INC. All Rights Reserved.
JPM DAVIS 7-22

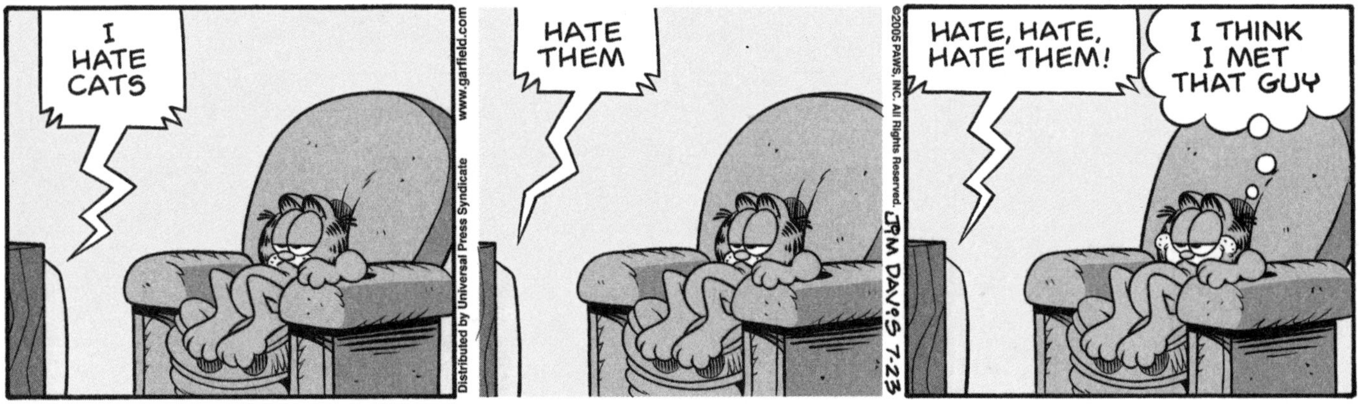
I HATE CATS
HATE THEM
HATE, HATE, HATE THEM!
I THINK I MET THAT GUY
www.garfield.com Distributed by Universal Press Syndicate
©2005 PAWS, INC. All Rights Reserved.
JPM DAVIS 7-23

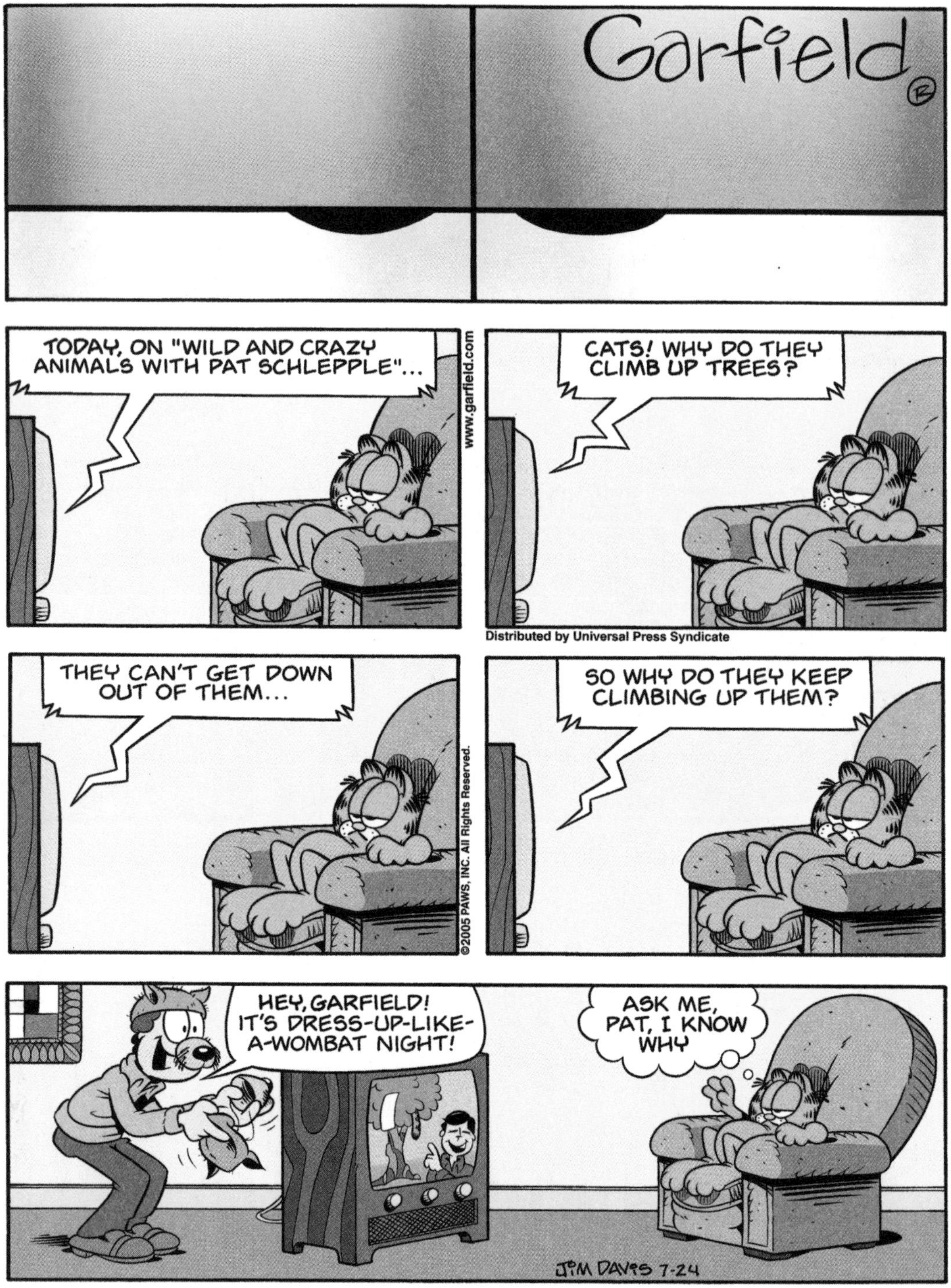
Garfield®
TODAY, ON "WILD AND CRAZY ANIMALS WITH PAT SCHLEPPLE"...
www.garfield.com
CATS! WHY DO THEY CLIMB UP TREES?
Distributed by Universal Press Syndicate
THEY CAN'T GET DOWN OUT OF THEM...
©2005 PAWS, INC. All Rights Reserved.
SO WHY DO THEY KEEP CLIMBING UP THEM?
HEY, GARFIELD! IT'S DRESS-UP-LIKE-A-WOMBAT NIGHT!
ASK ME, PAT, I KNOW WHY
JIM DAVIS 7-24

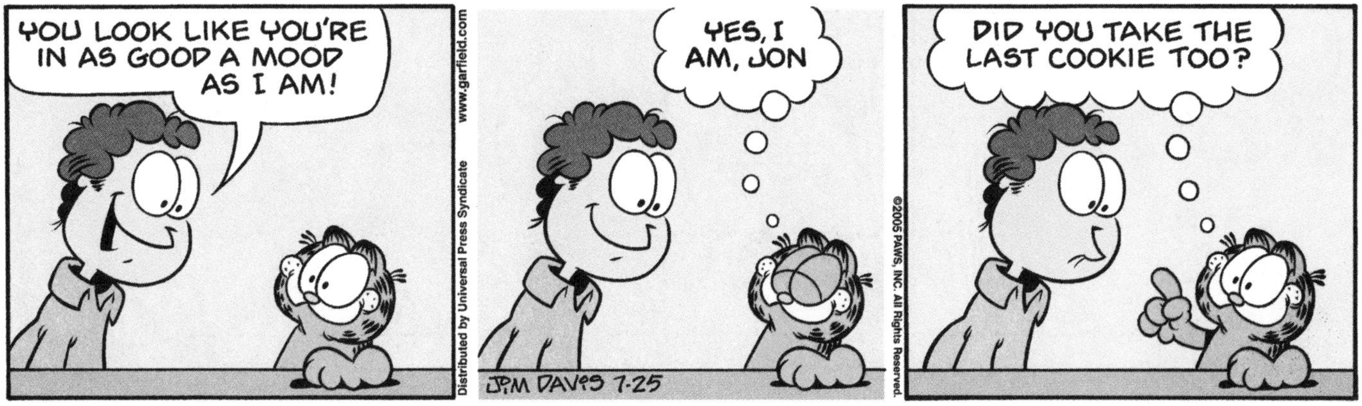
YOU LOOK LIKE YOU'RE IN AS GOOD A MOOD AS I AM!
YES, I AM, JON
DID YOU TAKE THE LAST COOKIE TOO?
JIM DAVIS 7-25
www.garfield.com
Distributed by Universal Press Syndicate
©2005 PAWS, INC. All Rights Reserved.

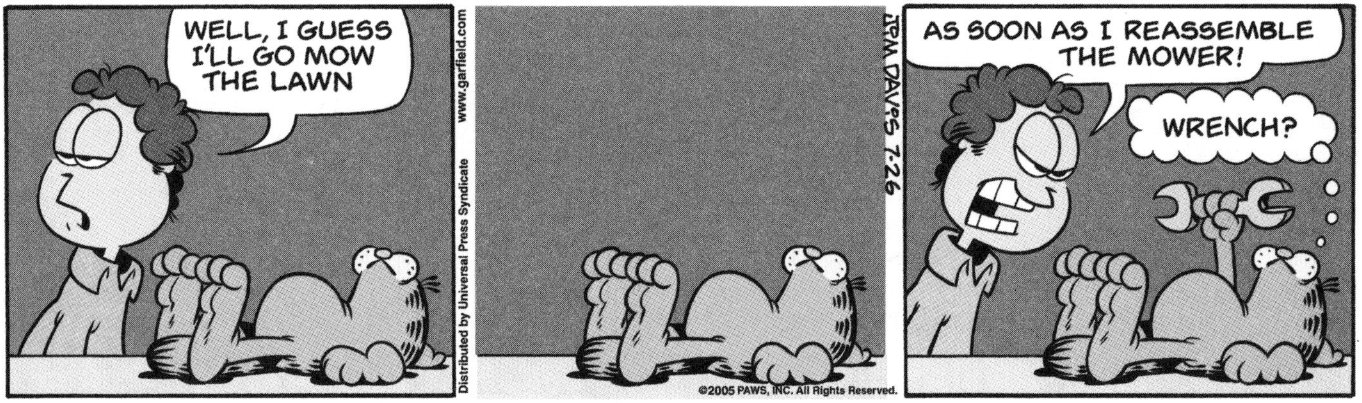
WELL, I GUESS I'LL GO MOW THE LAWN
AS SOON AS I REASSEMBLE THE MOWER!
WRENCH?
JIM DAVIS 7-26
www.garfield.com
Distributed by Universal Press Syndicate
©2005 PAWS, INC. All Rights Reserved.

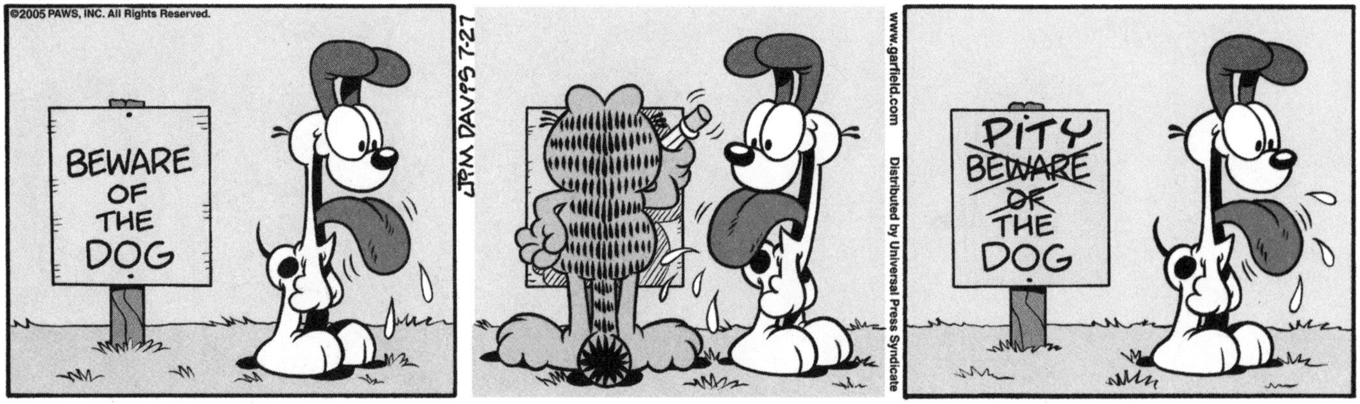
BEWARE OF THE DOG
PITY
BEWARE
OF
THE DOG
JIM DAVIS 7-27
©2005 PAWS, INC. All Rights Reserved.
www.garfield.com
Distributed by Universal Press Syndicate

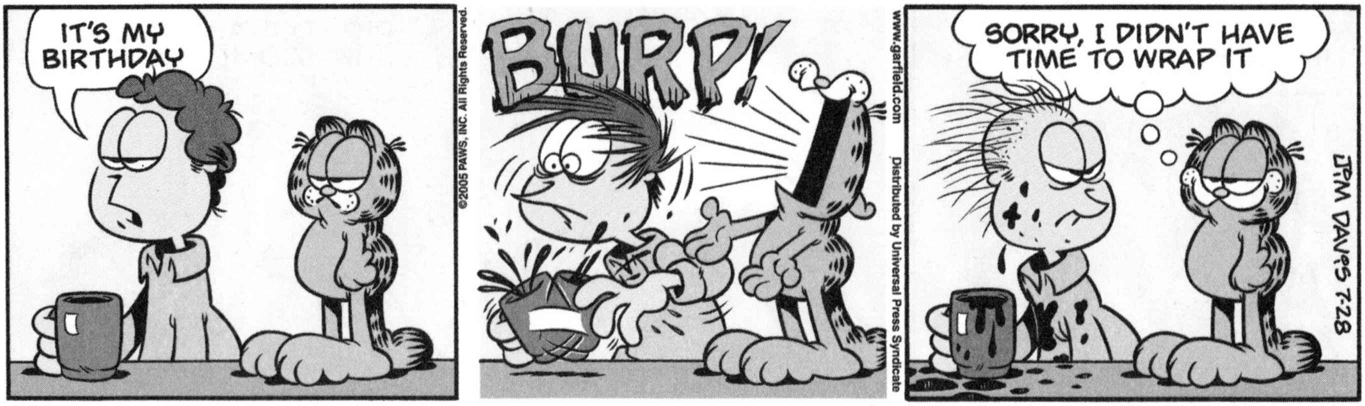
IT'S MY BIRTHDAY
BURP!
SORRY, I DIDN'T HAVE TIME TO WRAP IT
JPM DAVPS 7-28
©2005 PAWS, INC. All Rights Reserved.
Distributed by Universal Press Syndicate
www.garfield.com

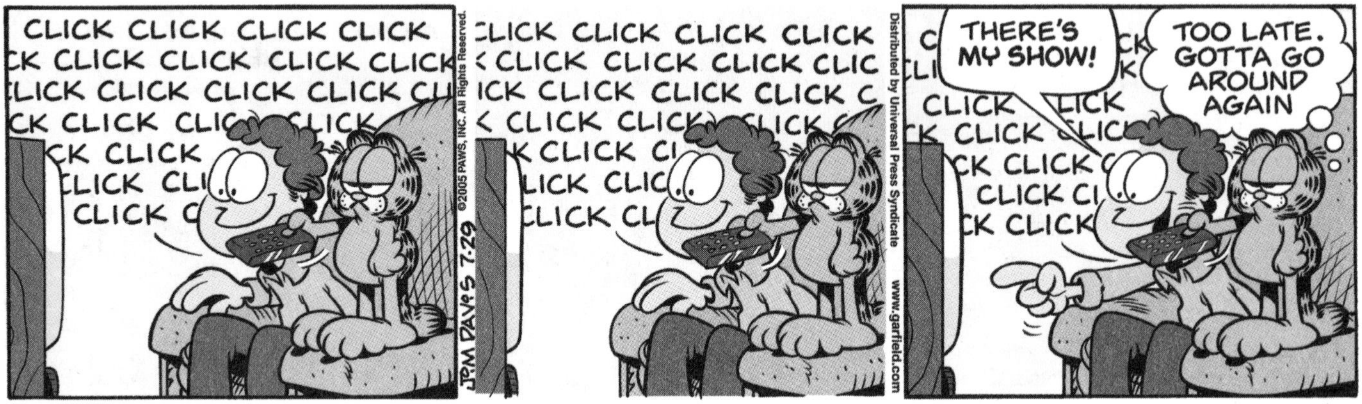
CLICK CLICK CLICK CLICK
THERE'S MY SHOW!
TOO LATE. GOTTA GO AROUND AGAIN
JPM DAVPS 7-29
©2005 PAWS, INC. All Rights Reserved.
Distributed by Universal Press Syndicate
www.garfield.com

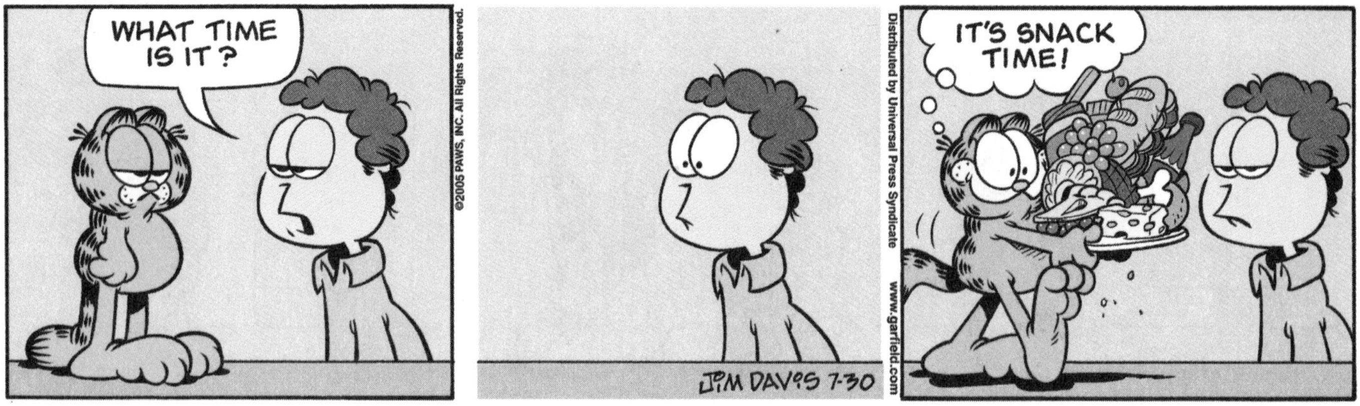
WHAT TIME IS IT?
IT'S SNACK TIME!
JPM DAVPS 7-30
©2005 PAWS, INC. All Rights Reserved.
Distributed by Universal Press Syndicate
www.garfield.com

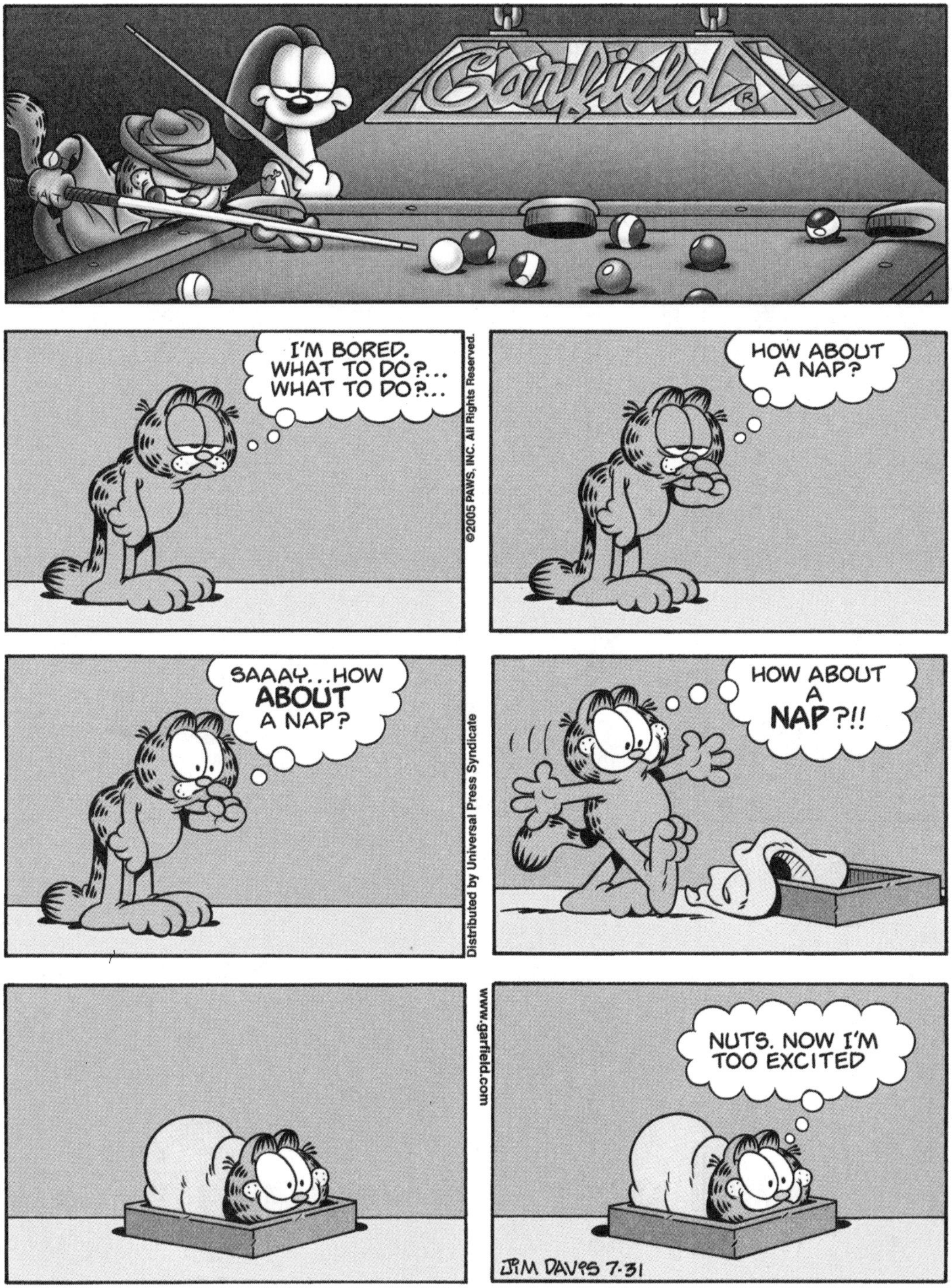
Garfield
I'M BORED. WHAT TO DO?... WHAT TO DO?...
©2005 PAWS, INC. All Rights Reserved.
HOW ABOUT A NAP?
SAAAY...HOW **ABOUT** A NAP?
Distributed by Universal Press Syndicate
HOW ABOUT A **NAP**?!!
www.garfield.com
NUTS. NOW I'M TOO EXCITED
JIM DAVIS 7-31

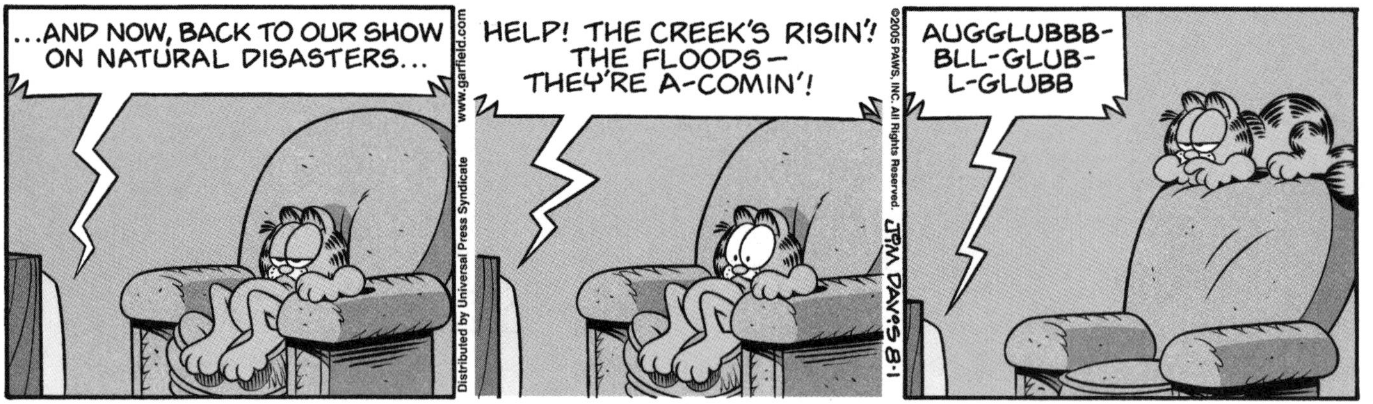
...AND NOW, BACK TO OUR SHOW ON NATURAL DISASTERS...
HELP! THE CREEK'S RISIN'! THE FLOODS— THEY'RE A-COMIN'!
AUGGLUBBB-BLL-GLUB-L-GLUBB

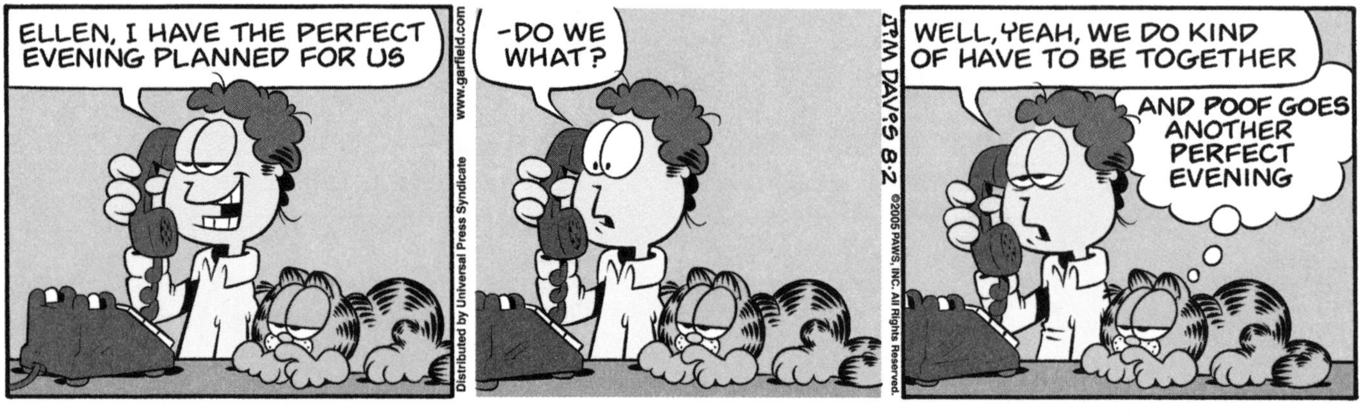
ELLEN, I HAVE THE PERFECT EVENING PLANNED FOR US
-DO WE WHAT?
WELL, YEAH, WE DO KIND OF HAVE TO BE TOGETHER
AND POOF GOES ANOTHER PERFECT EVENING

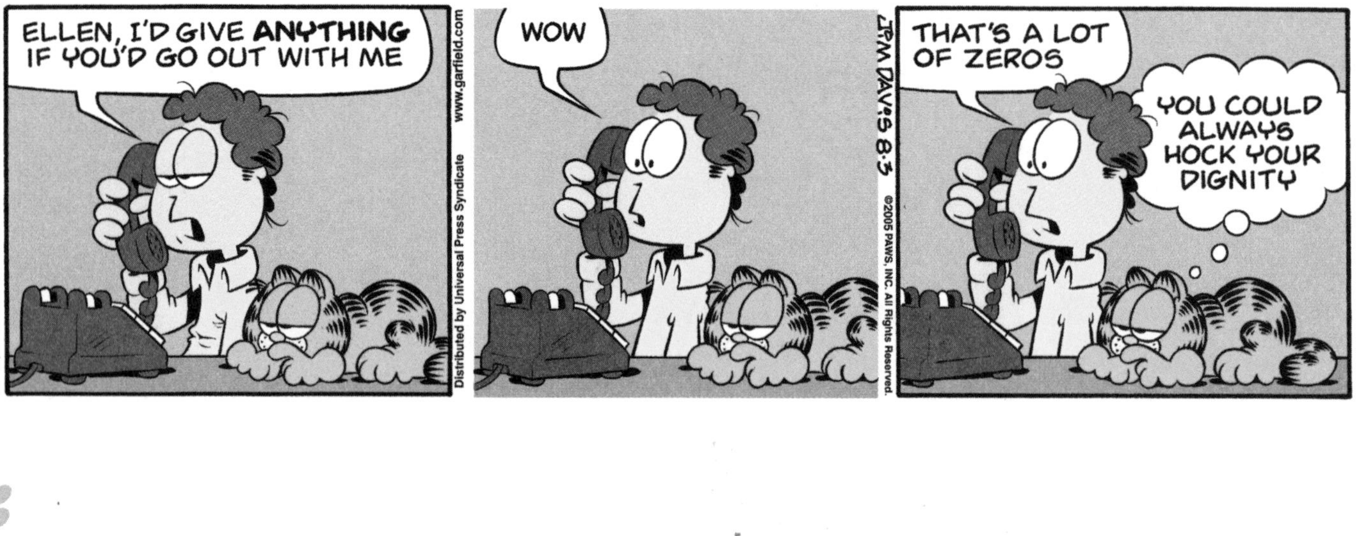
ELLEN, I'D GIVE **ANYTHING** IF YOU'D GO OUT WITH ME
WOW
THAT'S A LOT OF ZEROS
YOU COULD ALWAYS HOCK YOUR DIGNITY

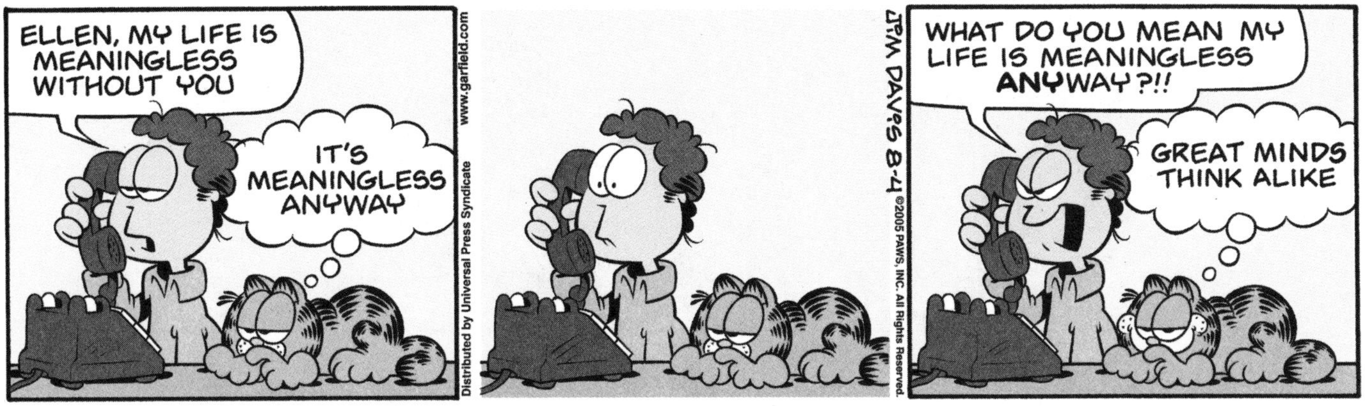
ELLEN, MY LIFE IS MEANINGLESS WITHOUT YOU
IT'S MEANINGLESS ANYWAY
WHAT DO YOU MEAN MY LIFE IS MEANINGLESS **ANY**WAY?!!
GREAT MINDS THINK ALIKE
Distributed by Universal Press Syndicate www.garfield.com
JIM DAVIS 8-4
©2005 PAWS, INC. All Rights Reserved.

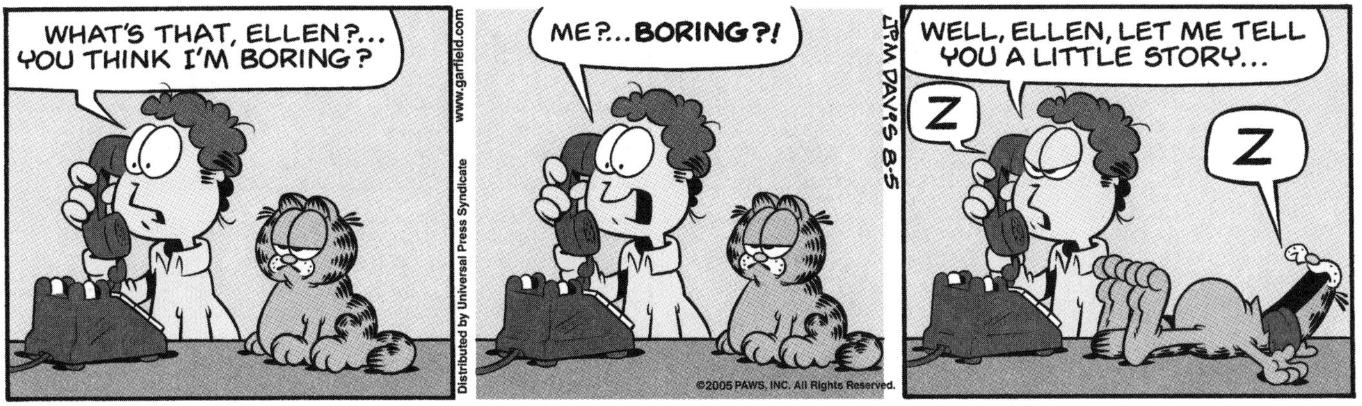
WHAT'S THAT, ELLEN?... YOU THINK I'M BORING?
ME?... **BORING?!**
WELL, ELLEN, LET ME TELL YOU A LITTLE STORY...
Z
Z
Distributed by Universal Press Syndicate www.garfield.com
JIM DAVIS 8-5
©2005 PAWS, INC. All Rights Reserved.

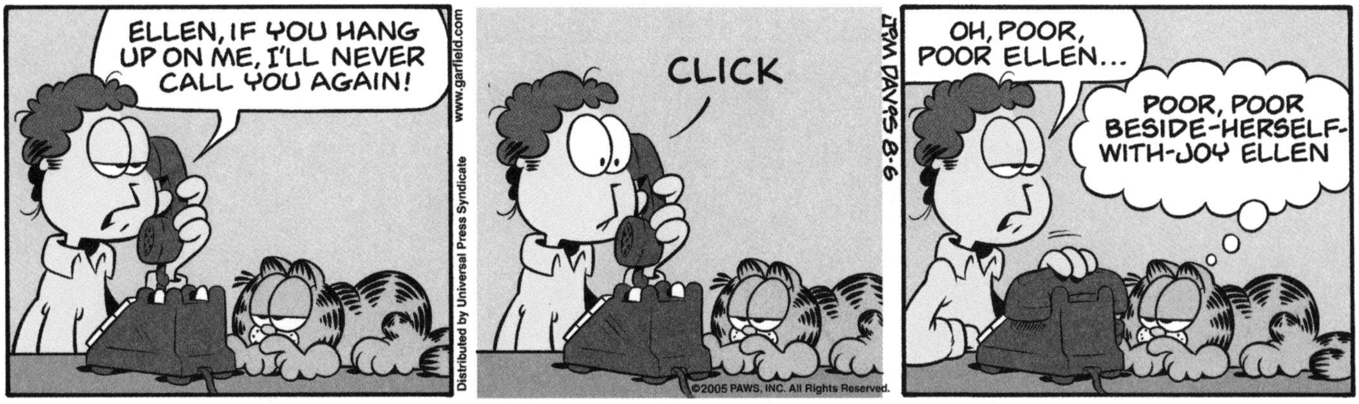
ELLEN, IF YOU HANG UP ON ME, I'LL NEVER CALL YOU AGAIN!
CLICK
OH, POOR, POOR ELLEN...
POOR, POOR BESIDE-HERSELF-WITH-JOY ELLEN
Distributed by Universal Press Syndicate www.garfield.com
JIM DAVIS 8-6
©2005 PAWS, INC. All Rights Reserved.

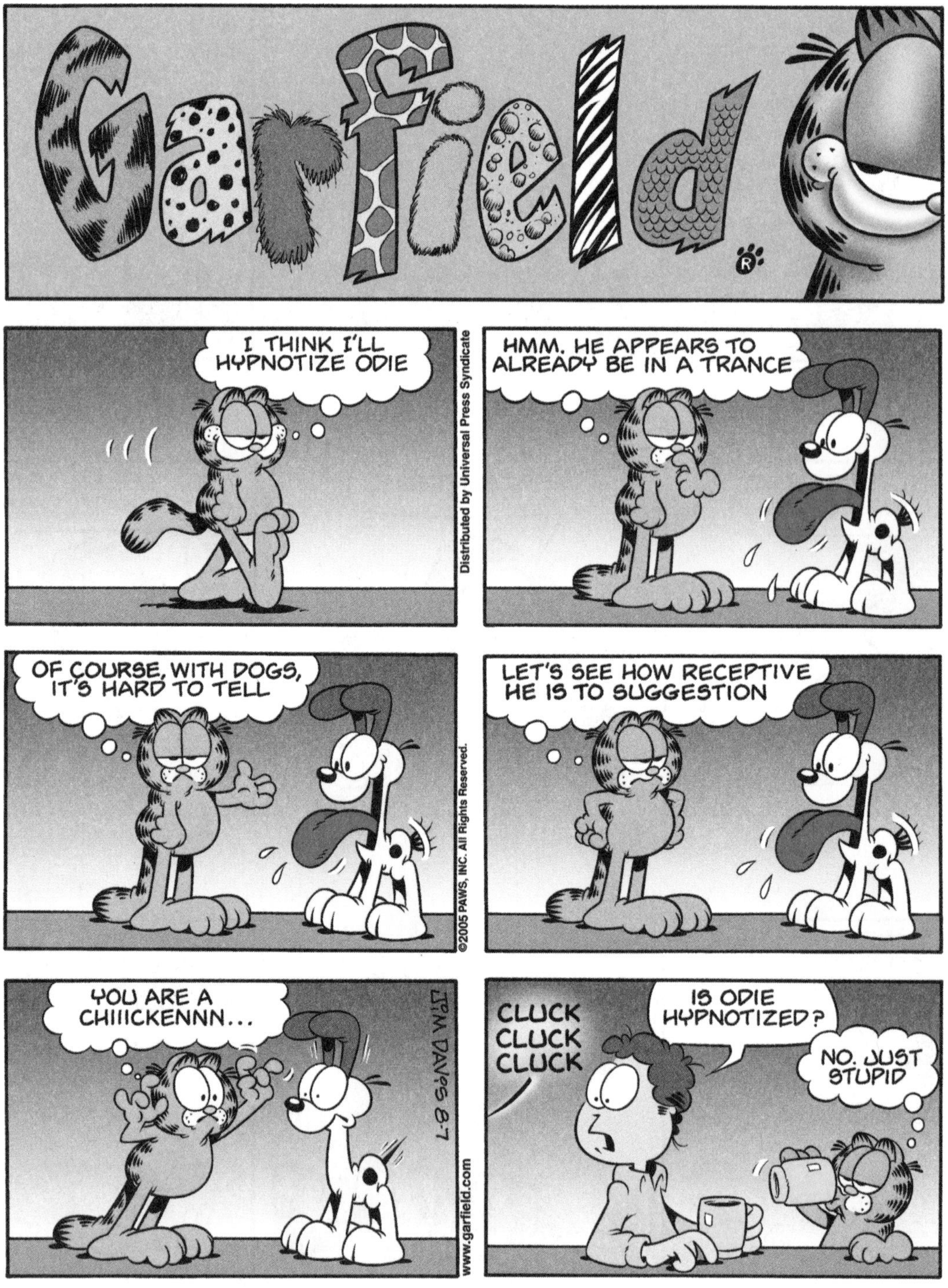
Garfield
I THINK I'LL HYPNOTIZE ODIE
HMM. HE APPEARS TO ALREADY BE IN A TRANCE
OF COURSE, WITH DOGS, IT'S HARD TO TELL
LET'S SEE HOW RECEPTIVE HE IS TO SUGGESTION
YOU ARE A CHIIICKENNN...
CLUCK CLUCK CLUCK
IS ODIE HYPNOTIZED?
NO. JUST STUPID
JIM DAVIS 8-7
Distributed by Universal Press Syndicate
©2005 PAWS, INC. All Rights Reserved.
www.garfield.com

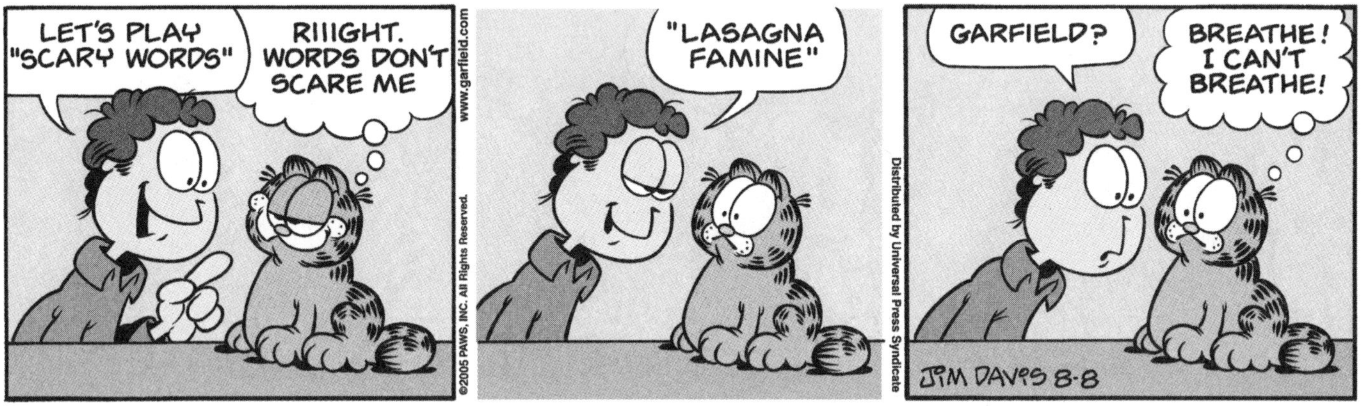
LET'S PLAY "SCARY WORDS"
RIIIGHT. WORDS DON'T SCARE ME
©2005 PAWS, INC. All Rights Reserved. www.garfield.com
"LASAGNA FAMINE"
Distributed by Universal Press Syndicate
GARFIELD?
BREATHE! I CAN'T BREATHE!
JIM DAVIS 8-8

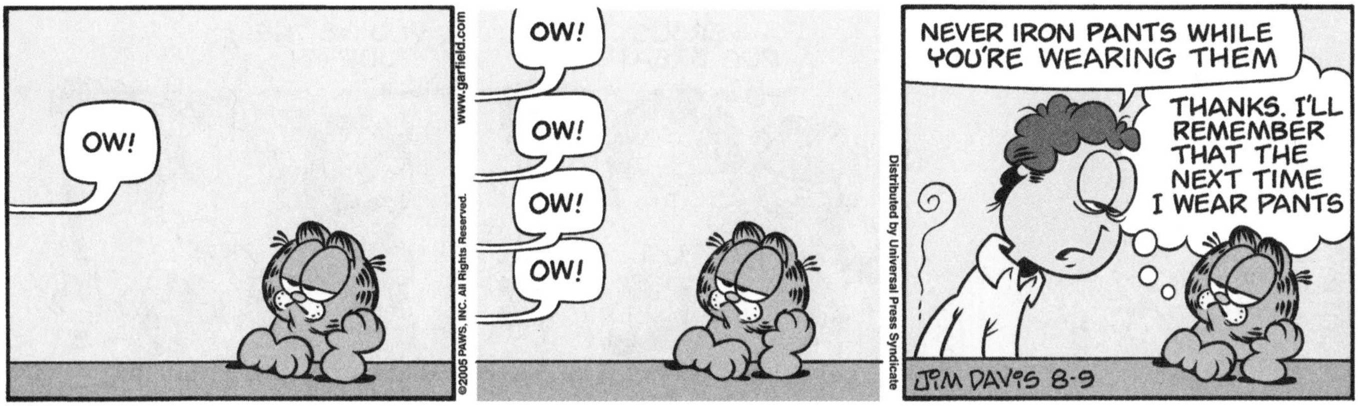
OW!
©2005 PAWS, INC. All Rights Reserved. www.garfield.com
OW!
OW!
OW!
OW!
Distributed by Universal Press Syndicate
NEVER IRON PANTS WHILE YOU'RE WEARING THEM
THANKS. I'LL REMEMBER THAT THE NEXT TIME I WEAR PANTS
JIM DAVIS 8-9

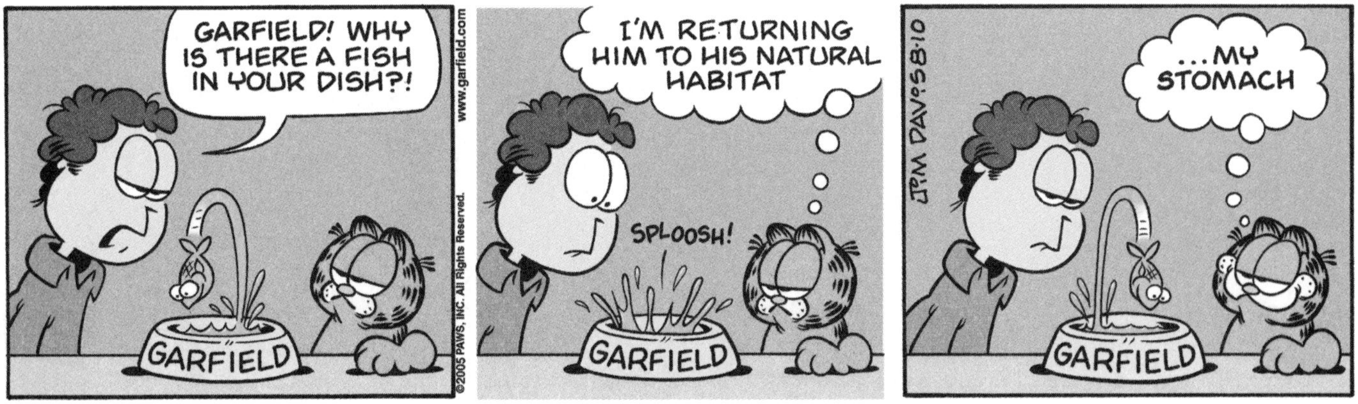
GARFIELD! WHY IS THERE A FISH IN YOUR DISH?!
GARFIELD
©2005 PAWS, INC. All Rights Reserved. www.garfield.com
I'M RETURNING HIM TO HIS NATURAL HABITAT
SPLOOSH!
GARFIELD
JIM DAVIS 8-10
...MY STOMACH
GARFIELD

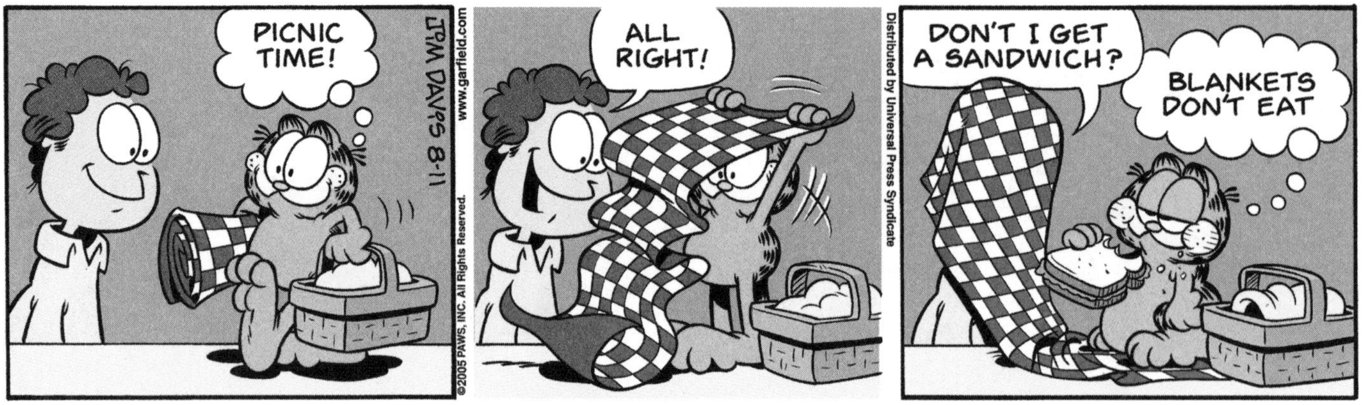
PICNIC TIME!
JIM DAVIS 8-11
www.garfield.com
©2005 PAWS, INC. All Rights Reserved.
ALL RIGHT!
Distributed by Universal Press Syndicate
DON'T I GET A SANDWICH?
BLANKETS DON'T EAT

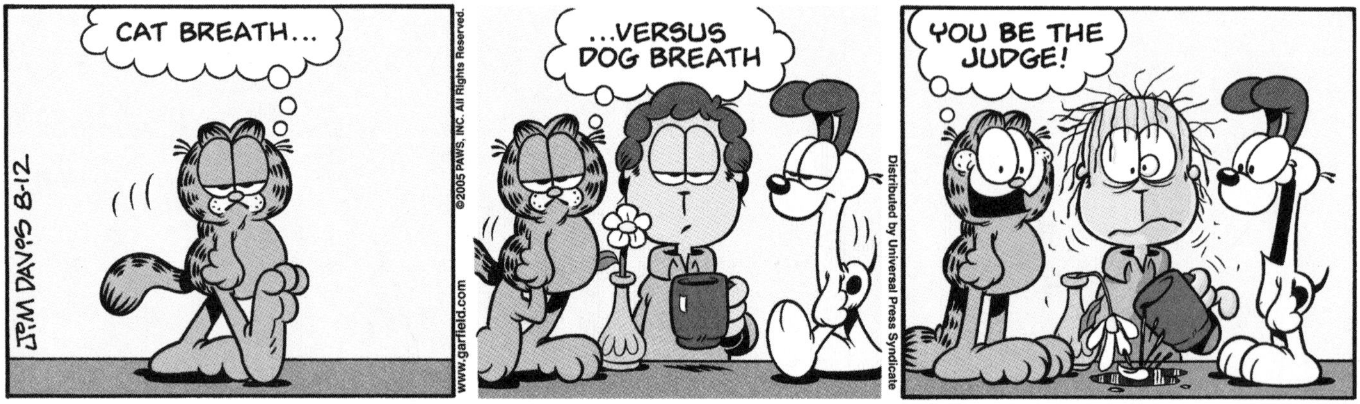
CAT BREATH...
JIM DAVIS 8-12
©2005 PAWS, INC. All Rights Reserved.
www.garfield.com
...VERSUS DOG BREATH
Distributed by Universal Press Syndicate
YOU BE THE JUDGE!

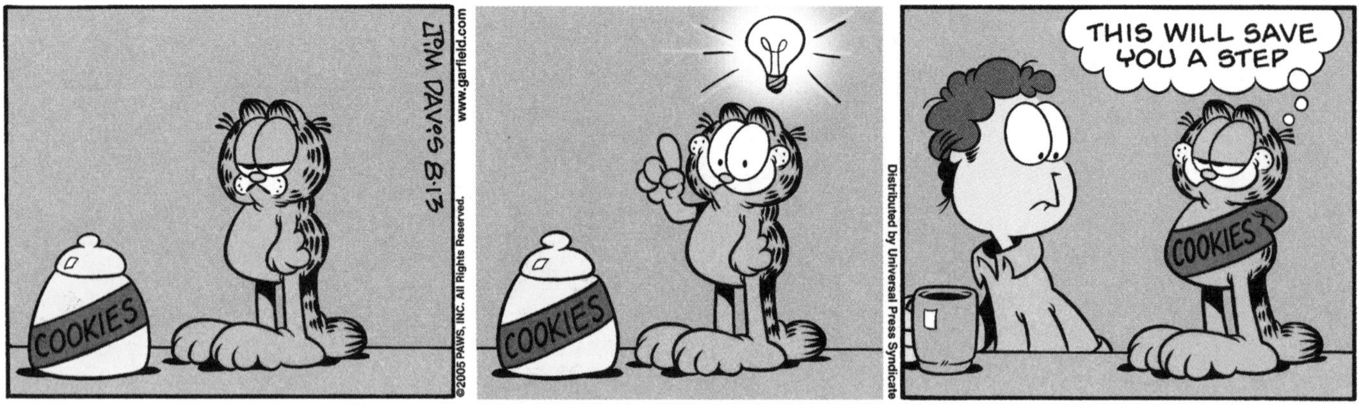
COOKIES
JIM DAVIS 8-13
www.garfield.com
©2005 PAWS, INC. All Rights Reserved.
COOKIES
Distributed by Universal Press Syndicate
THIS WILL SAVE YOU A STEP
COOKIES

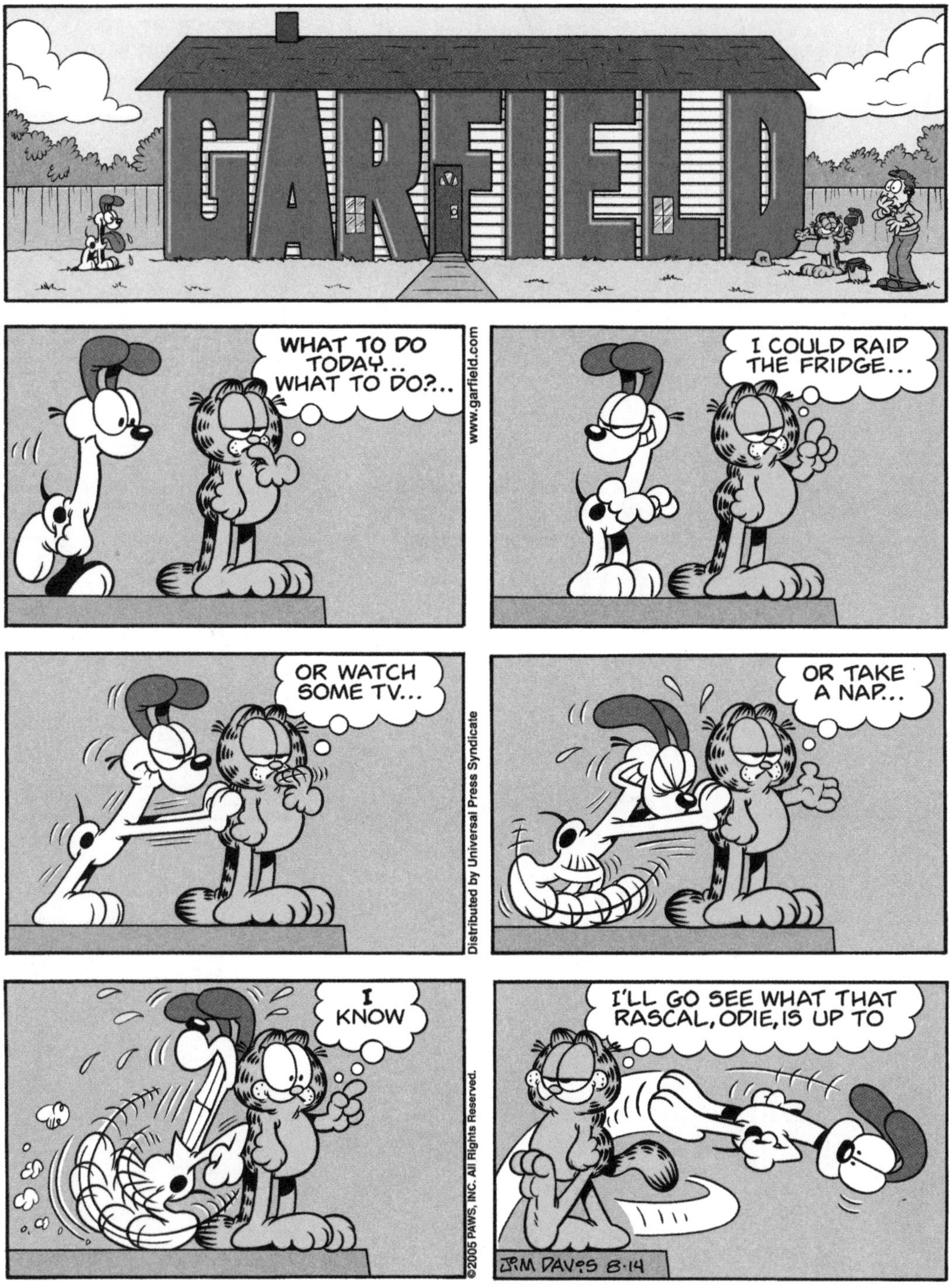
GARFIELD
WHAT TO DO TODAY... WHAT TO DO?...
I COULD RAID THE FRIDGE...
OR WATCH SOME TV...
OR TAKE A NAP...
I KNOW
I'LL GO SEE WHAT THAT RASCAL, ODIE, IS UP TO
JIM DAVIS 8-14
www.garfield.com
Distributed by Universal Press Syndicate
©2005 PAWS, INC. All Rights Reserved.

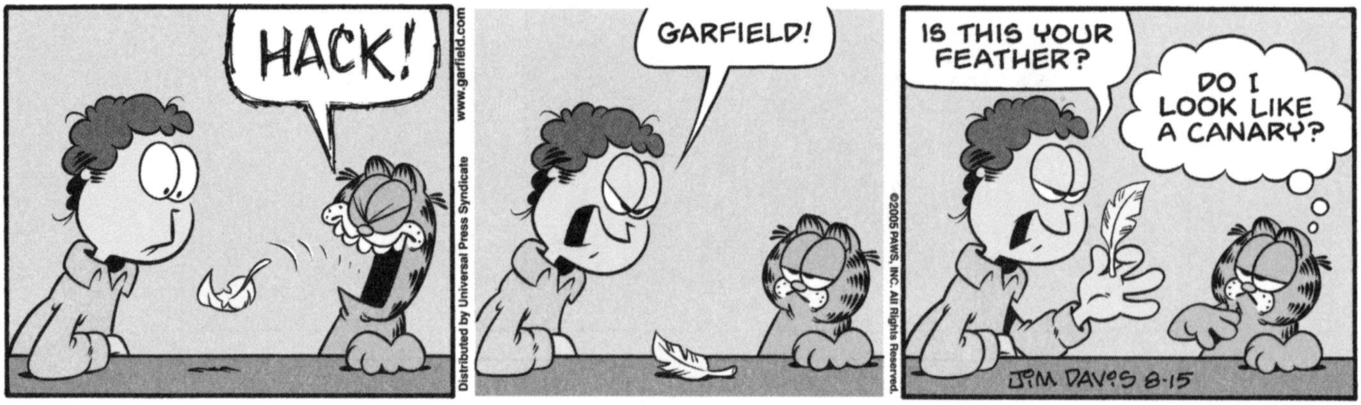
HACK!
GARFIELD!
IS THIS YOUR FEATHER?
DO I LOOK LIKE A CANARY?
JIM DAVIS 8-15
www.garfield.com Distributed by Universal Press Syndicate
©2005 PAWS, INC. All Rights Reserved.

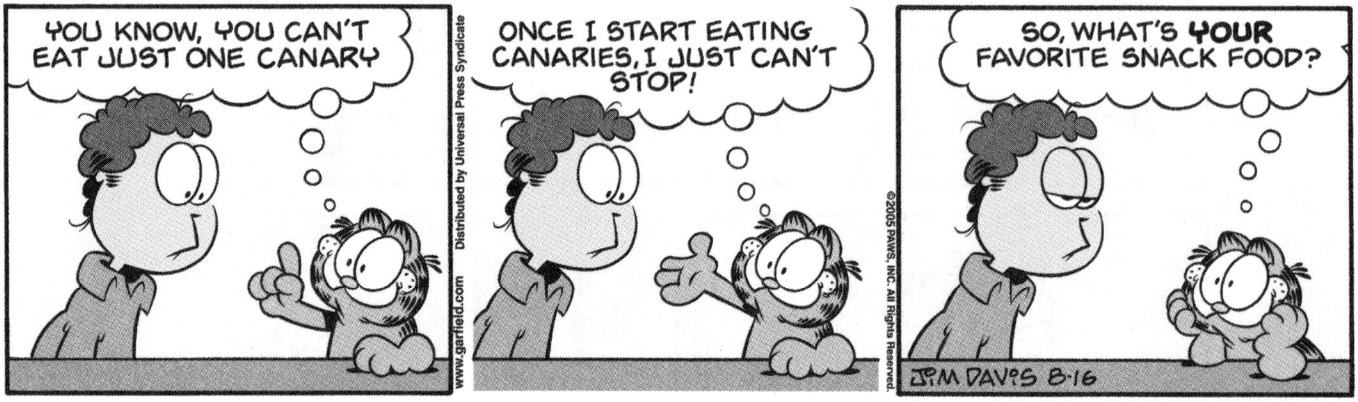
YOU KNOW, YOU CAN'T EAT JUST ONE CANARY
ONCE I START EATING CANARIES, I JUST CAN'T STOP!
SO, WHAT'S **YOUR** FAVORITE SNACK FOOD?
JIM DAVIS 8-16
Distributed by Universal Press Syndicate www.garfield.com
©2005 PAWS, INC. All Rights Reserved.

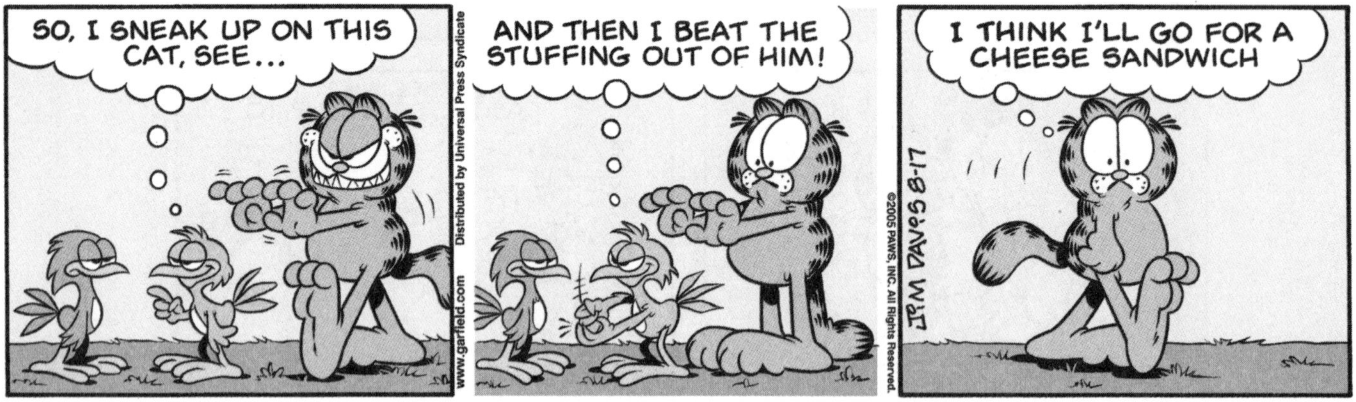
SO, I SNEAK UP ON THIS CAT, SEE...
AND THEN I BEAT THE STUFFING OUT OF HIM!
I THINK I'LL GO FOR A CHEESE SANDWICH
JIM DAVIS 8-17
Distributed by Universal Press Syndicate www.garfield.com
©2005 PAWS, INC. All Rights Reserved.

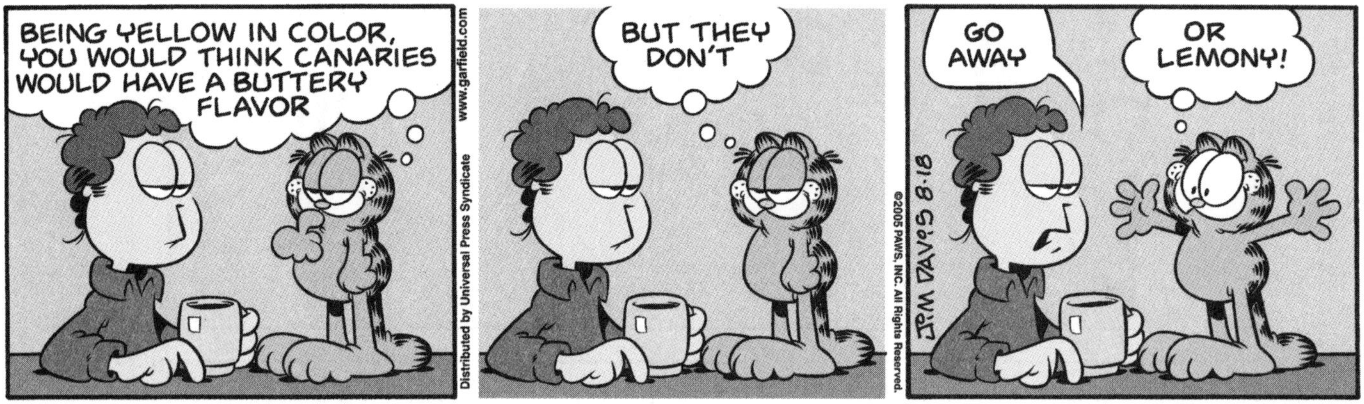
BEING YELLOW IN COLOR, YOU WOULD THINK CANARIES WOULD HAVE A BUTTERY FLAVOR
www.garfield.com
Distributed by Universal Press Syndicate
BUT THEY DON'T
©2005 PAWS, INC. All Rights Reserved.
GO AWAY
OR LEMONY!
JPM DAVIS 8-18

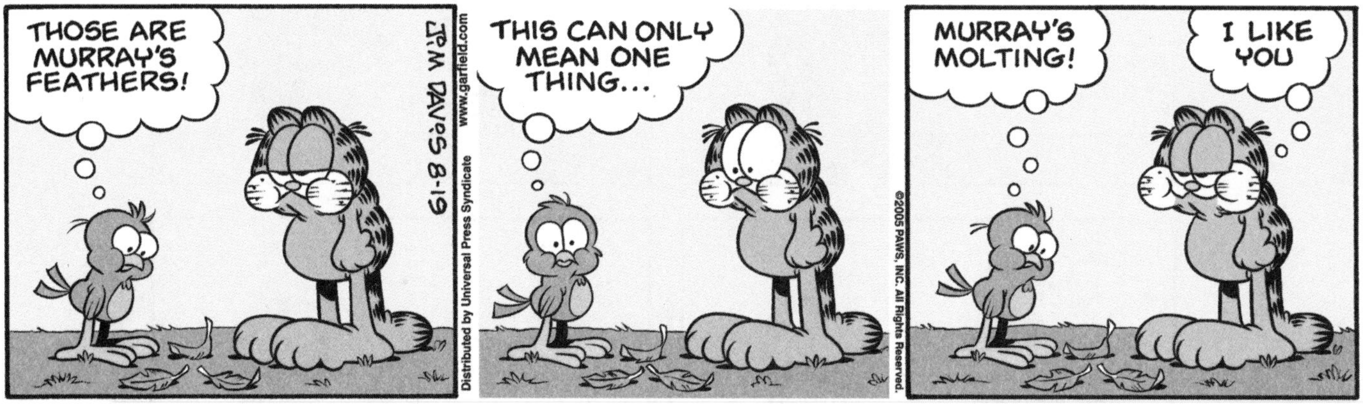
THOSE ARE MURRAY'S FEATHERS!
JPM DAVIS 8-19
www.garfield.com
Distributed by Universal Press Syndicate
THIS CAN ONLY MEAN ONE THING...
©2005 PAWS, INC. All Rights Reserved.
MURRAY'S MOLTING!
I LIKE YOU

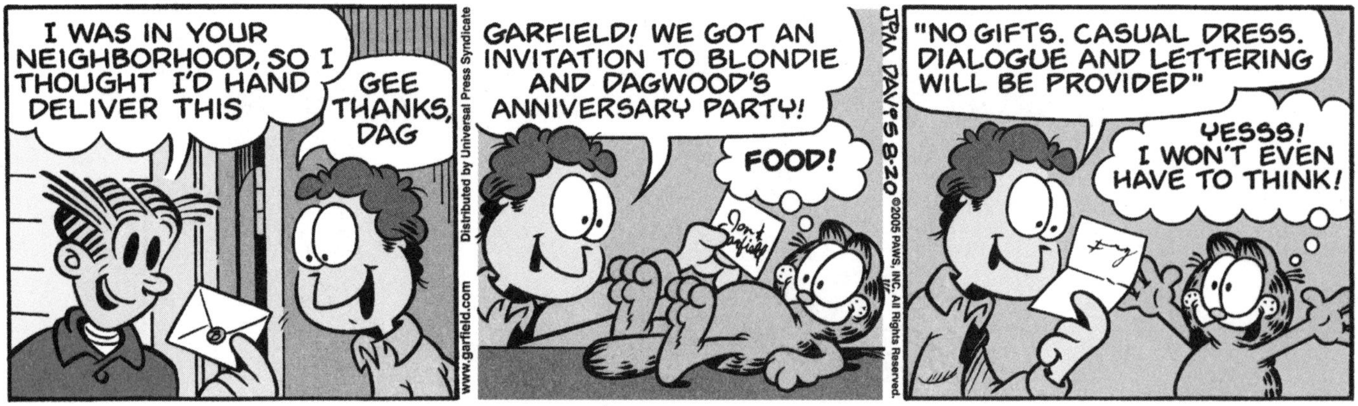
I WAS IN YOUR NEIGHBORHOOD, SO I THOUGHT I'D HAND DELIVER THIS
GEE THANKS, DAG
Distributed by Universal Press Syndicate
www.garfield.com
GARFIELD! WE GOT AN INVITATION TO BLONDIE AND DAGWOOD'S ANNIVERSARY PARTY!
FOOD!
JPM DAVIS 8-20
©2005 PAWS, INC. All Rights Reserved.
"NO GIFTS. CASUAL DRESS. DIALOGUE AND LETTERING WILL BE PROVIDED"
YESSS! I WON'T EVEN HAVE TO THINK!

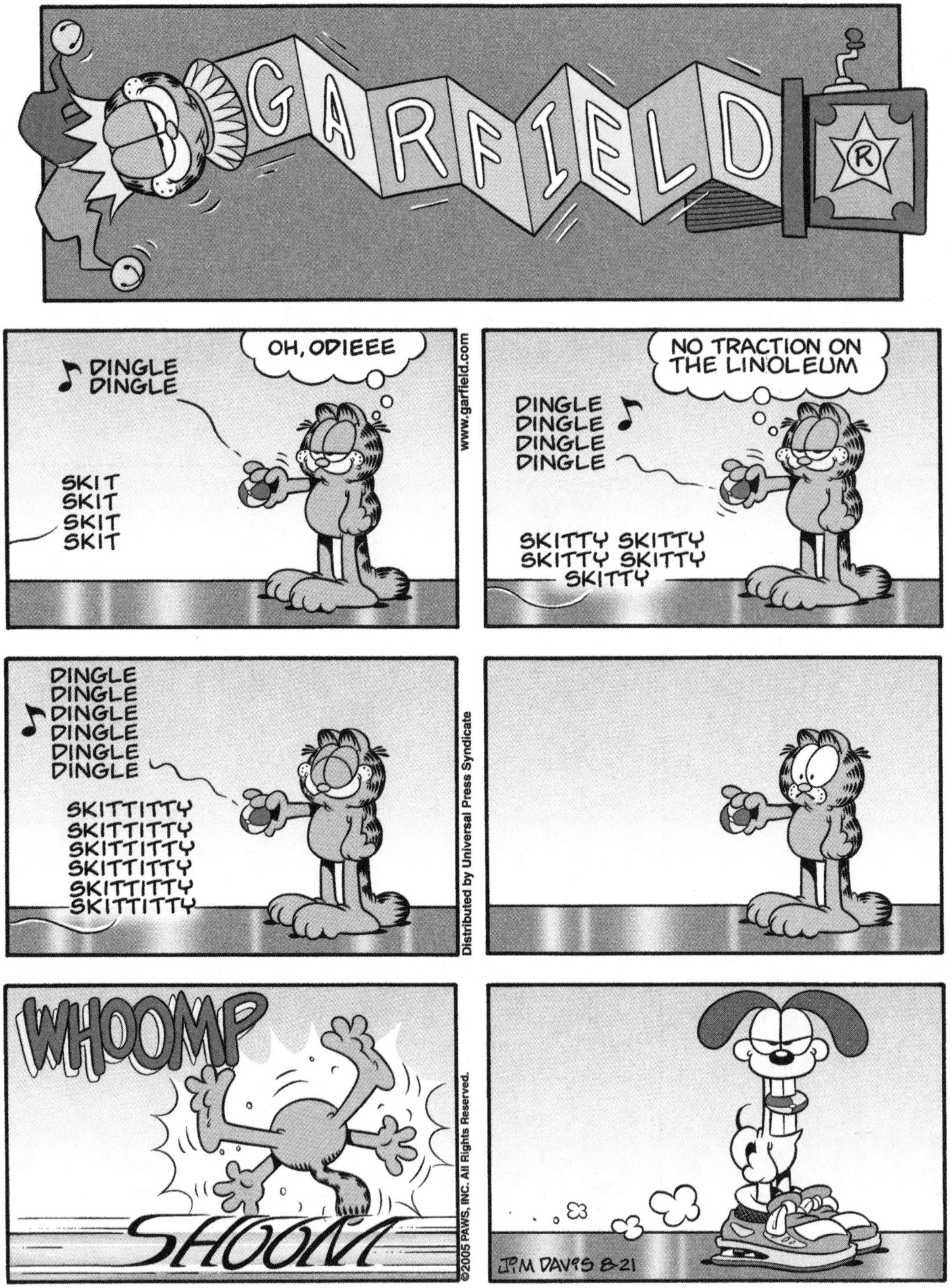
GARFIELD
DINGLE DINGLE
OH, ODIEEE
SKIT SKIT SKIT SKIT
www.garfield.com
DINGLE DINGLE DINGLE DINGLE
NO TRACTION ON THE LINOLEUM
SKITTY SKITTY SKITTY SKITTY SKITTY
DINGLE DINGLE DINGLE DINGLE DINGLE DINGLE
SKITTITTY SKITTITTY SKITTITTY SKITTITTY SKITTITTY SKITTITTY
Distributed by Universal Press Syndicate
WHOOMP
SHOOM
©2005 PAWS, INC. All Rights Reserved.
JIM DAVIS 8-21

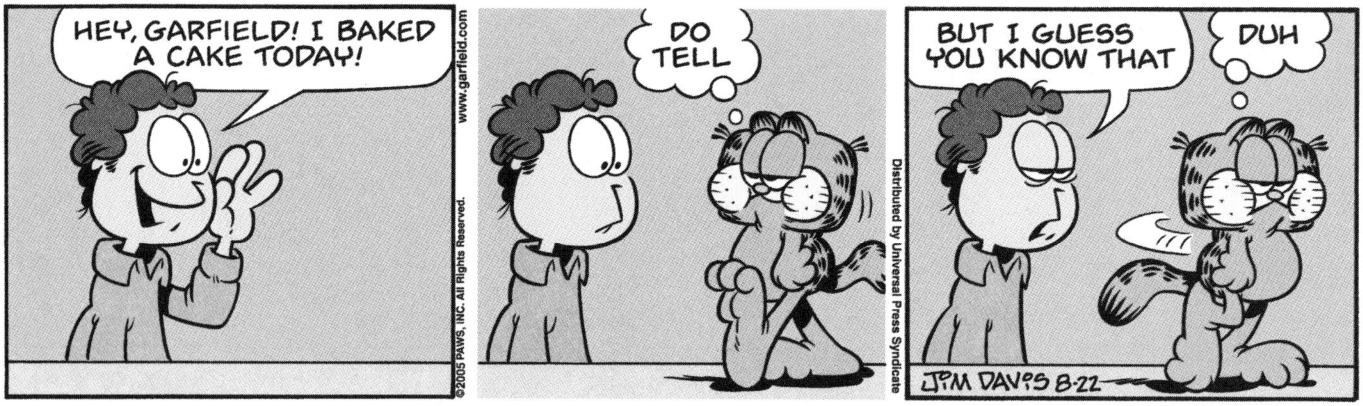
HEY, GARFIELD! I BAKED A CAKE TODAY!
DO TELL
BUT I GUESS YOU KNOW THAT
DUH
©2005 PAWS, INC. All Rights Reserved.
www.garfield.com
Distributed by Universal Press Syndicate

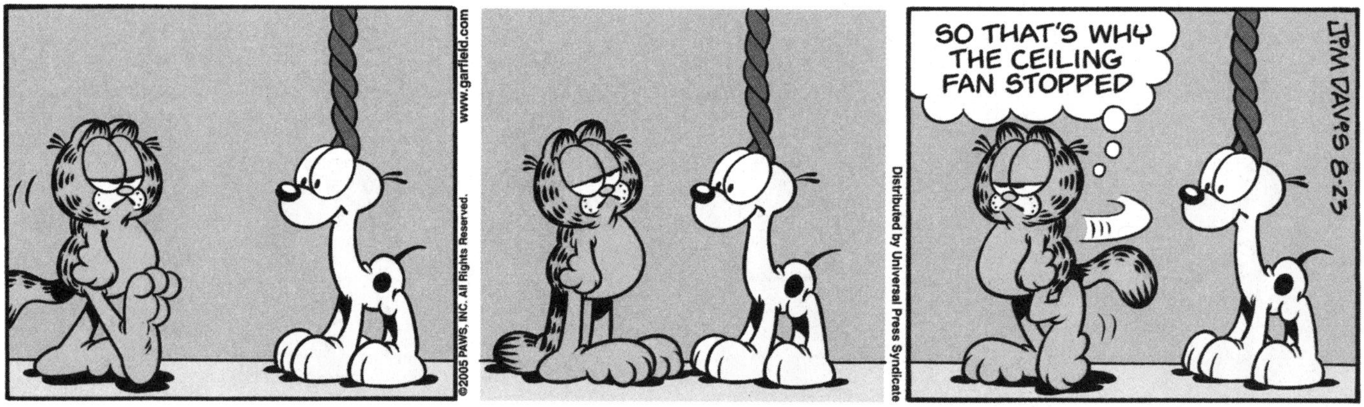
SO THAT'S WHY THE CEILING FAN STOPPED
©2005 PAWS, INC. All Rights Reserved.
www.garfield.com
Distributed by Universal Press Syndicate

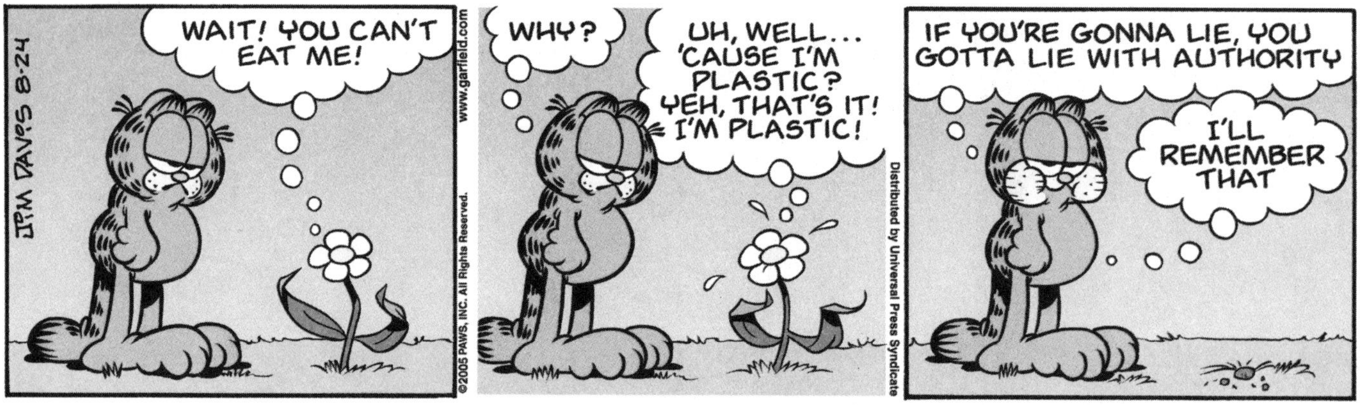
WAIT! YOU CAN'T EAT ME!
WHY?
UH, WELL... 'CAUSE I'M PLASTIC? YEH, THAT'S IT! I'M PLASTIC!
IF YOU'RE GONNA LIE, YOU GOTTA LIE WITH AUTHORITY
I'LL REMEMBER THAT
©2005 PAWS, INC. All Rights Reserved.
www.garfield.com
Distributed by Universal Press Syndicate

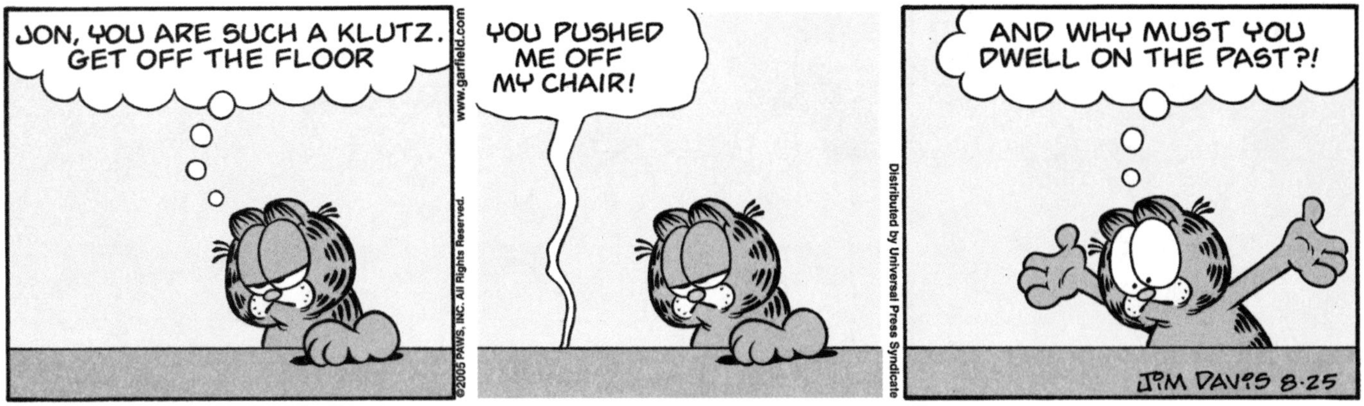
JON, YOU ARE SUCH A KLUTZ. GET OFF THE FLOOR
©2005 PAWS, INC. All Rights Reserved. www.garfield.com
YOU PUSHED ME OFF MY CHAIR!
Distributed by Universal Press Syndicate
AND WHY MUST YOU DWELL ON THE PAST?!
JIM DAVIS 8-25

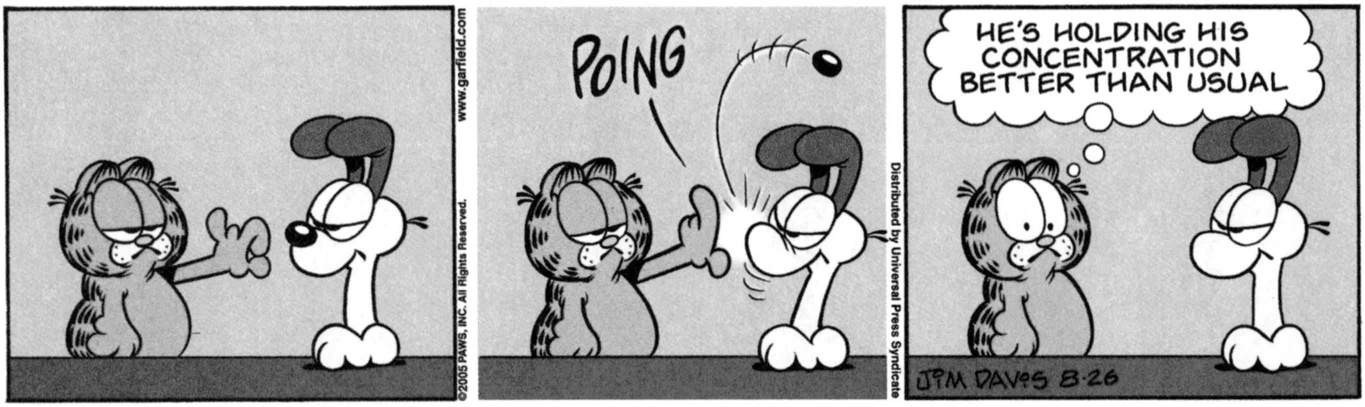
©2005 PAWS, INC. All Rights Reserved. www.garfield.com
POING
Distributed by Universal Press Syndicate
HE'S HOLDING HIS CONCENTRATION BETTER THAN USUAL
JIM DAVIS 8-26

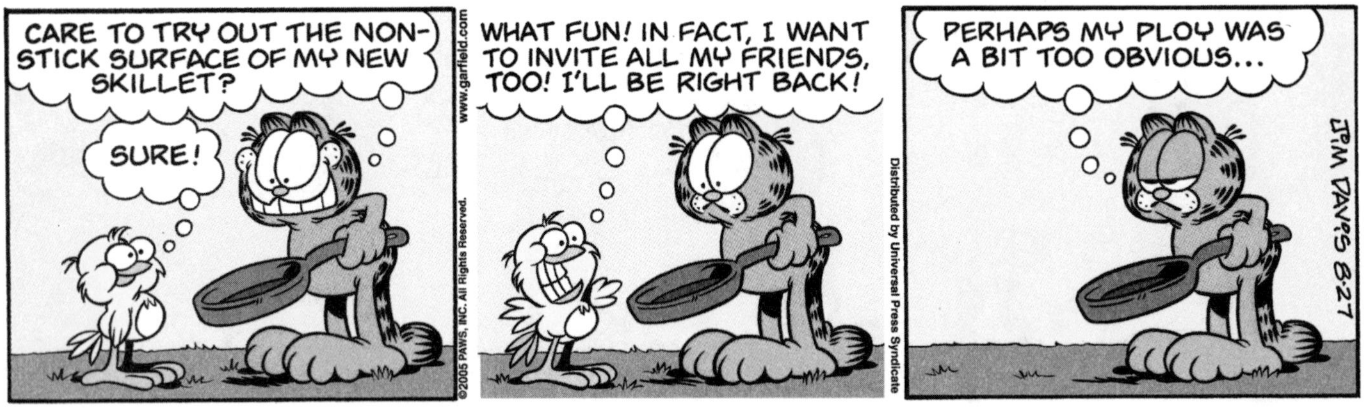
CARE TO TRY OUT THE NON-STICK SURFACE OF MY NEW SKILLET?
SURE!
©2005 PAWS, INC. All Rights Reserved. www.garfield.com
WHAT FUN! IN FACT, I WANT TO INVITE ALL MY FRIENDS, TOO! I'LL BE RIGHT BACK!
Distributed by Universal Press Syndicate
PERHAPS MY PLOY WAS A BIT TOO OBVIOUS...
JIM DAVIS 8-27

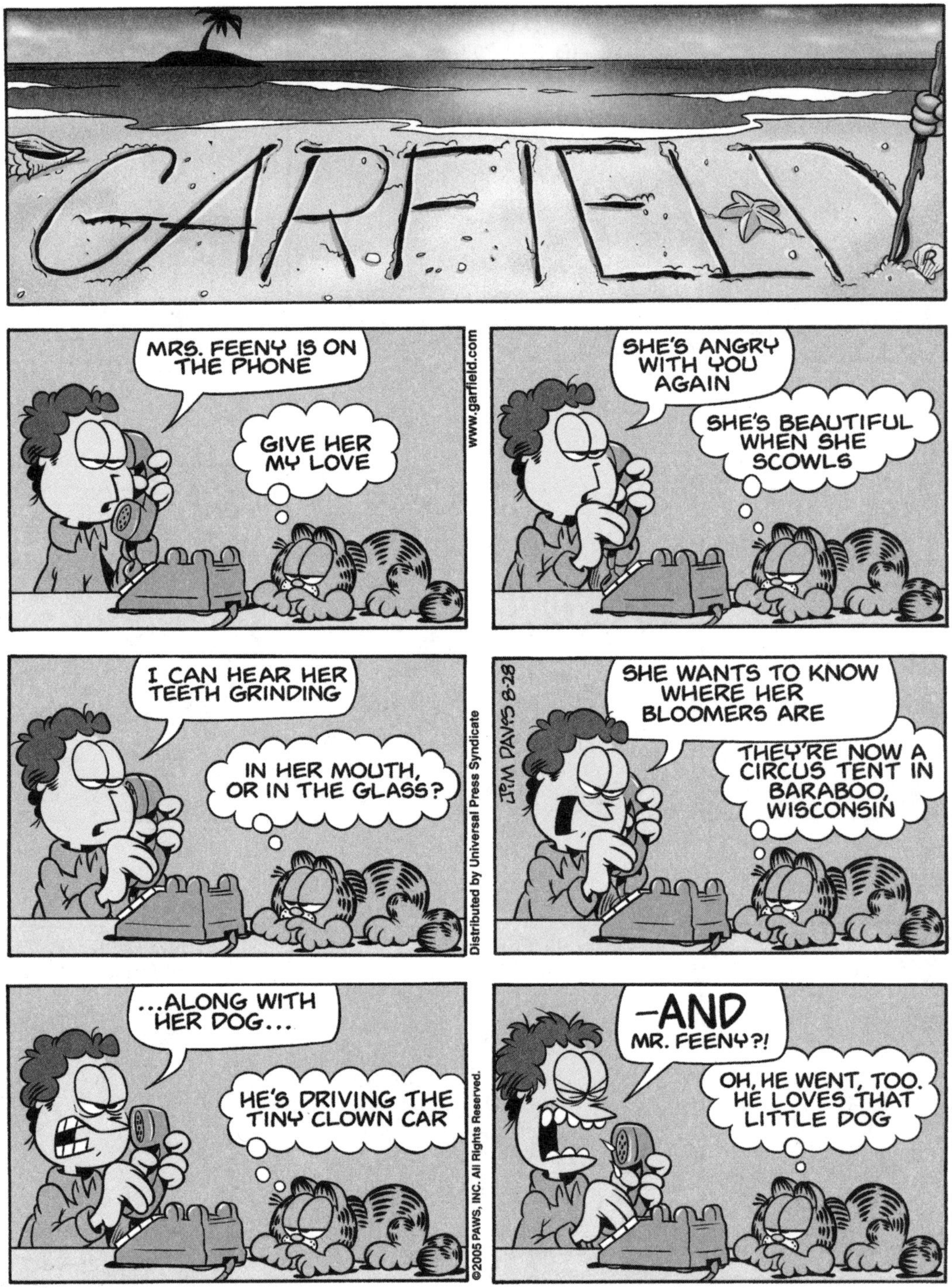
GARFIELD
MRS. FEENY IS ON THE PHONE
GIVE HER MY LOVE
www.garfield.com
SHE'S ANGRY WITH YOU AGAIN
SHE'S BEAUTIFUL WHEN SHE SCOWLS
I CAN HEAR HER TEETH GRINDING
IN HER MOUTH, OR IN THE GLASS?
Distributed by Universal Press Syndicate
JPM DAVPS 8-28
SHE WANTS TO KNOW WHERE HER BLOOMERS ARE
THEY'RE NOW A CIRCUS TENT IN BARABOO, WISCONSIN
...ALONG WITH HER DOG...
HE'S DRIVING THE TINY CLOWN CAR
©2005 PAWS, INC. All Rights Reserved.
–AND MR. FEENY?!
OH, HE WENT, TOO. HE LOVES THAT LITTLE DOG

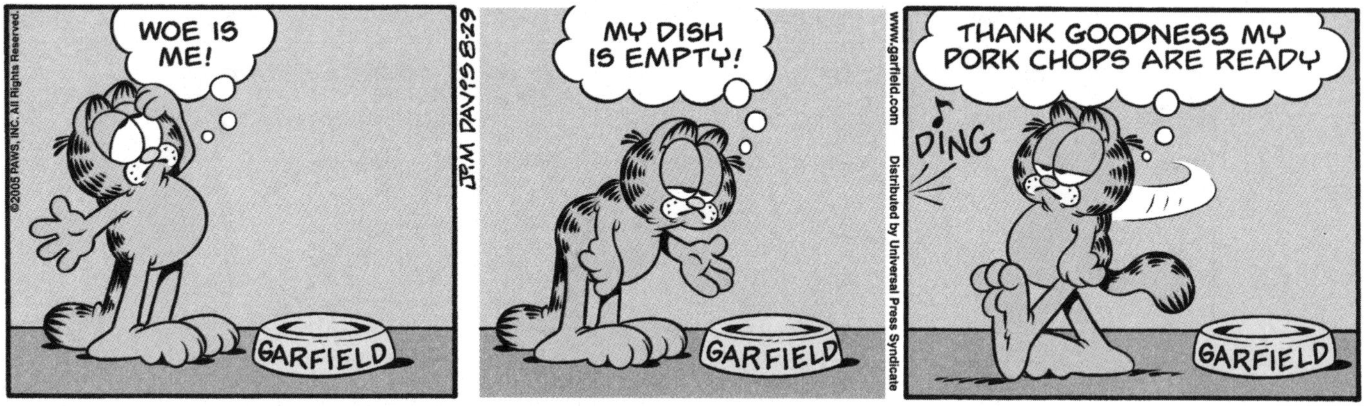
WOE IS ME!
MY DISH IS EMPTY!
THANK GOODNESS MY PORK CHOPS ARE READY
DING
GARFIELD
JPM DAVIS 8-29
©2005 PAWS, INC. All Rights Reserved.
www.garfield.com Distributed by Universal Press Syndicate

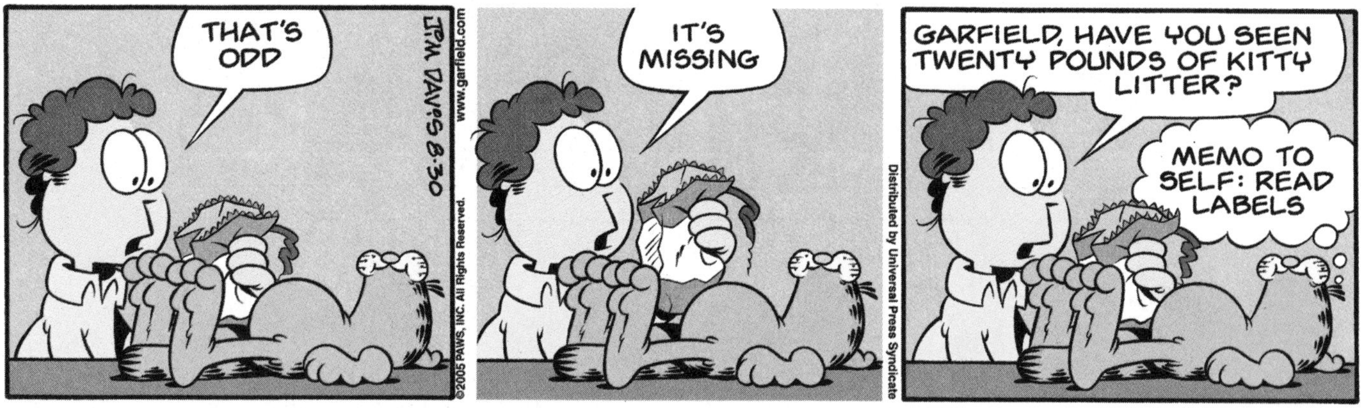
THAT'S ODD
IT'S MISSING
GARFIELD, HAVE YOU SEEN TWENTY POUNDS OF KITTY LITTER?
MEMO TO SELF: READ LABELS
JPM DAVIS 8-30
©2005 PAWS, INC. All Rights Reserved. www.garfield.com
Distributed by Universal Press Syndicate

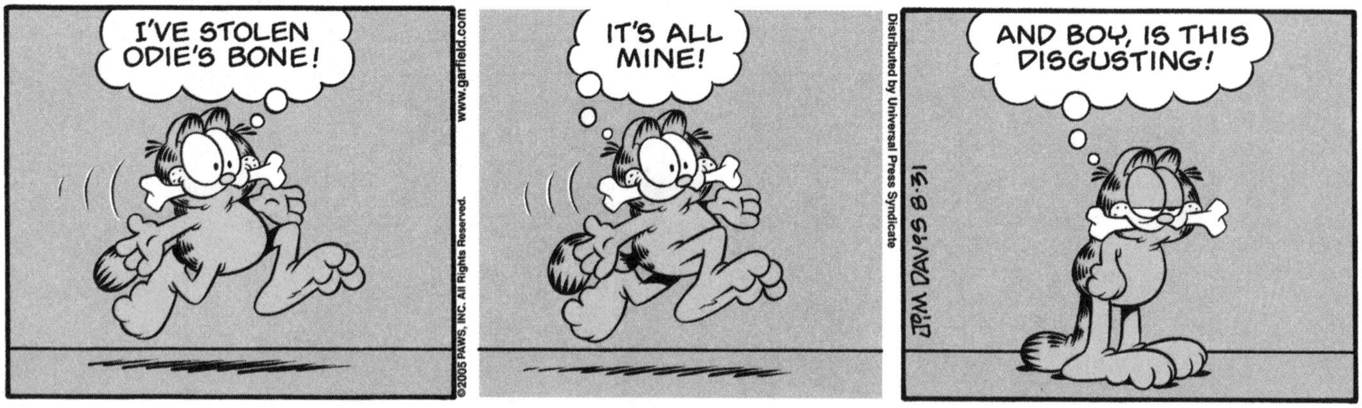
I'VE STOLEN ODIE'S BONE!
IT'S ALL MINE!
AND BOY, IS THIS DISGUSTING!
JPM DAVIS 8-31
©2005 PAWS, INC. All Rights Reserved. www.garfield.com
Distributed by Universal Press Syndicate

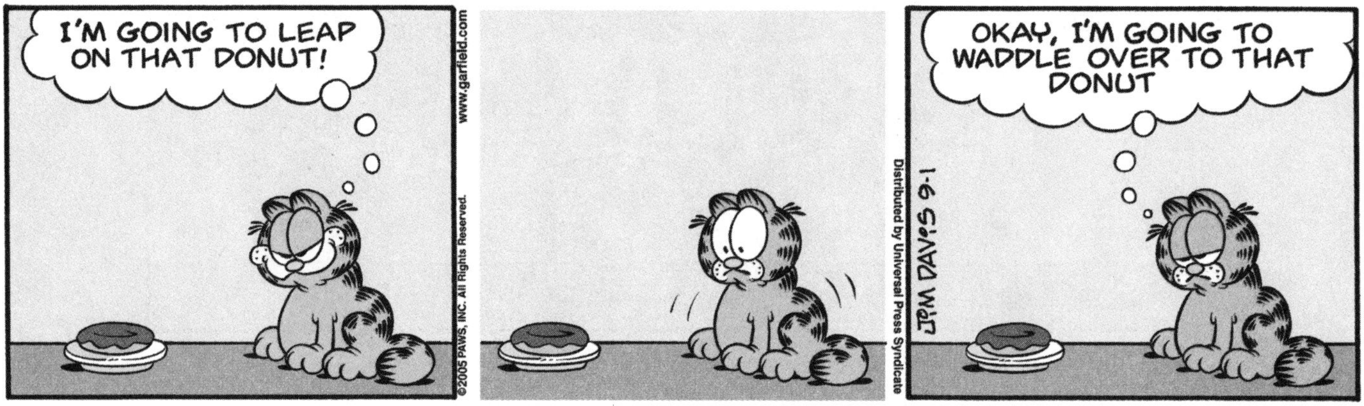
I'M GOING TO LEAP ON THAT DONUT!
OKAY, I'M GOING TO WADDLE OVER TO THAT DONUT
JPM DAVPS 9-1
©2005 PAWS, INC. All Rights Reserved. www.garfield.com
Distributed by Universal Press Syndicate

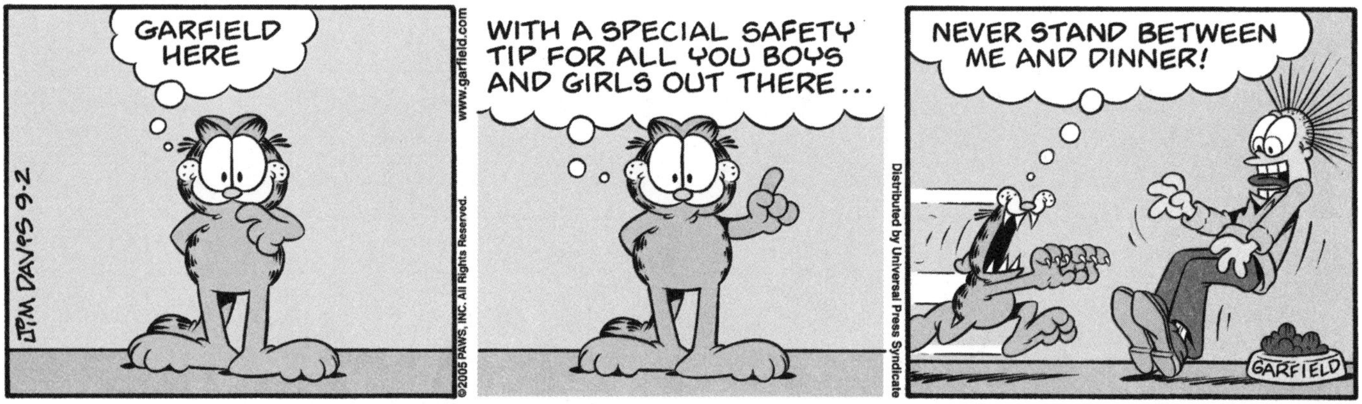
GARFIELD HERE
WITH A SPECIAL SAFETY TIP FOR ALL YOU BOYS AND GIRLS OUT THERE...
NEVER STAND BETWEEN ME AND DINNER!
GARFIELD
JPM DAVPS 9-2
©2005 PAWS, INC. All Rights Reserved. www.garfield.com
Distributed by Universal Press Syndicate

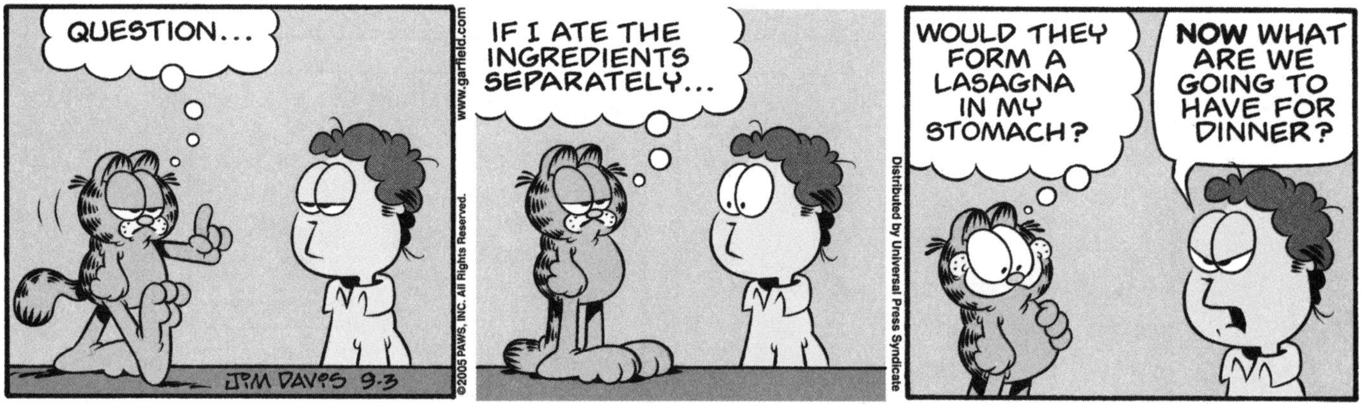
QUESTION...
IF I ATE THE INGREDIENTS SEPARATELY...
WOULD THEY FORM A LASAGNA IN MY STOMACH?
NOW WHAT ARE WE GOING TO HAVE FOR DINNER?
JPM DAVPS 9-3
©2005 PAWS, INC. All Rights Reserved. www.garfield.com
Distributed by Universal Press Syndicate

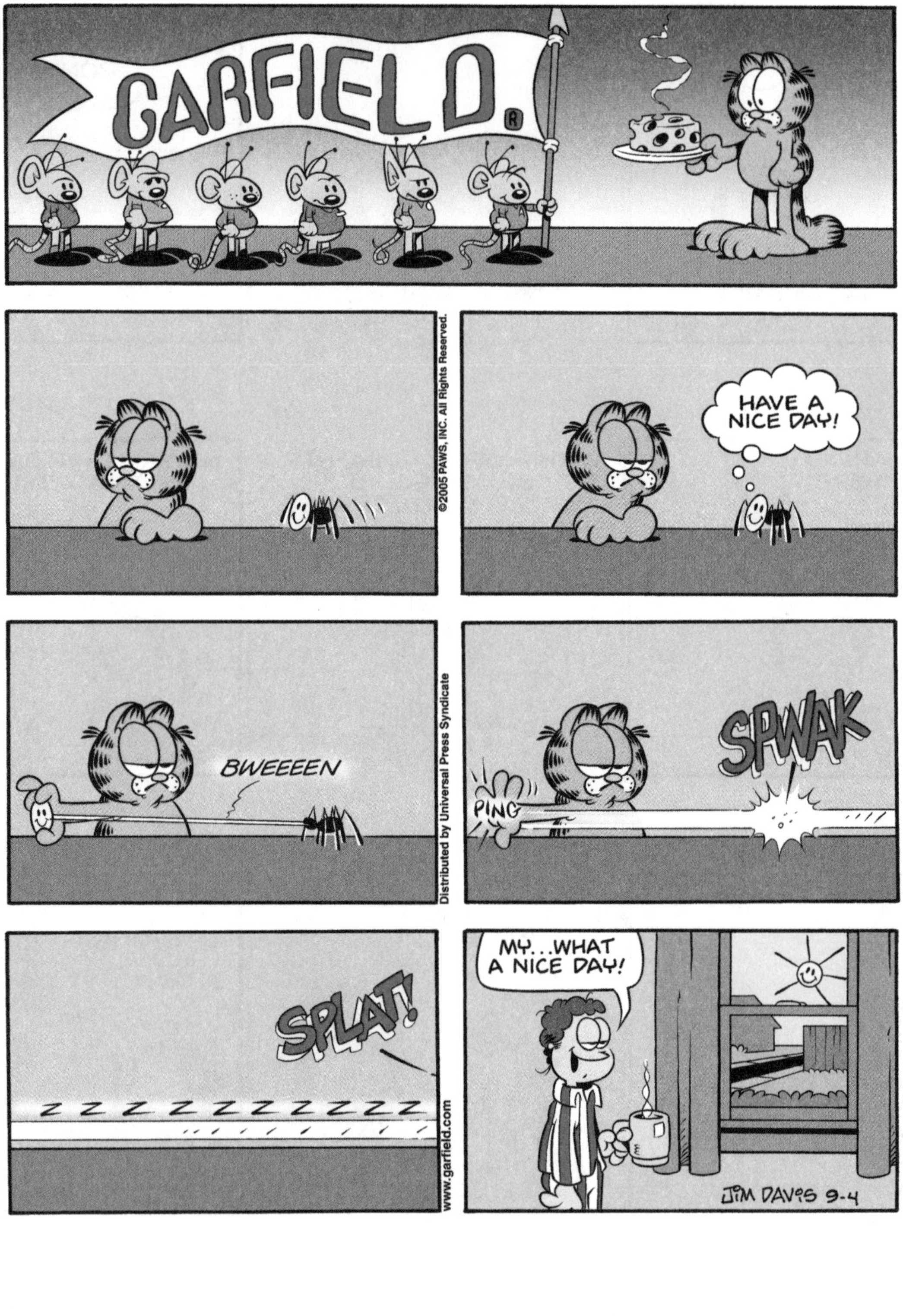
GARFIELD
©2005 PAWS, INC. All Rights Reserved.
HAVE A NICE DAY!
Distributed by Universal Press Syndicate
BWEEEEN
PING
SPWAK
SPLAT!
Z Z Z Z Z Z Z Z Z Z Z Z Z Z
www.garfield.com
MY...WHAT A NICE DAY!
JIM DAVIS 9-4

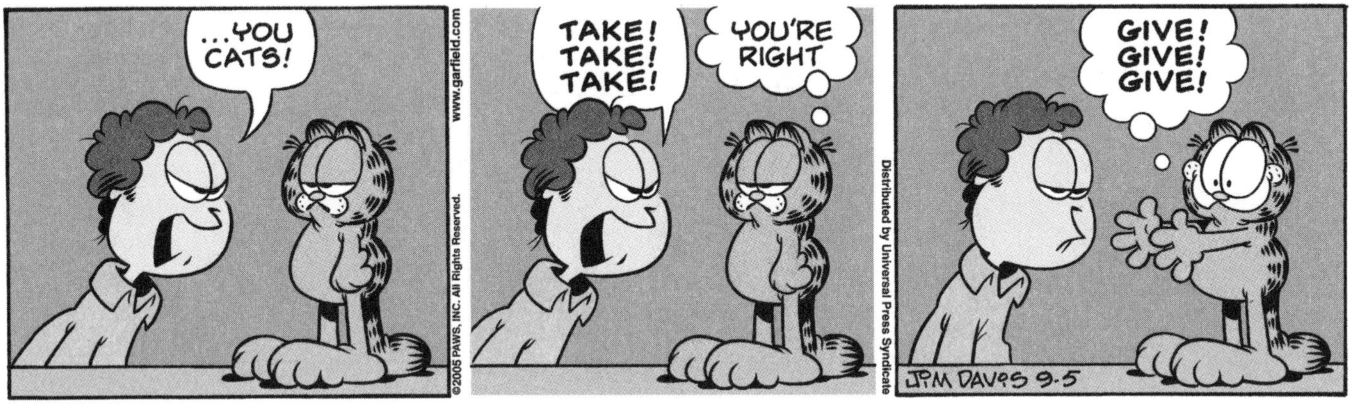
...YOU CATS!
TAKE! TAKE! TAKE!
YOU'RE RIGHT
GIVE! GIVE! GIVE!
©2005 PAWS, INC. All Rights Reserved. www.garfield.com
Distributed by Universal Press Syndicate
JIM DAVIS 9-5

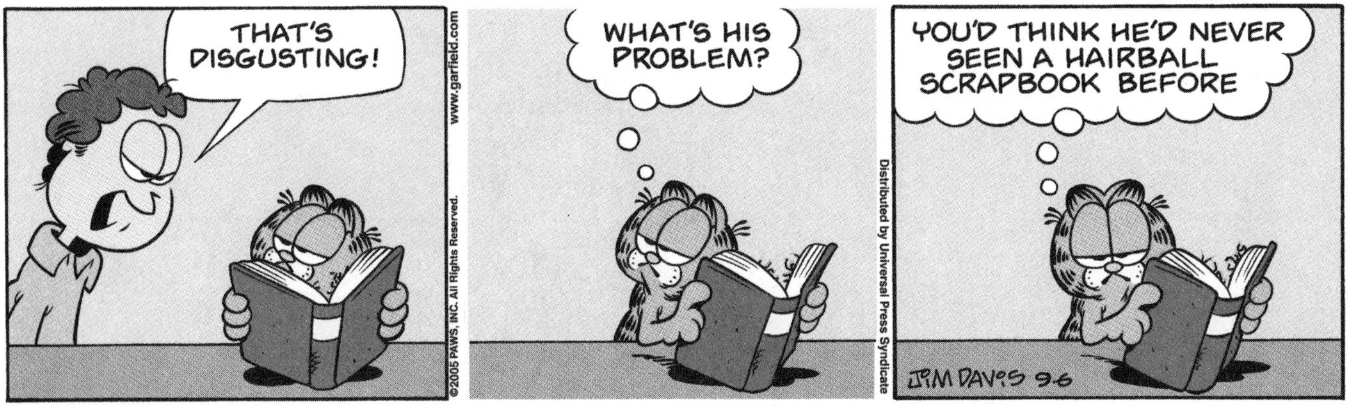
THAT'S DISGUSTING!
WHAT'S HIS PROBLEM?
YOU'D THINK HE'D NEVER SEEN A HAIRBALL SCRAPBOOK BEFORE
©2005 PAWS, INC. All Rights Reserved. www.garfield.com
Distributed by Universal Press Syndicate
JIM DAVIS 9-6

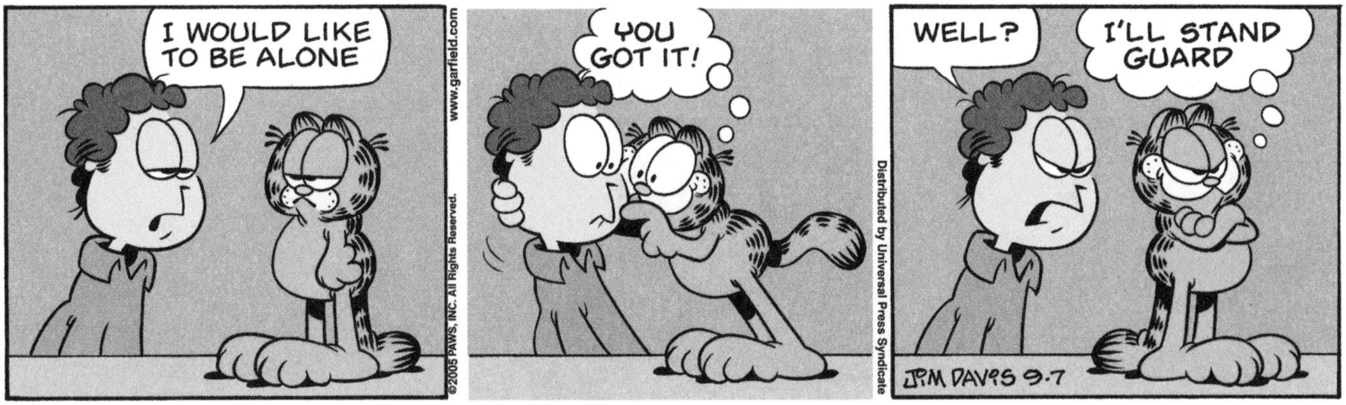
I WOULD LIKE TO BE ALONE
YOU GOT IT!
WELL?
I'LL STAND GUARD
©2005 PAWS, INC. All Rights Reserved. www.garfield.com
Distributed by Universal Press Syndicate
JIM DAVIS 9-7

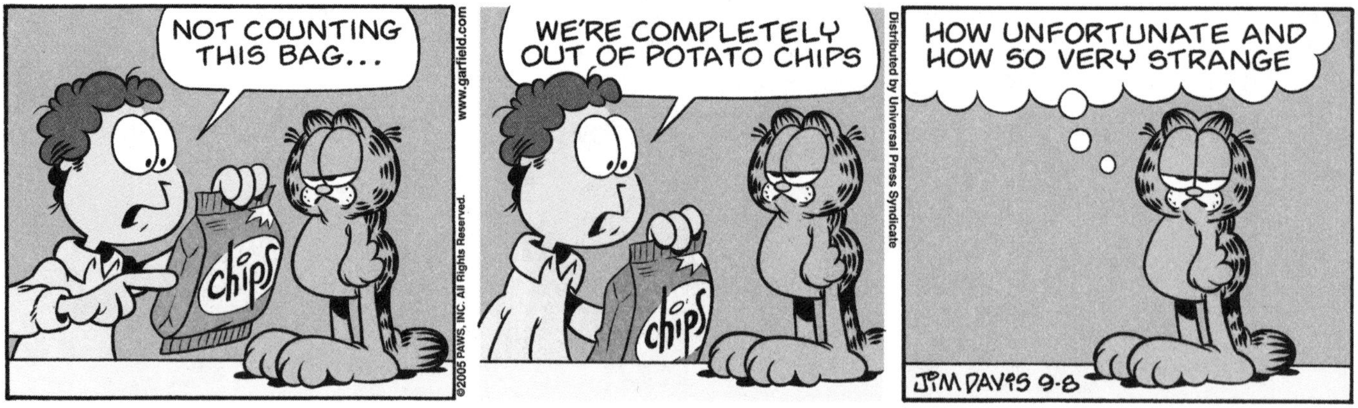
NOT COUNTING THIS BAG...
chips
©2005 PAWS, INC. All Rights Reserved. www.garfield.com
WE'RE COMPLETELY OUT OF POTATO CHIPS
chips
Distributed by Universal Press Syndicate
HOW UNFORTUNATE AND HOW SO VERY STRANGE
JIM DAVIS 9-8

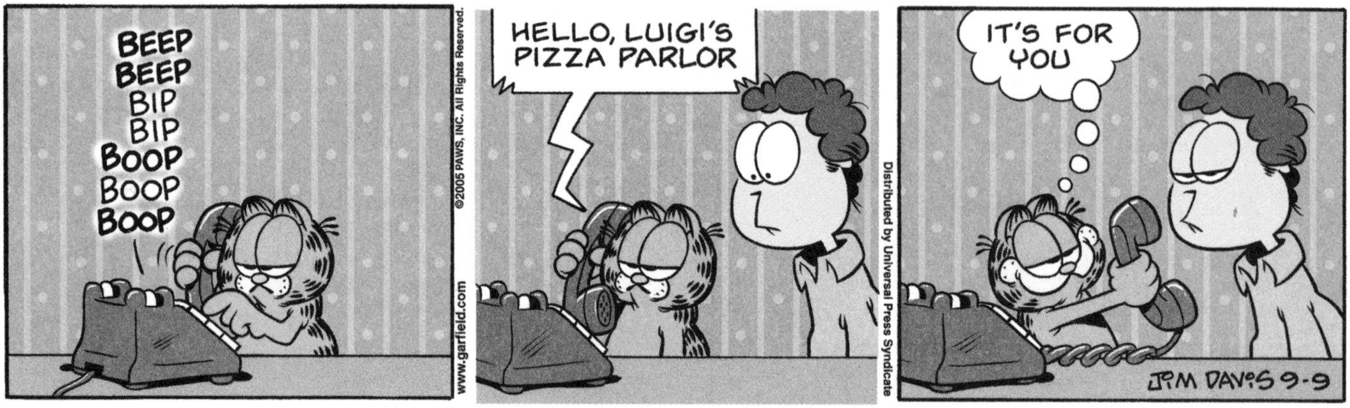
BEEP
BEEP
BIP
BIP
BOOP
BOOP
BOOP
www.garfield.com ©2005 PAWS, INC. All Rights Reserved.
HELLO, LUIGI'S PIZZA PARLOR
Distributed by Universal Press Syndicate
IT'S FOR YOU
JIM DAVIS 9-9

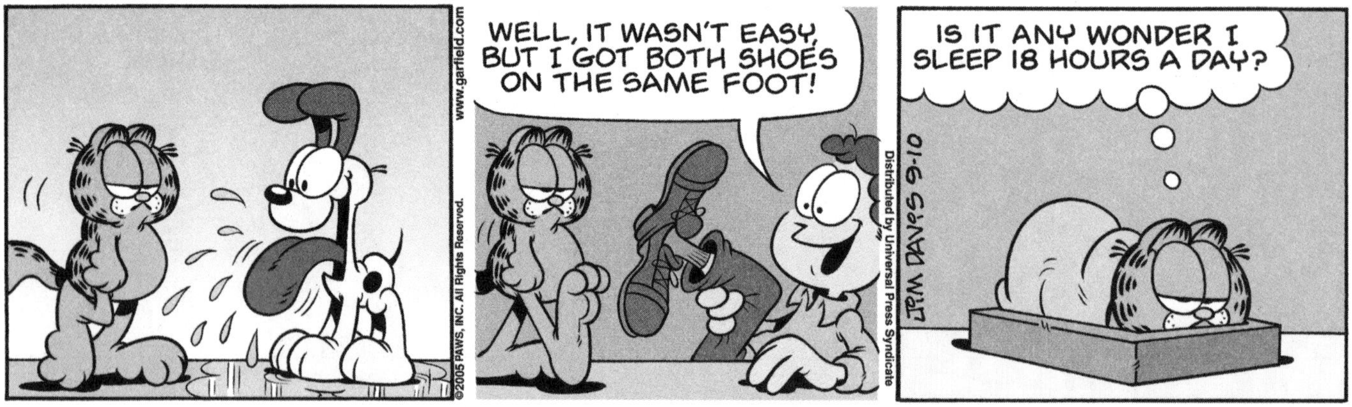
©2005 PAWS, INC. All Rights Reserved. www.garfield.com
WELL, IT WASN'T EASY, BUT I GOT BOTH SHOES ON THE SAME FOOT!
Distributed by Universal Press Syndicate
IS IT ANY WONDER I SLEEP 18 HOURS A DAY?
JIM DAVIS 9-10

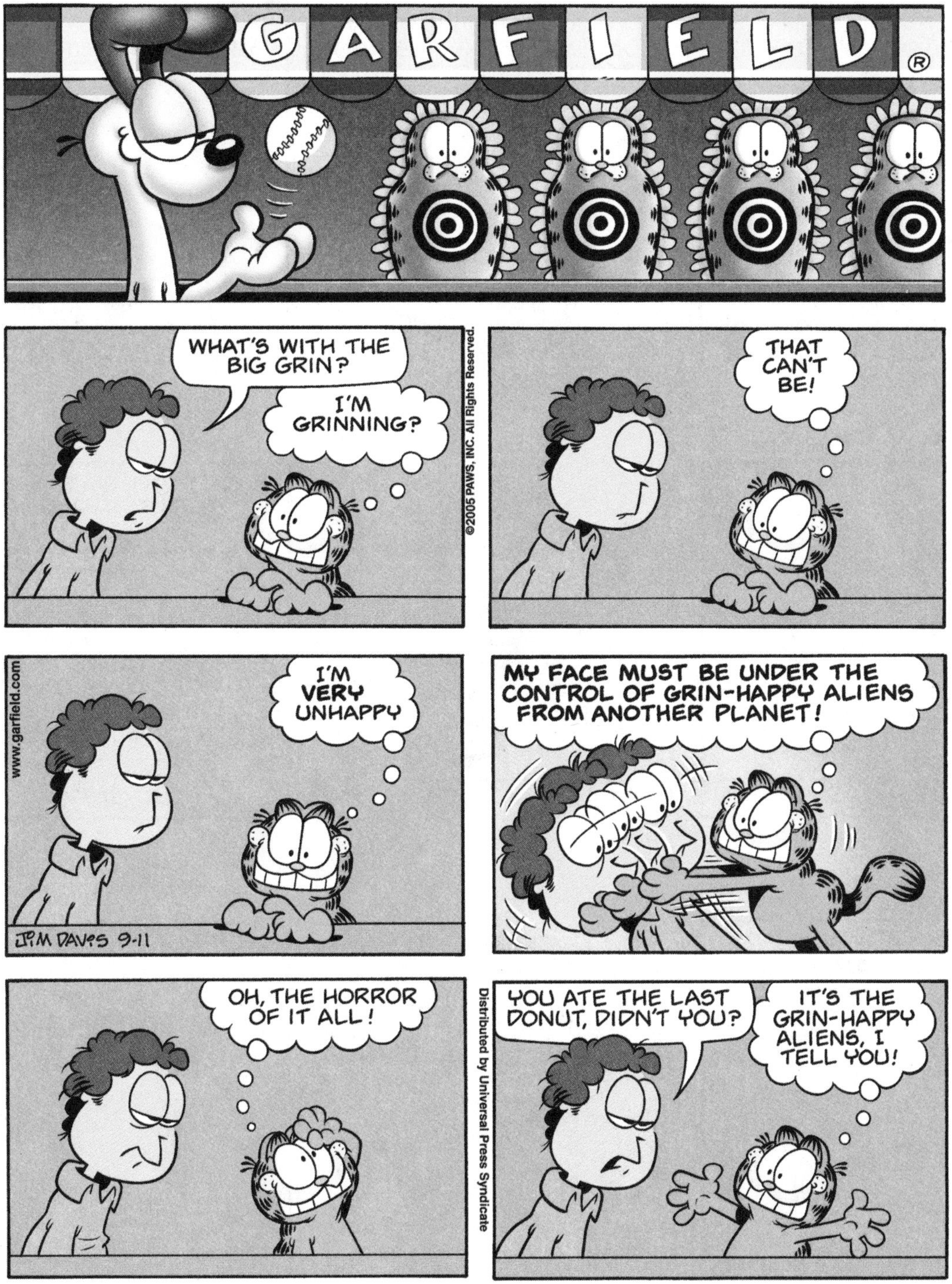

GARFIELD®
WHAT'S WITH THE BIG GRIN?
I'M GRINNING?
©2005 PAWS, INC. All Rights Reserved.
THAT CAN'T BE!
www.garfield.com
I'M VERY UNHAPPY
JIM DAVIS 9-11
MY FACE MUST BE UNDER THE CONTROL OF GRIN-HAPPY ALIENS FROM ANOTHER PLANET!
OH, THE HORROR OF IT ALL!
Distributed by Universal Press Syndicate
YOU ATE THE LAST DONUT, DIDN'T YOU?
IT'S THE GRIN-HAPPY ALIENS, I TELL YOU!

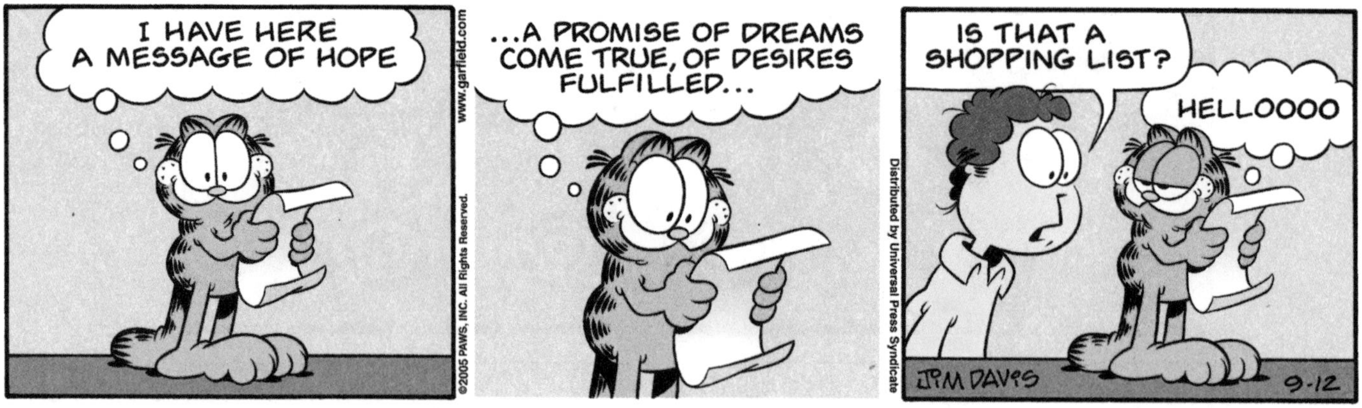
I HAVE HERE A MESSAGE OF HOPE
www.garfield.com
©2005 PAWS, INC. All Rights Reserved.
...A PROMISE OF DREAMS COME TRUE, OF DESIRES FULFILLED...
Distributed by Universal Press Syndicate
IS THAT A SHOPPING LIST?
HELLOOOO
JIM DAVIS 9-12

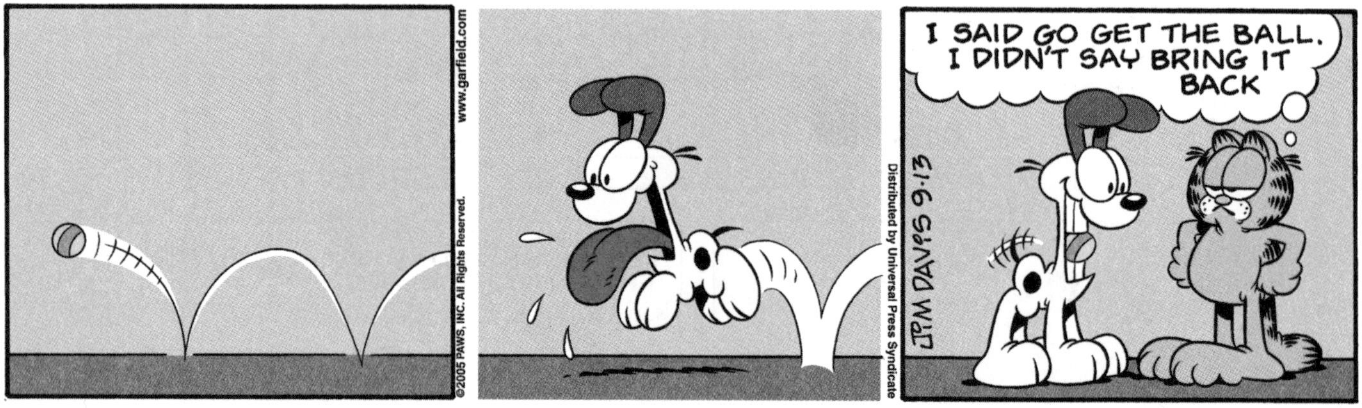
www.garfield.com
©2005 PAWS, INC. All Rights Reserved.
Distributed by Universal Press Syndicate
JIM DAVIS 9-13
I SAID GO GET THE BALL. I DIDN'T SAY BRING IT BACK

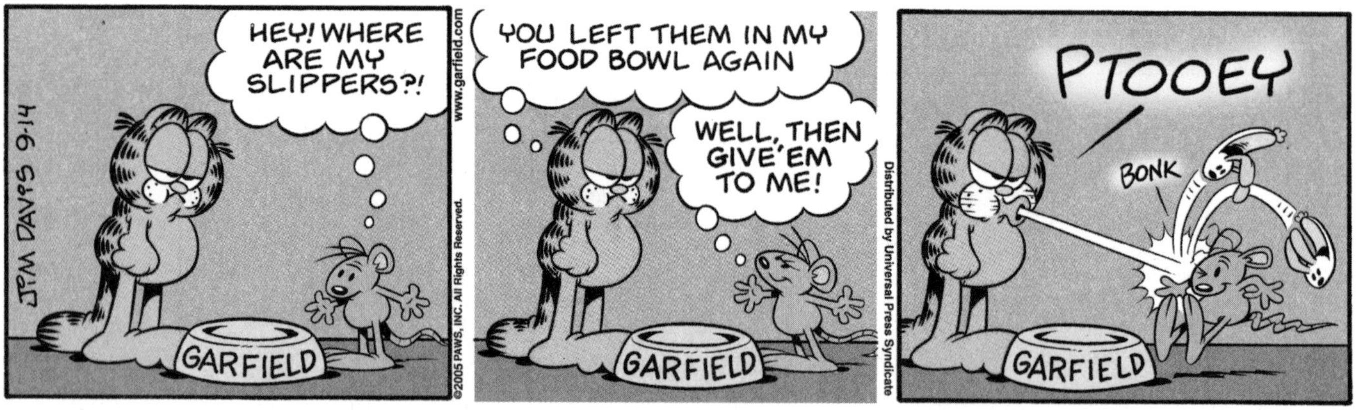
JIM DAVIS 9-14
HEY! WHERE ARE MY SLIPPERS?!
GARFIELD
www.garfield.com
©2005 PAWS, INC. All Rights Reserved.
YOU LEFT THEM IN MY FOOD BOWL AGAIN
WELL, THEN GIVE'EM TO ME!
GARFIELD
Distributed by Universal Press Syndicate
PTOOEY
BONK
GARFIELD

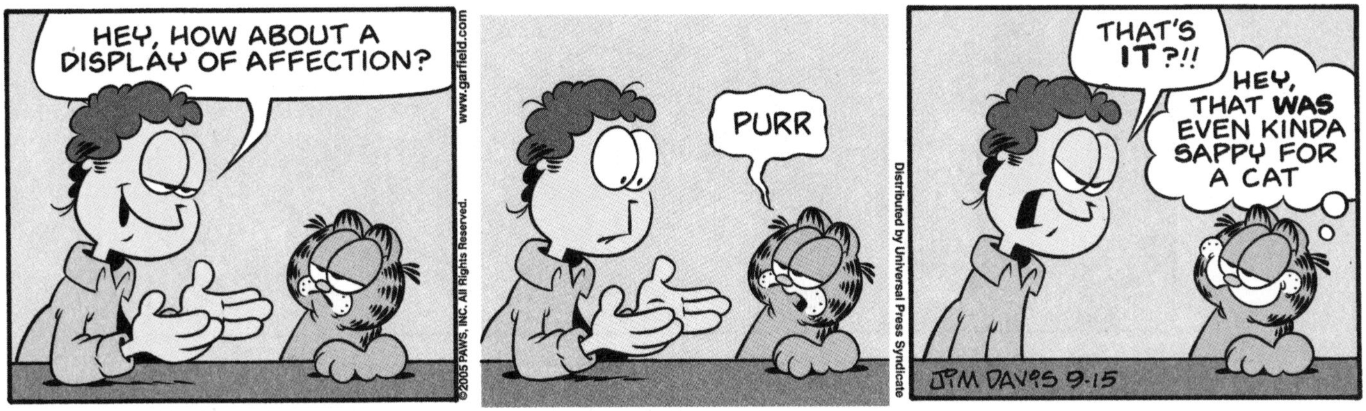
HEY, HOW ABOUT A DISPLAY OF AFFECTION?
PURR
THAT'S **IT**?!!
HEY, THAT **WAS** EVEN KINDA SAPPY FOR A CAT
JIM DAVIS 9-15
©2005 PAWS, INC. All Rights Reserved. www.garfield.com
Distributed by Universal Press Syndicate

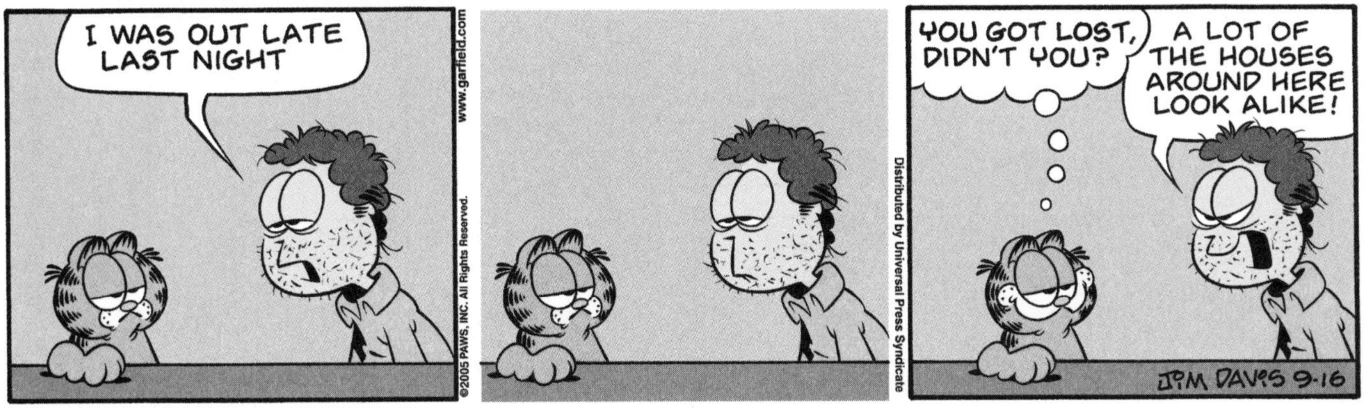
I WAS OUT LATE LAST NIGHT
YOU GOT LOST, DIDN'T YOU?
A LOT OF THE HOUSES AROUND HERE LOOK ALIKE!
JIM DAVIS 9-16
©2005 PAWS, INC. All Rights Reserved. www.garfield.com
Distributed by Universal Press Syndicate

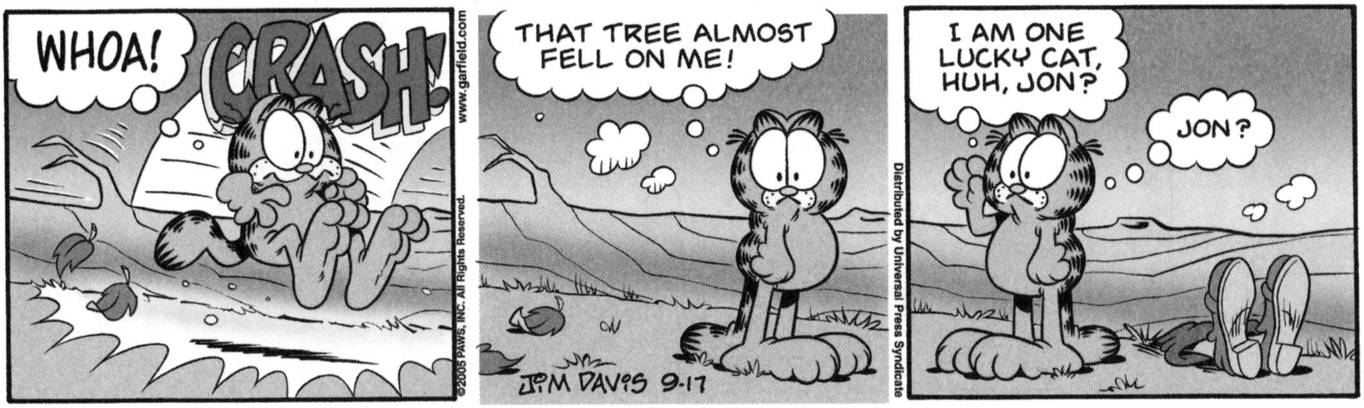
WHOA!
CRASH!
THAT TREE ALMOST FELL ON ME!
JIM DAVIS 9-17
I AM ONE LUCKY CAT, HUH, JON?
JON?
©2005 PAWS, INC. All Rights Reserved. www.garfield.com
Distributed by Universal Press Syndicate

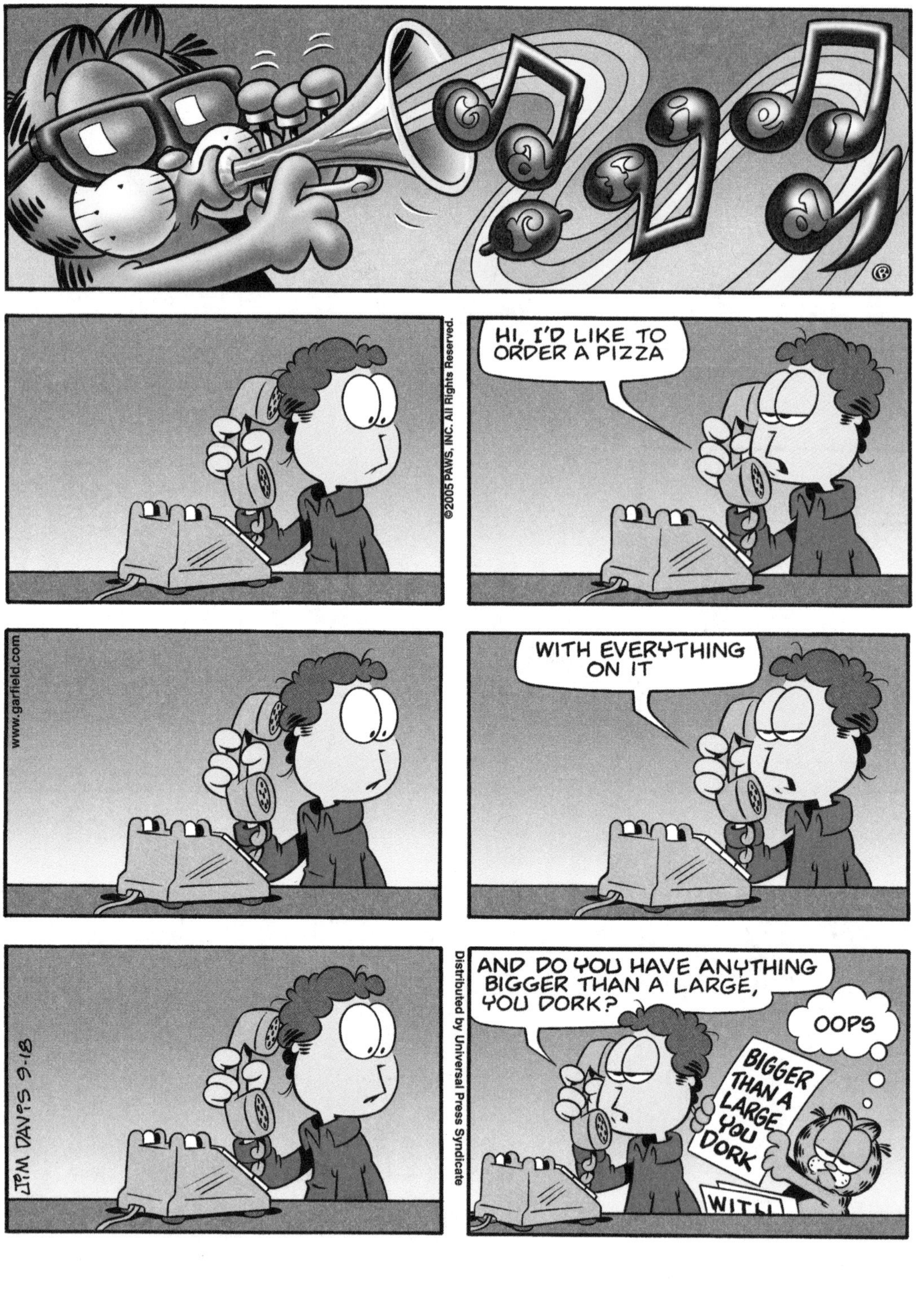
Garfield ®
©2005 PAWS, INC. All Rights Reserved.
HI, I'D LIKE TO ORDER A PIZZA
www.garfield.com
WITH EVERYTHING ON IT
JIM DAVIS 9-18
Distributed by Universal Press Syndicate
AND DO YOU HAVE ANYTHING BIGGER THAN A LARGE, YOU DORK?
OOPS
BIGGER THAN A LARGE YOU DORK
WITH

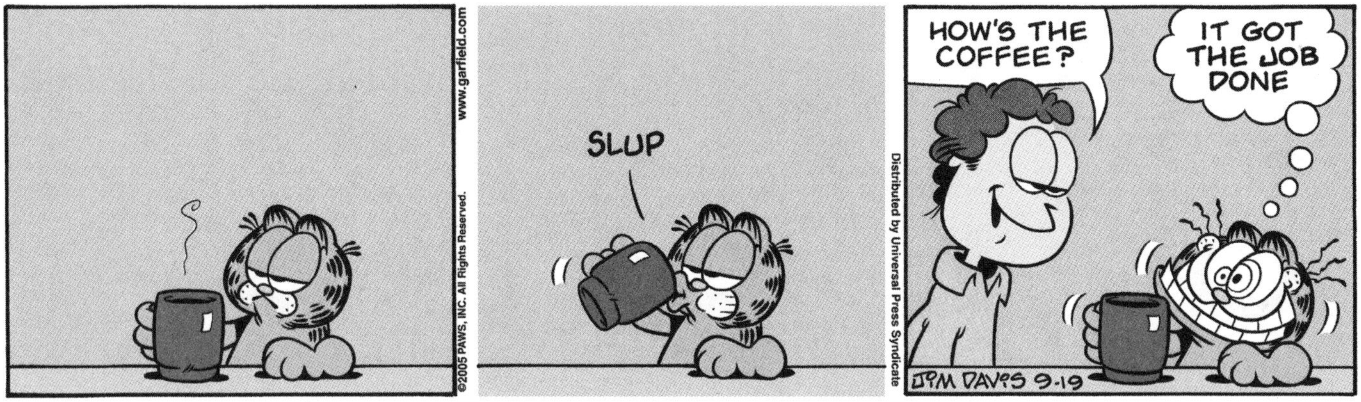
©2005 PAWS, INC. All Rights Reserved.
www.garfield.com
SLUP
Distributed by Universal Press Syndicate
HOW'S THE COFFEE?
IT GOT THE JOB DONE
JIM DAVIS 9-19

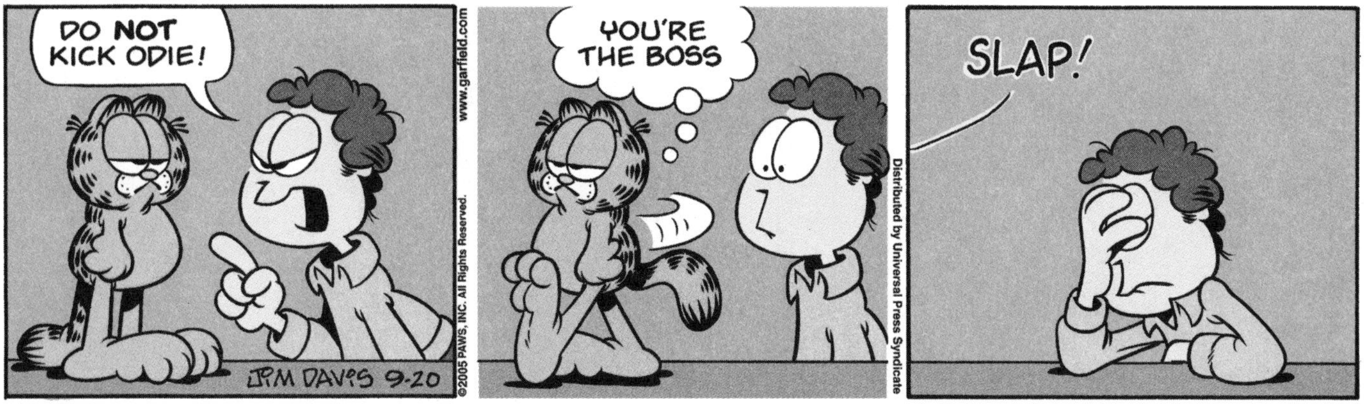
DO NOT KICK ODIE!
JIM DAVIS 9-20
©2005 PAWS, INC. All Rights Reserved.
www.garfield.com
YOU'RE THE BOSS
Distributed by Universal Press Syndicate
SLAP!

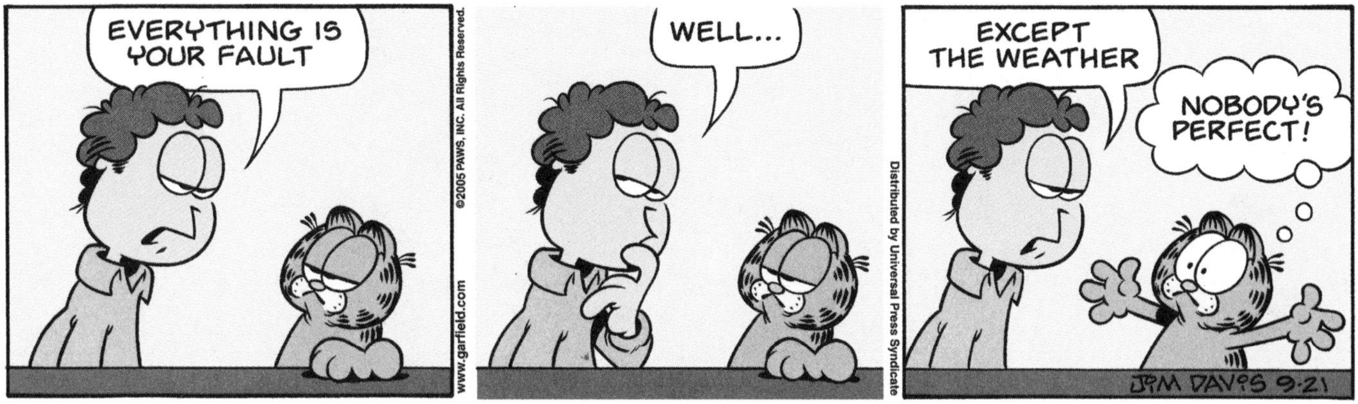
EVERYTHING IS YOUR FAULT
©2005 PAWS, INC. All Rights Reserved.
www.garfield.com
WELL...
Distributed by Universal Press Syndicate
EXCEPT THE WEATHER
NOBODY'S PERFECT!
JIM DAVIS 9-21

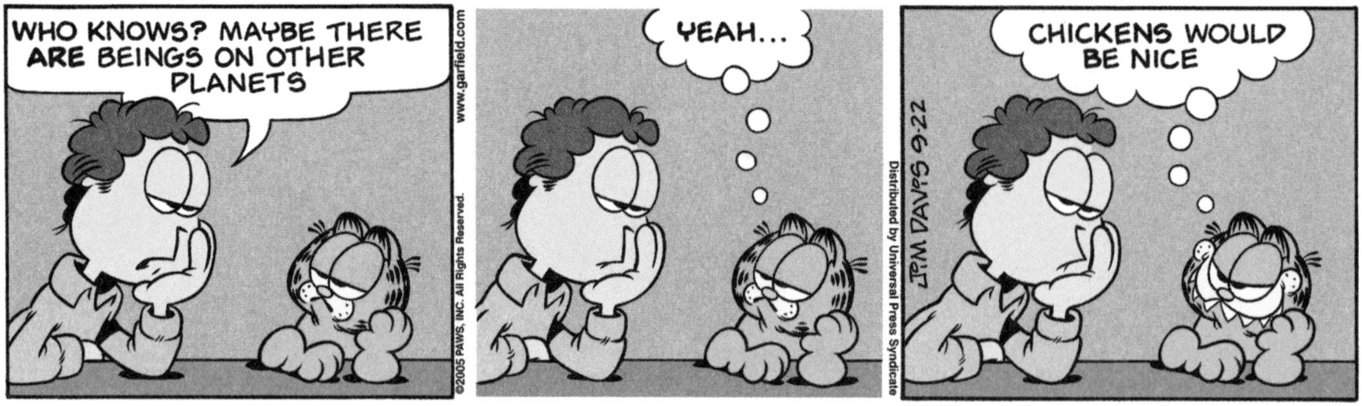
WHO KNOWS? MAYBE THERE ARE BEINGS ON OTHER PLANETS
YEAH...
CHICKENS WOULD BE NICE
©2005 PAWS, INC. All Rights Reserved.
www.garfield.com
Distributed by Universal Press Syndicate
JIM DAVIS 9-22

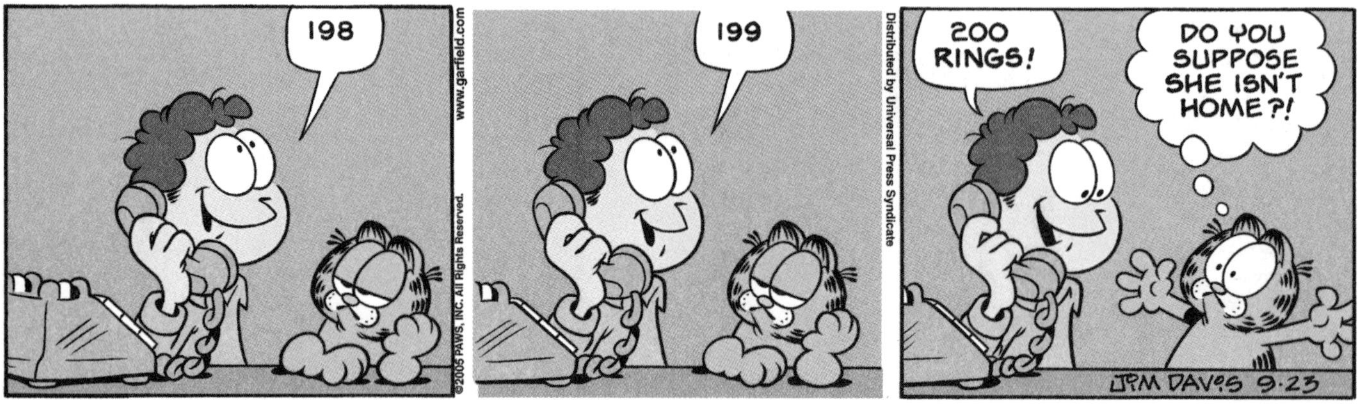
198
199
200 RINGS!
DO YOU SUPPOSE SHE ISN'T HOME?!
©2005 PAWS, INC. All Rights Reserved.
www.garfield.com
Distributed by Universal Press Syndicate
JIM DAVIS 9-23

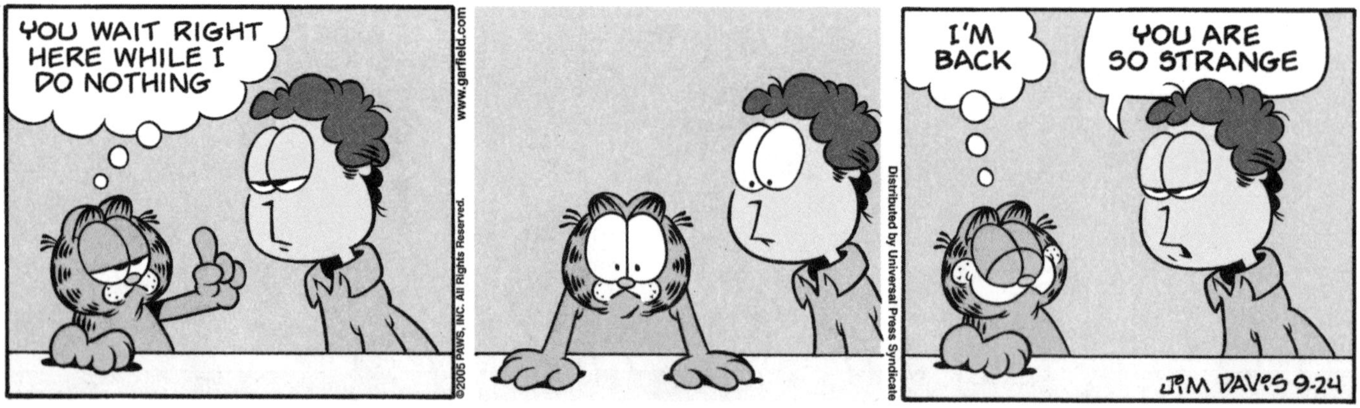
YOU WAIT RIGHT HERE WHILE I DO NOTHING
I'M BACK
YOU ARE SO STRANGE
©2005 PAWS, INC. All Rights Reserved.
www.garfield.com
Distributed by Universal Press Syndicate
JIM DAVIS 9-24

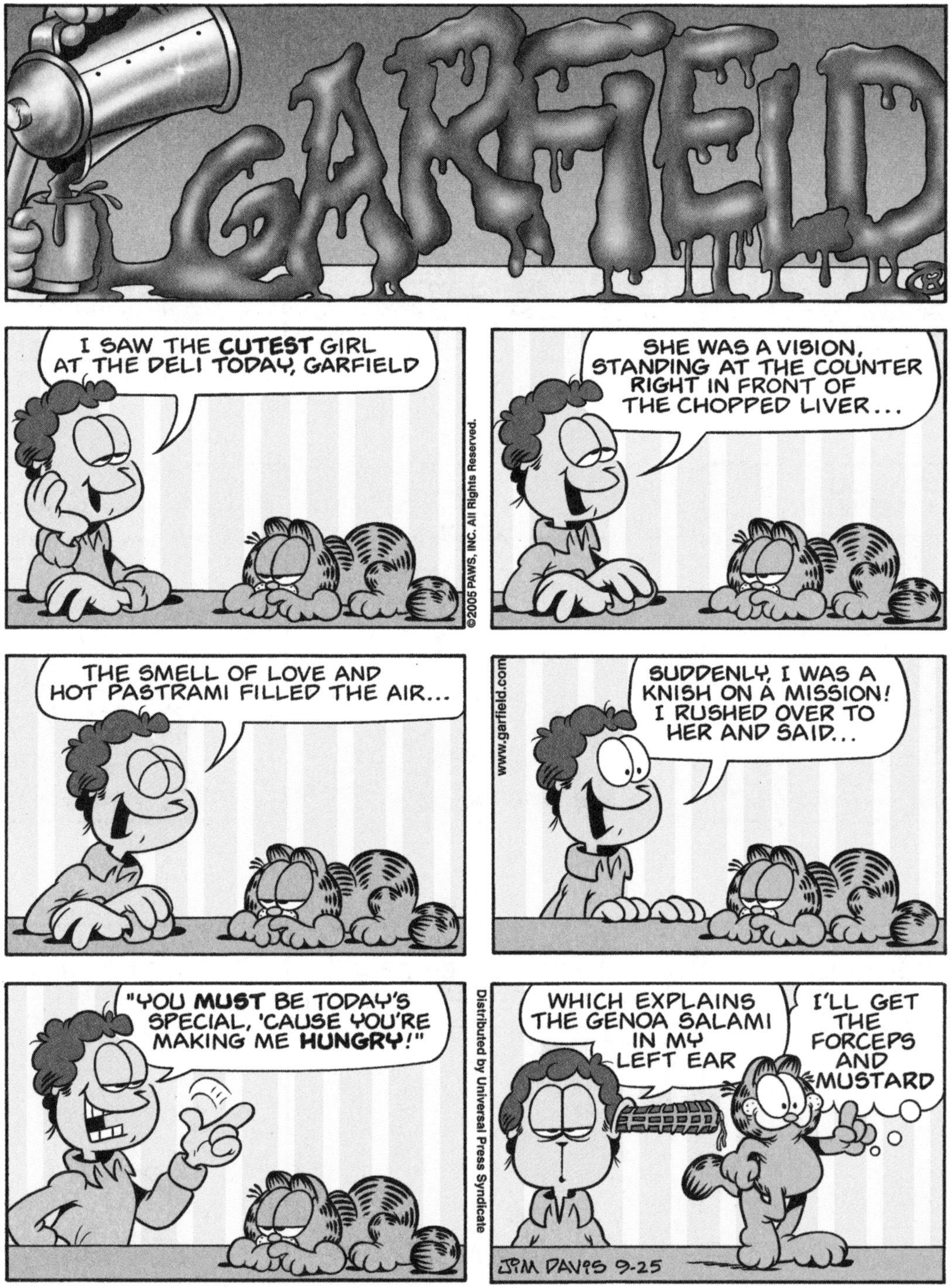
GARFIELD
I SAW THE CUTEST GIRL AT THE DELI TODAY, GARFIELD
SHE WAS A VISION, STANDING AT THE COUNTER RIGHT IN FRONT OF THE CHOPPED LIVER...
THE SMELL OF LOVE AND HOT PASTRAMI FILLED THE AIR...
SUDDENLY, I WAS A KNISH ON A MISSION! I RUSHED OVER TO HER AND SAID...
"YOU MUST BE TODAY'S SPECIAL, 'CAUSE YOU'RE MAKING ME HUNGRY!"
WHICH EXPLAINS THE GENOA SALAMI IN MY LEFT EAR
I'LL GET THE FORCEPS AND MUSTARD
JIM DAVIS 9-25
©2005 PAWS, INC. All Rights Reserved.
www.garfield.com
Distributed by Universal Press Syndicate

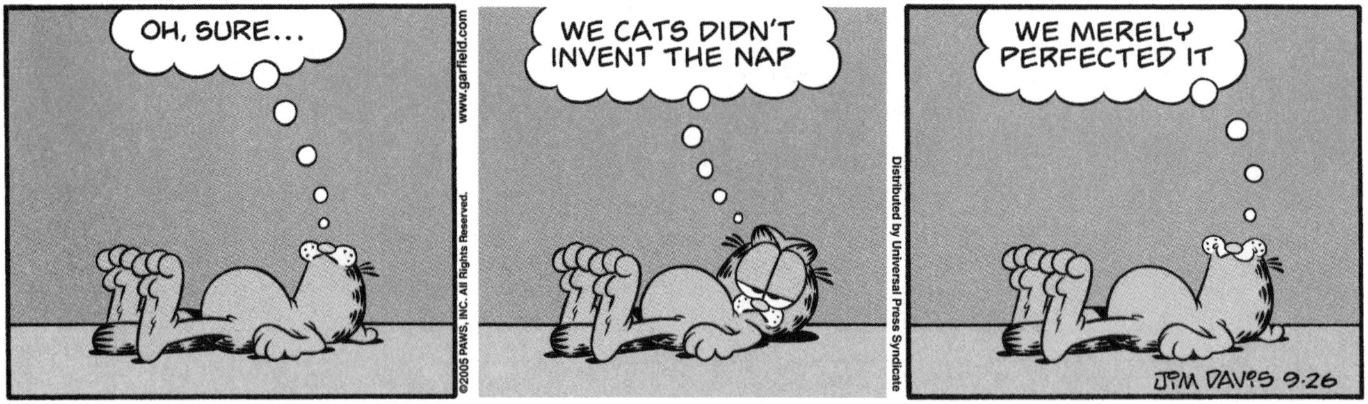
OH, SURE...
WE CATS DIDN'T INVENT THE NAP
WE MERELY PERFECTED IT
JIM DAVIS 9-26
©2005 PAWS, INC. All Rights Reserved. www.garfield.com
Distributed by Universal Press Syndicate

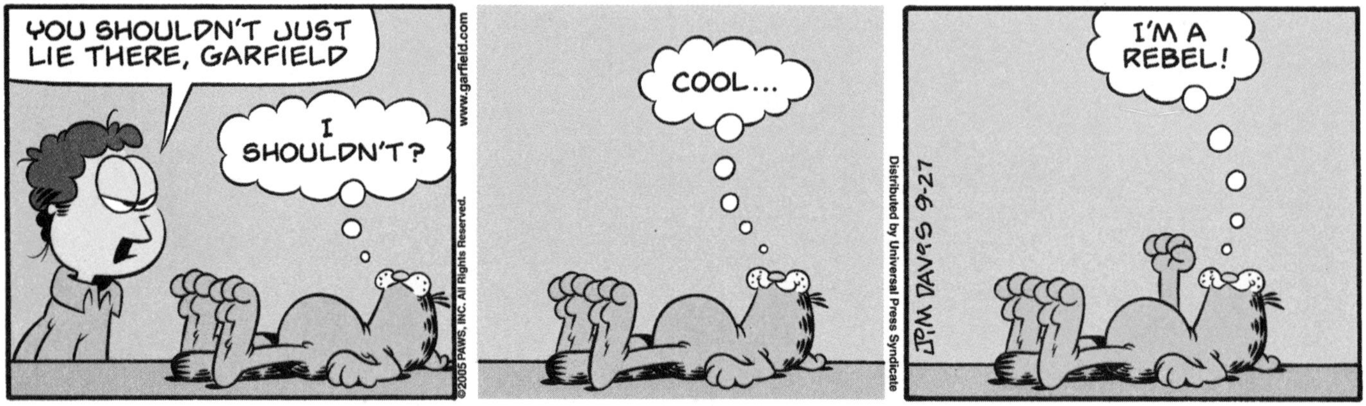
YOU SHOULDN'T JUST LIE THERE, GARFIELD
I SHOULDN'T?
COOL...
I'M A REBEL!
JIM DAVIS 9-27
©2005 PAWS, INC. All Rights Reserved. www.garfield.com
Distributed by Universal Press Syndicate

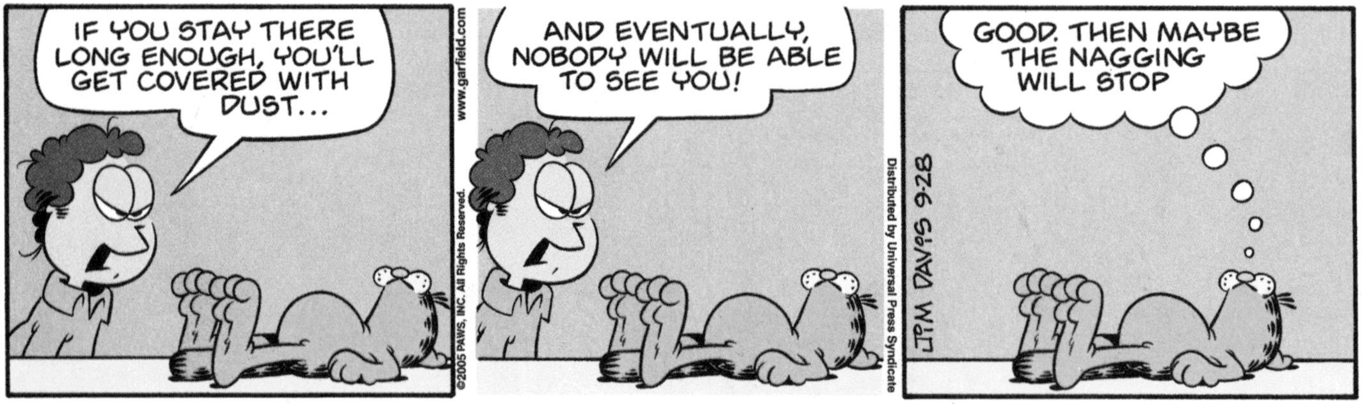
IF YOU STAY THERE LONG ENOUGH, YOU'LL GET COVERED WITH DUST...
AND EVENTUALLY, NOBODY WILL BE ABLE TO SEE YOU!
GOOD. THEN MAYBE THE NAGGING WILL STOP
JIM DAVIS 9-28
©2005 PAWS, INC. All Rights Reserved. www.garfield.com
Distributed by Universal Press Syndicate

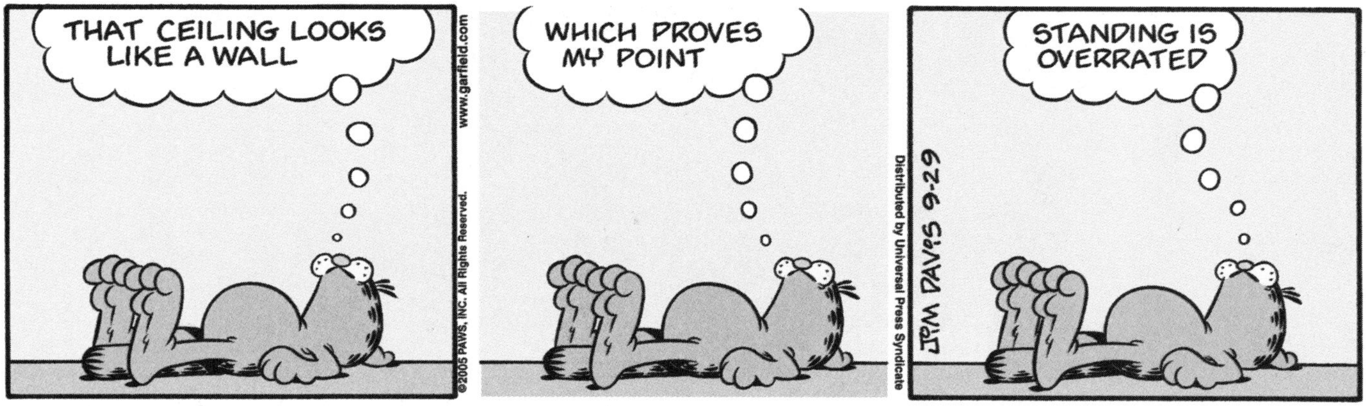
THAT CEILING LOOKS LIKE A WALL
WHICH PROVES MY POINT
STANDING IS OVERRATED
JPM DAVPS 9-29
©2005 PAWS, INC. All Rights Reserved.
www.garfield.com
Distributed by Universal Press Syndicate

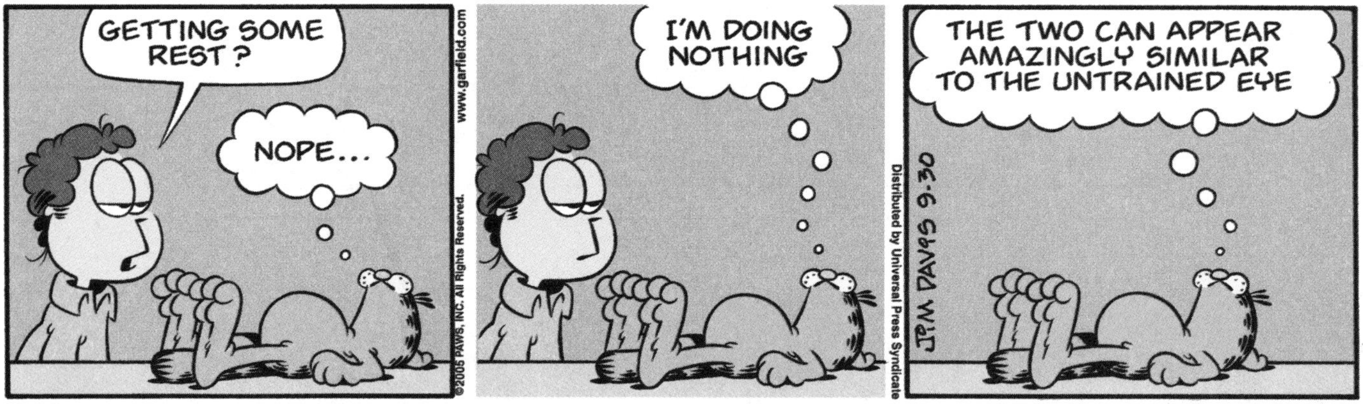
GETTING SOME REST?
NOPE...
I'M DOING NOTHING
THE TWO CAN APPEAR AMAZINGLY SIMILAR TO THE UNTRAINED EYE
JPM DAVPS 9-30
©2005 PAWS, INC. All Rights Reserved.
www.garfield.com
Distributed by Universal Press Syndicate

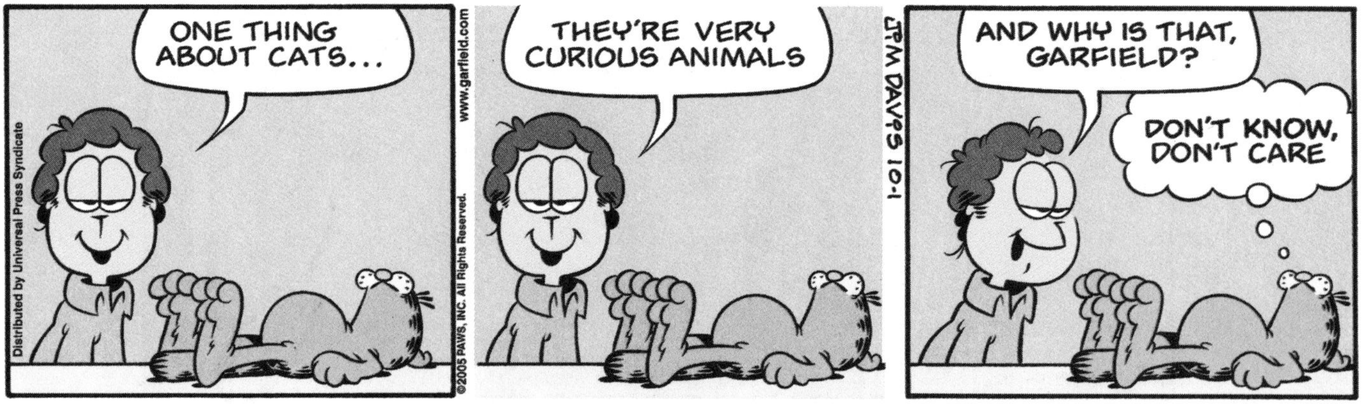
ONE THING ABOUT CATS...
THEY'RE VERY CURIOUS ANIMALS
AND WHY IS THAT, GARFIELD?
DON'T KNOW, DON'T CARE
JPM DAVPS 10-1
©2005 PAWS, INC. All Rights Reserved.
www.garfield.com
Distributed by Universal Press Syndicate

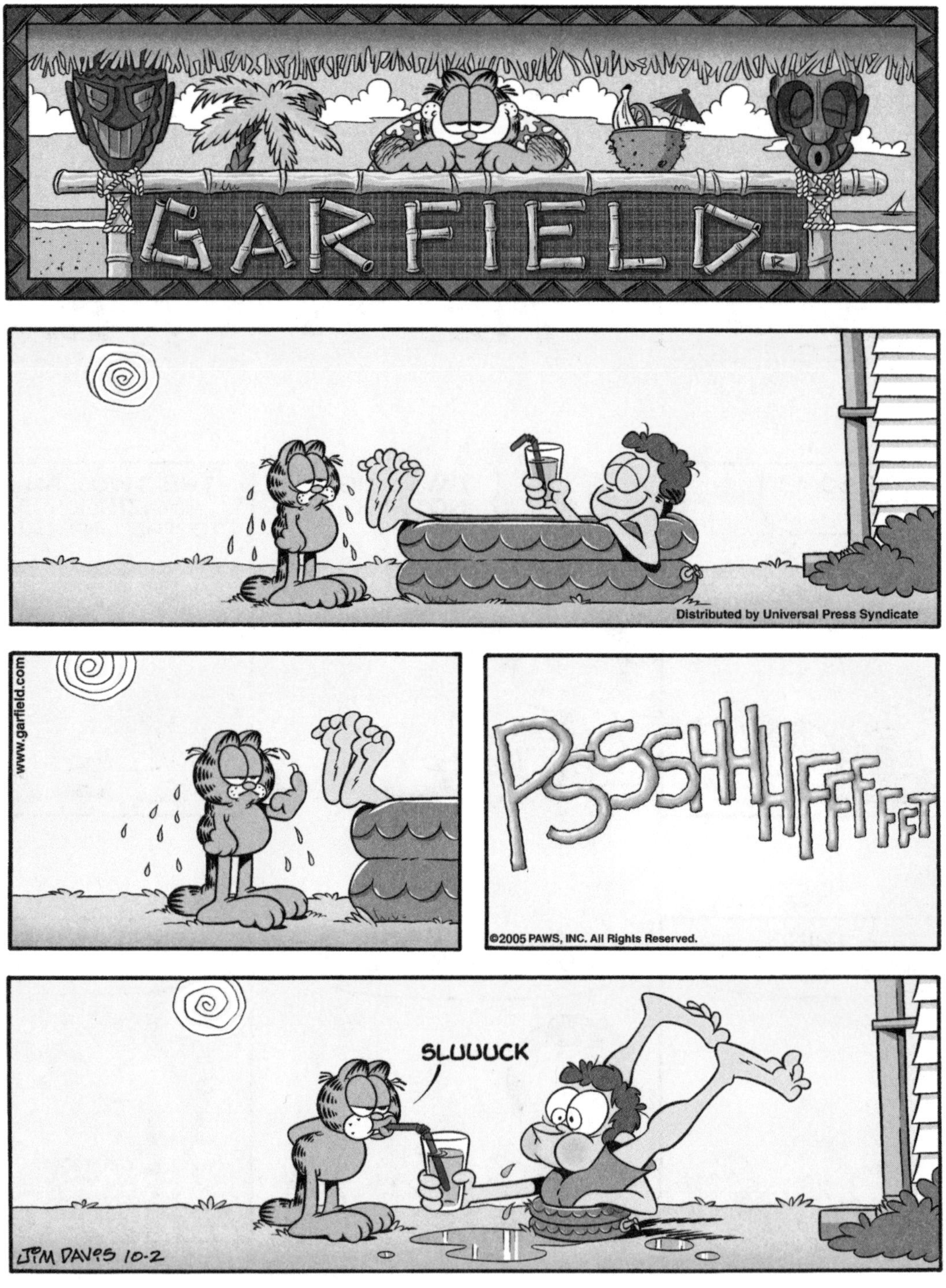
GARFIELD
Distributed by Universal Press Syndicate
www.garfield.com
PSSSSHHHFFFFFFT
©2005 PAWS, INC. All Rights Reserved.
SLUUUCK
JIM DAVIS 10-2

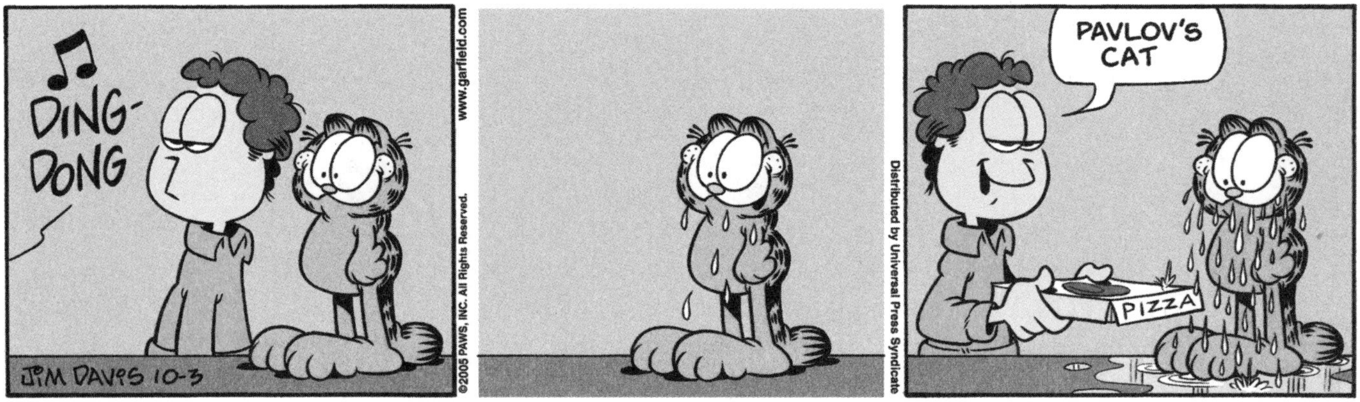
DING-DONG
JIM DAVIS 10-3
www.garfield.com
©2005 PAWS, INC. All Rights Reserved.
Distributed by Universal Press Syndicate
PAVLOV'S CAT
PIZZA

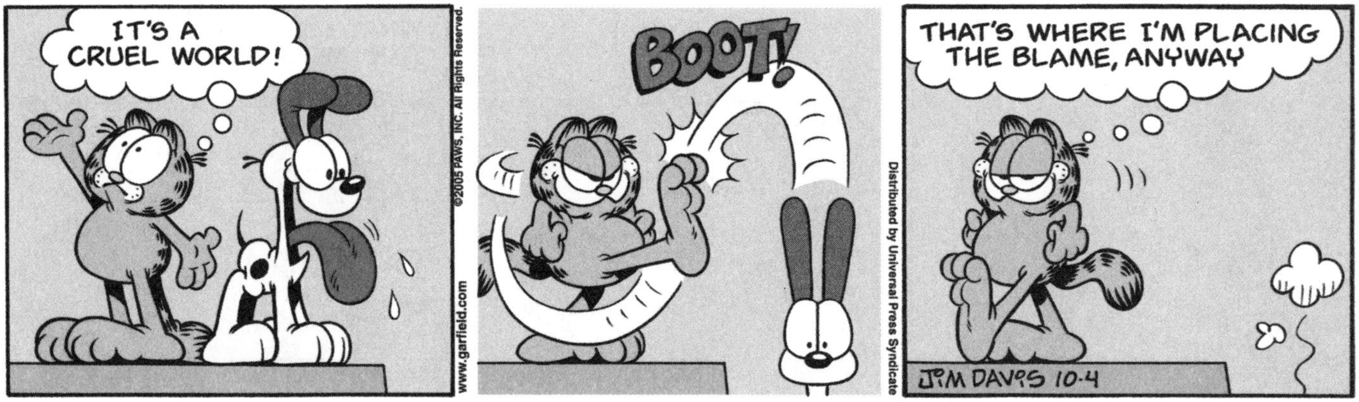
IT'S A CRUEL WORLD!
©2005 PAWS, INC. All Rights Reserved.
www.garfield.com
BOOT!
Distributed by Universal Press Syndicate
THAT'S WHERE I'M PLACING THE BLAME, ANYWAY
JIM DAVIS 10-4

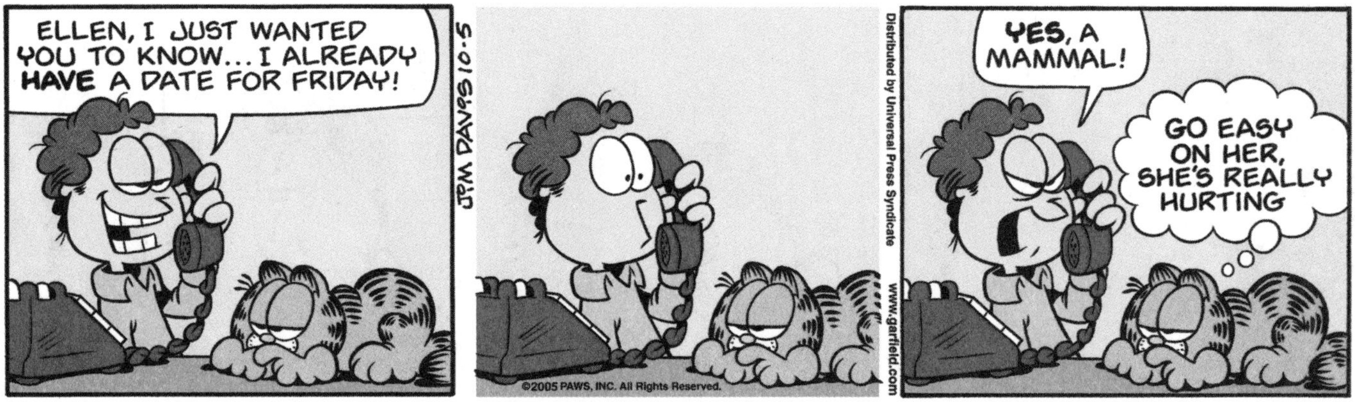
ELLEN, I JUST WANTED YOU TO KNOW... I ALREADY **HAVE** A DATE FOR FRIDAY!
JIM DAVIS 10-5
©2005 PAWS, INC. All Rights Reserved.
Distributed by Universal Press Syndicate
www.garfield.com
YES, A MAMMAL!
GO EASY ON HER, SHE'S REALLY HURTING

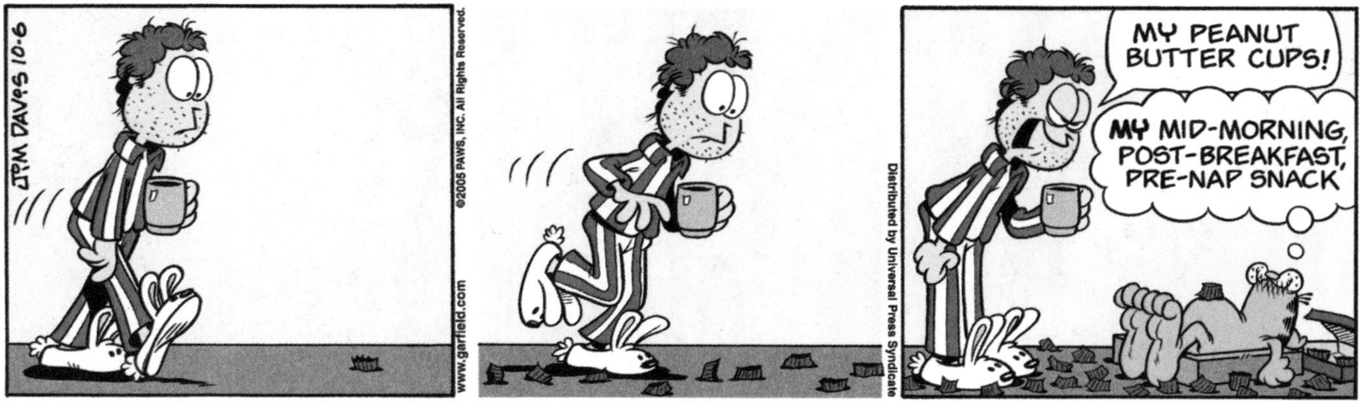
JIM DAVIS 10-6
MY PEANUT BUTTER CUPS!
MY MID-MORNING, POST-BREAKFAST, PRE-NAP SNACK
©2005 PAWS, INC. All Rights Reserved.
www.garfield.com
Distributed by Universal Press Syndicate

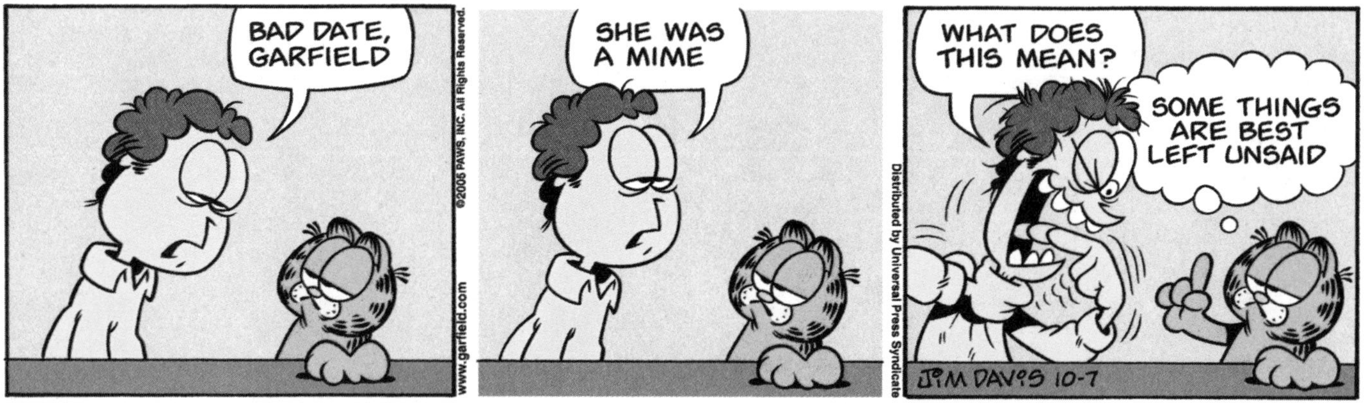
BAD DATE, GARFIELD
SHE WAS A MIME
WHAT DOES THIS MEAN?
SOME THINGS ARE BEST LEFT UNSAID
JIM DAVIS 10-7
©2005 PAWS, INC. All Rights Reserved.
www.garfield.com
Distributed by Universal Press Syndicate

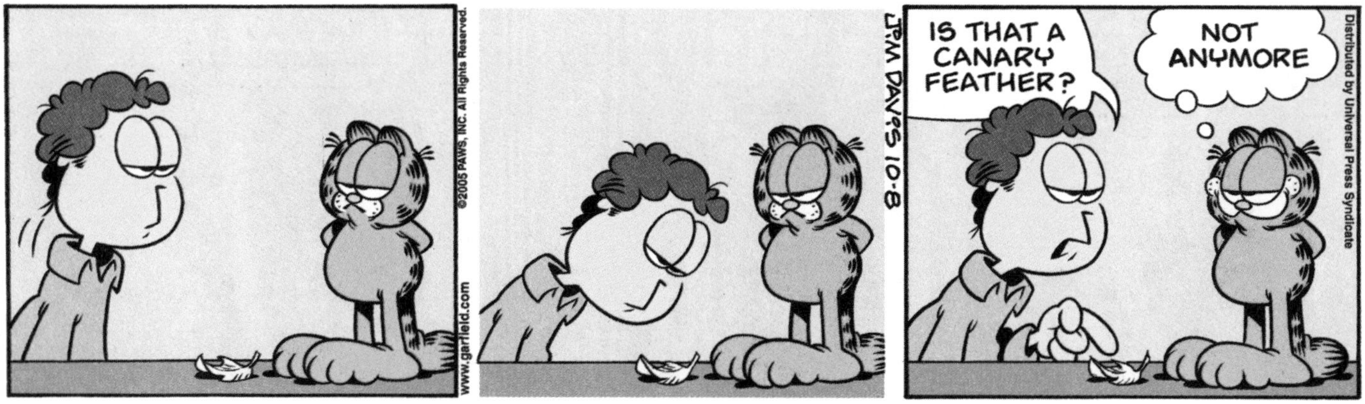
JIM DAVIS 10-8
IS THAT A CANARY FEATHER?
NOT ANYMORE
©2005 PAWS, INC. All Rights Reserved.
www.garfield.com
Distributed by Universal Press Syndicate

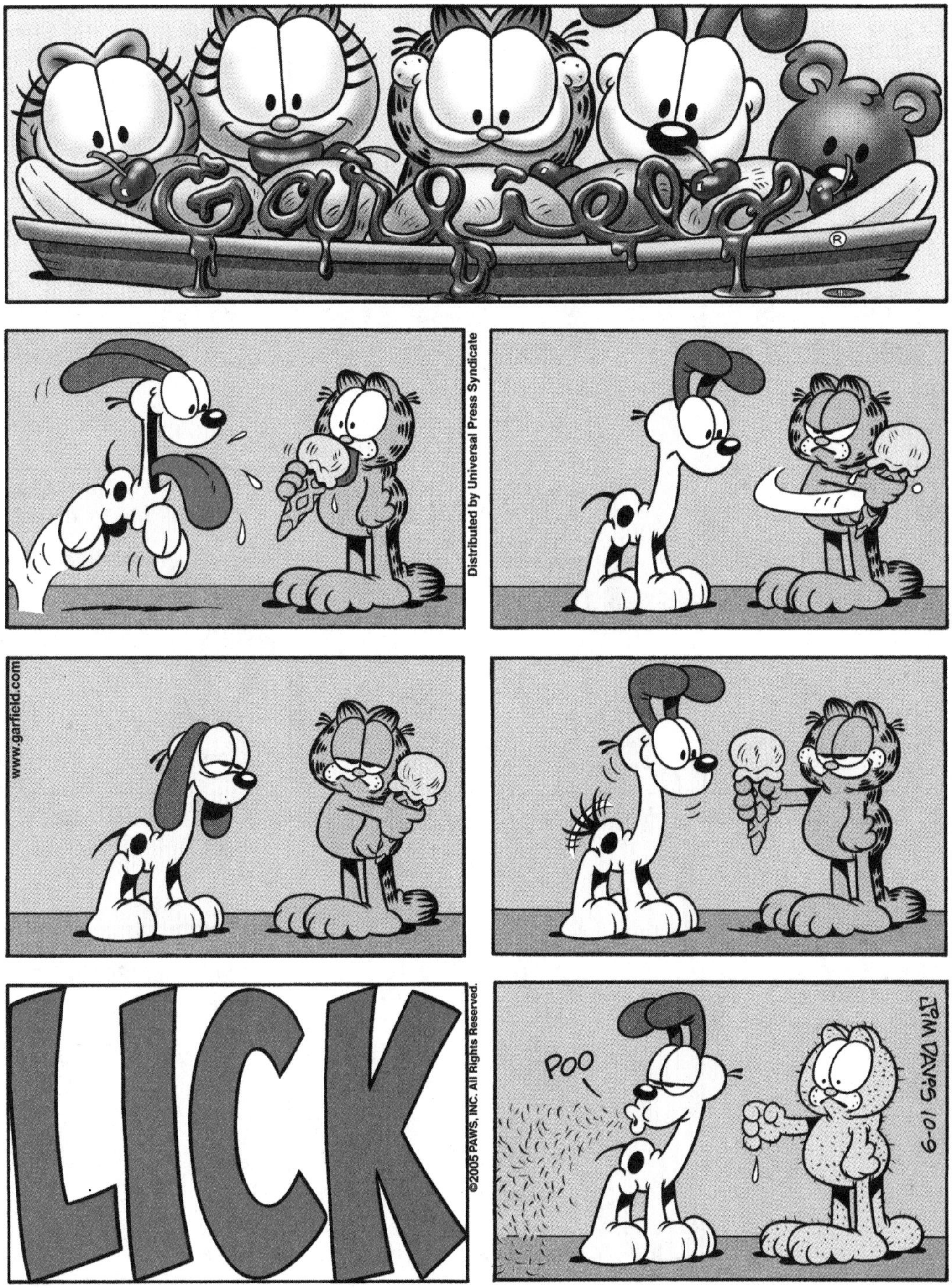
Garfield
Distributed by Universal Press Syndicate
www.garfield.com
LICK
©2005 PAWS, INC. All Rights Reserved.
POO
JIM DAVIS 10-9

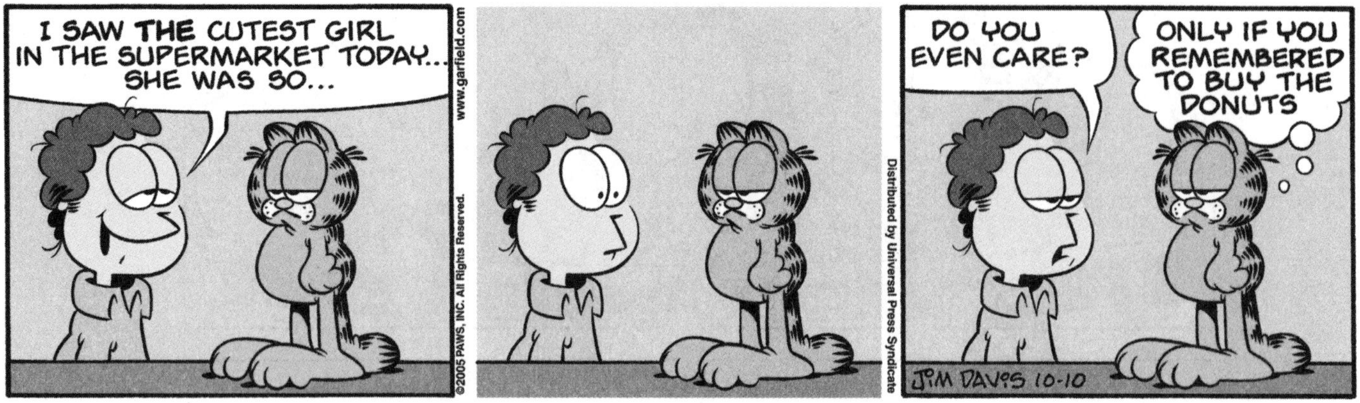
I SAW THE CUTEST GIRL IN THE SUPERMARKET TODAY... SHE WAS SO...
www.garfield.com
©2005 PAWS, INC. All Rights Reserved.
Distributed by Universal Press Syndicate
DO YOU EVEN CARE?
ONLY IF YOU REMEMBERED TO BUY THE DONUTS
JIM DAVIS 10-10

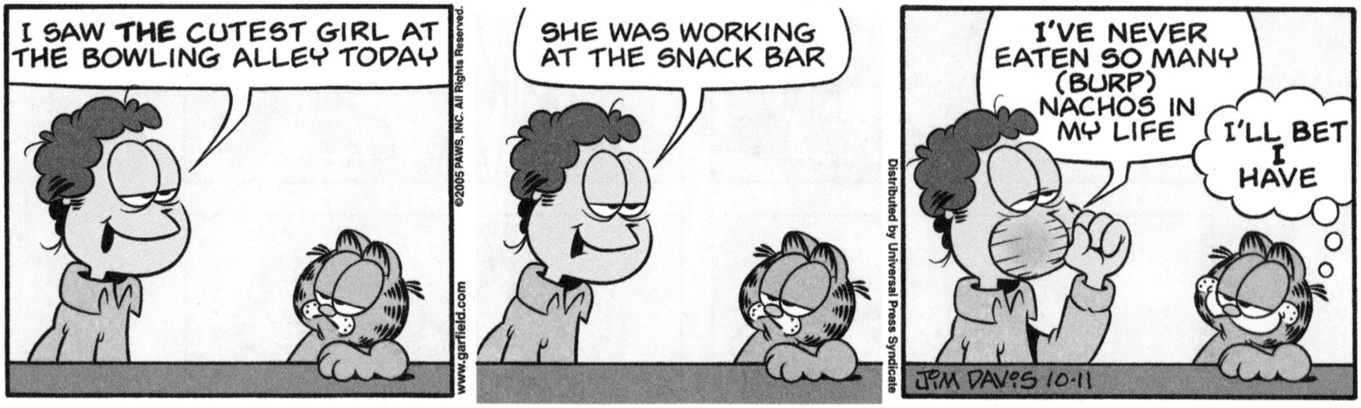
I SAW THE CUTEST GIRL AT THE BOWLING ALLEY TODAY
©2005 PAWS, INC. All Rights Reserved.
www.garfield.com
SHE WAS WORKING AT THE SNACK BAR
Distributed by Universal Press Syndicate
I'VE NEVER EATEN SO MANY (BURP) NACHOS IN MY LIFE
I'LL BET I HAVE
JIM DAVIS 10-11

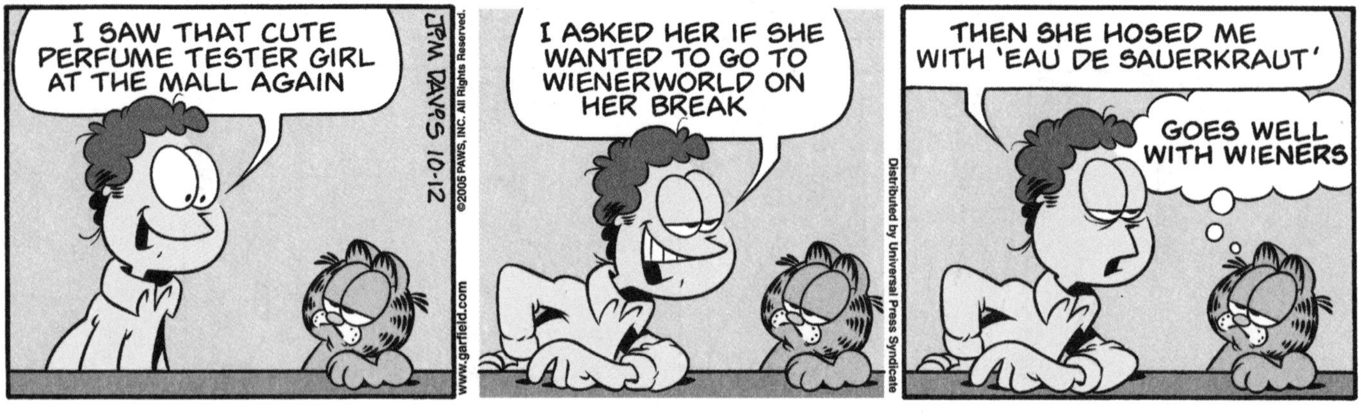
I SAW THAT CUTE PERFUME TESTER GIRL AT THE MALL AGAIN
JIM DAVIS 10-12
©2005 PAWS, INC. All Rights Reserved.
www.garfield.com
I ASKED HER IF SHE WANTED TO GO TO WIENERWORLD ON HER BREAK
Distributed by Universal Press Syndicate
THEN SHE HOSED ME WITH 'EAU DE SAUERKRAUT'
GOES WELL WITH WIENERS

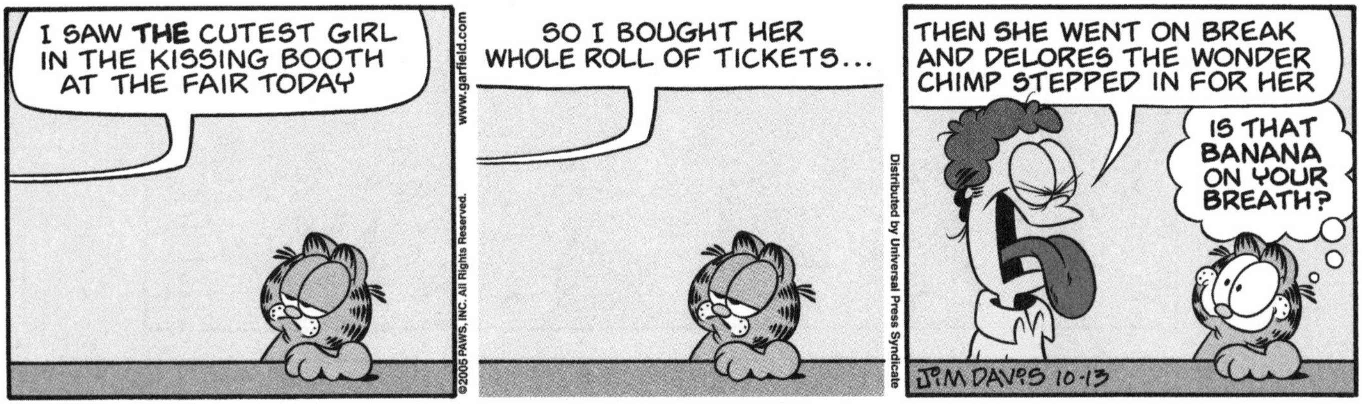
I SAW THE CUTEST GIRL IN THE KISSING BOOTH AT THE FAIR TODAY
SO I BOUGHT HER WHOLE ROLL OF TICKETS...
THEN SHE WENT ON BREAK AND DELORES THE WONDER CHIMP STEPPED IN FOR HER
IS THAT BANANA ON YOUR BREATH?
JIM DAVIS 10-13
©2005 PAWS, INC. All Rights Reserved. www.garfield.com
Distributed by Universal Press Syndicate

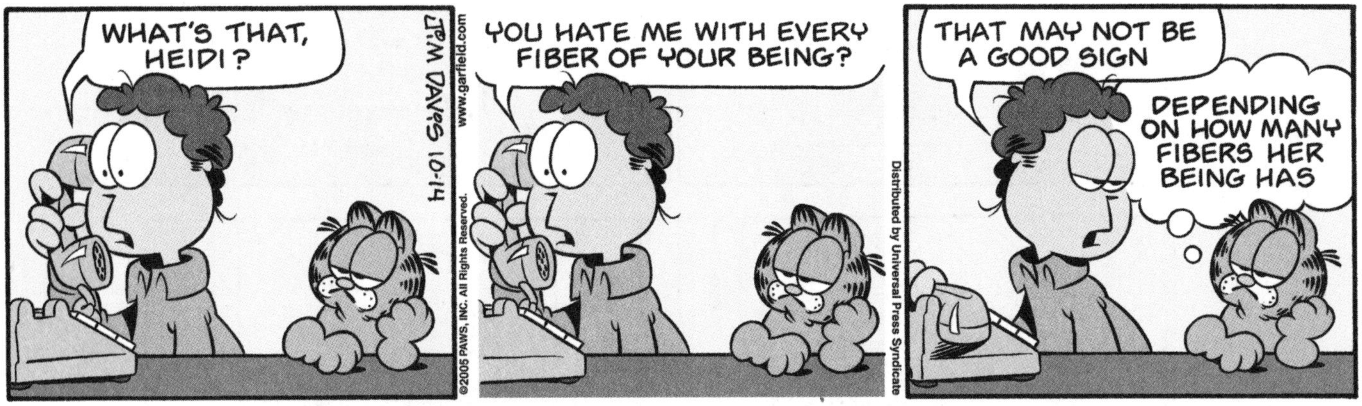
WHAT'S THAT, HEIDI?
YOU HATE ME WITH EVERY FIBER OF YOUR BEING?
THAT MAY NOT BE A GOOD SIGN
DEPENDING ON HOW MANY FIBERS HER BEING HAS
JIM DAVIS 10-14
©2005 PAWS, INC. All Rights Reserved. www.garfield.com
Distributed by Universal Press Syndicate

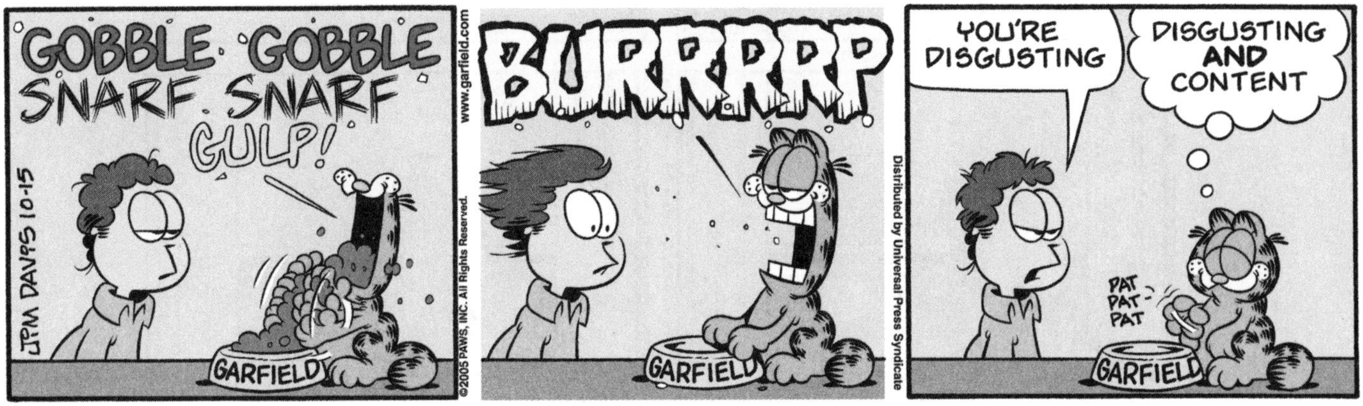
GOBBLE GOBBLE
SNARF SNARF
GULP!
GARFIELD
BURRRRP
GARFIELD
YOU'RE DISGUSTING
DISGUSTING AND CONTENT
PAT PAT PAT
GARFIELD
JIM DAVIS 10-15
©2005 PAWS, INC. All Rights Reserved. www.garfield.com
Distributed by Universal Press Syndicate

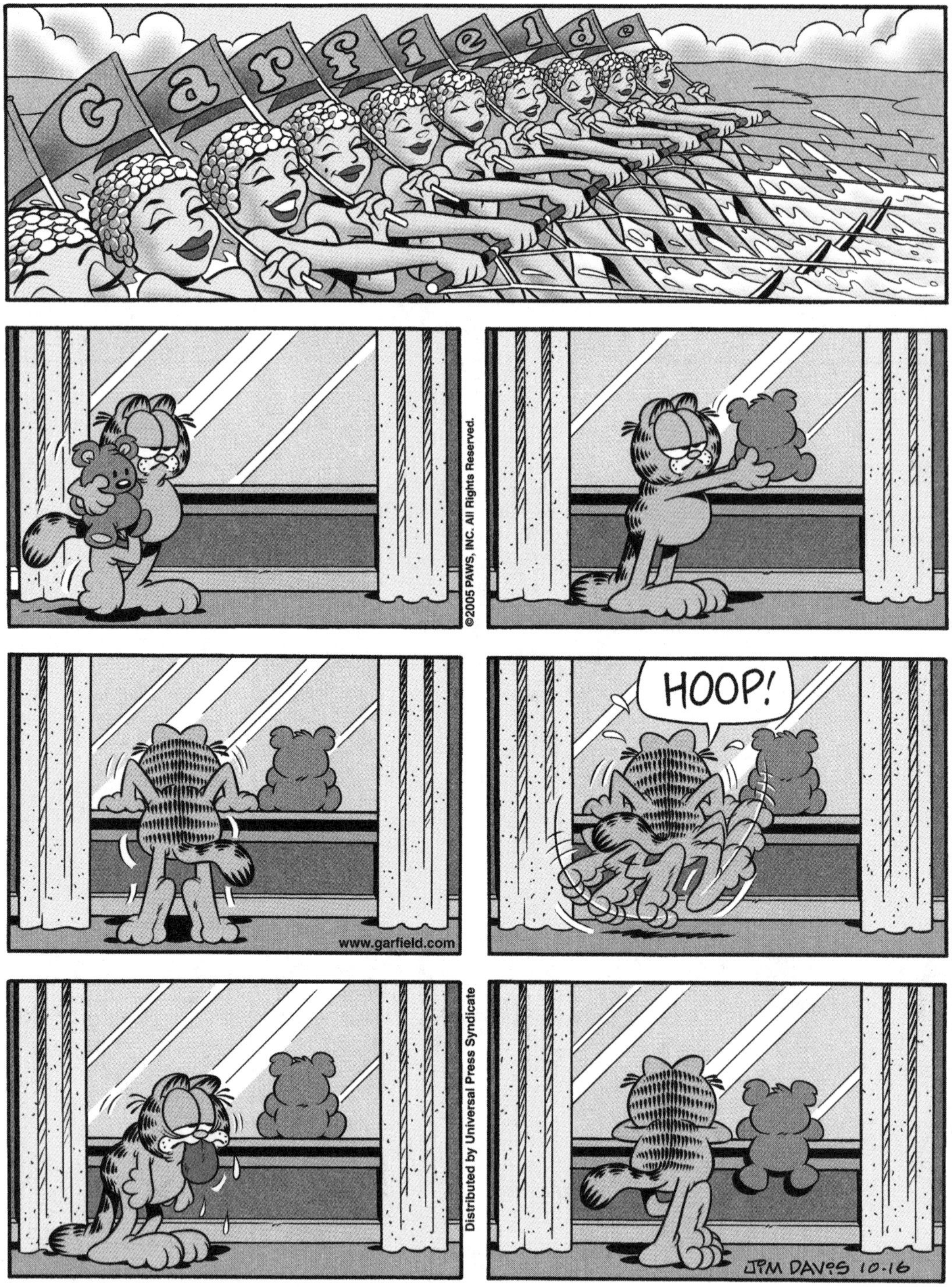
Garfield®
©2005 PAWS, INC. All Rights Reserved.
HOOP!
www.garfield.com
Distributed by Universal Press Syndicate
JIM DAVIS 10-16

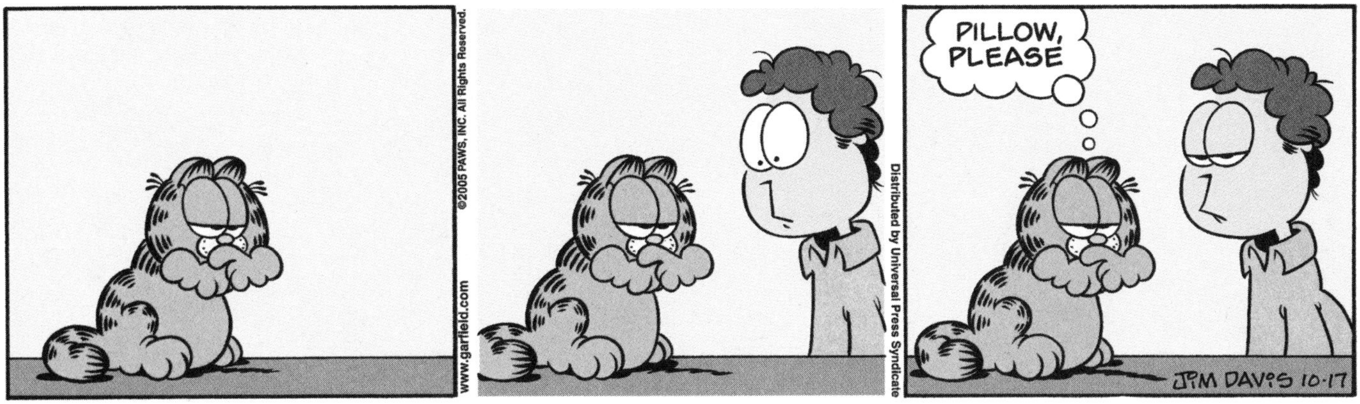
PILLOW, PLEASE
JIM DAVIS 10-17
©2005 PAWS, INC. All Rights Reserved.
www.garfield.com
Distributed by Universal Press Syndicate

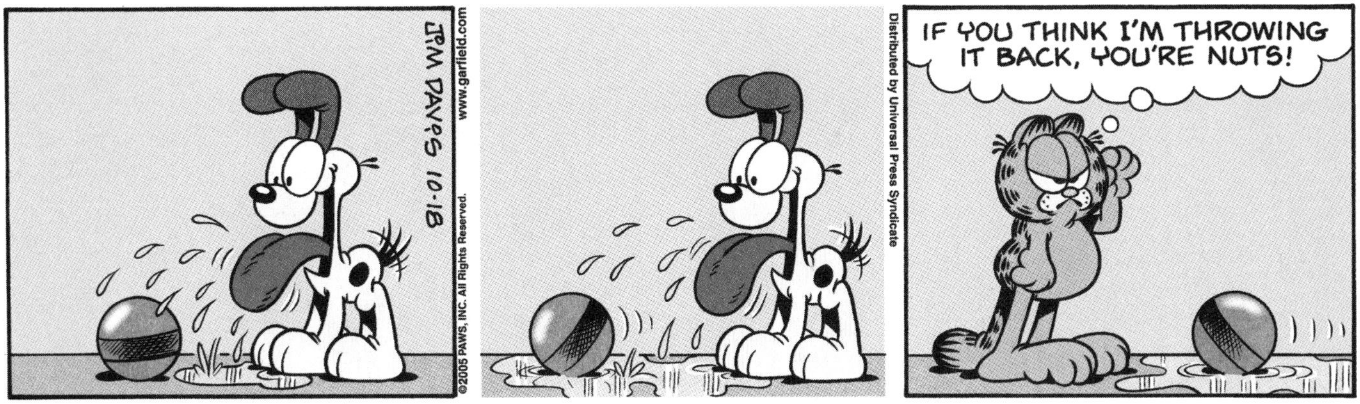
JIM DAVIS 10-18
IF YOU THINK I'M THROWING IT BACK, YOU'RE NUTS!
©2005 PAWS, INC. All Rights Reserved.
www.garfield.com
Distributed by Universal Press Syndicate

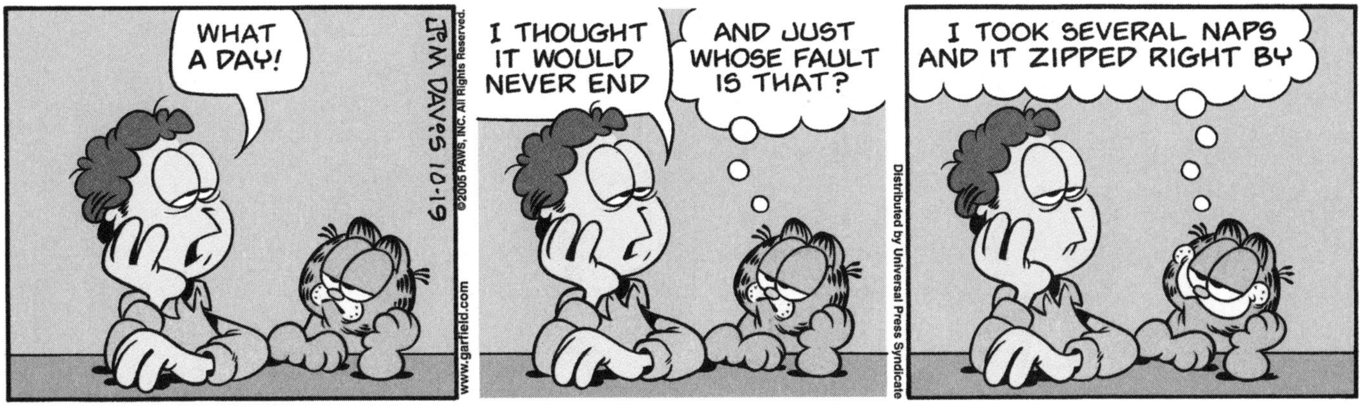
WHAT A DAY!
JIM DAVIS 10-19
I THOUGHT IT WOULD NEVER END
AND JUST WHOSE FAULT IS THAT?
I TOOK SEVERAL NAPS AND IT ZIPPED RIGHT BY
©2005 PAWS, INC. All Rights Reserved.
www.garfield.com
Distributed by Universal Press Syndicate

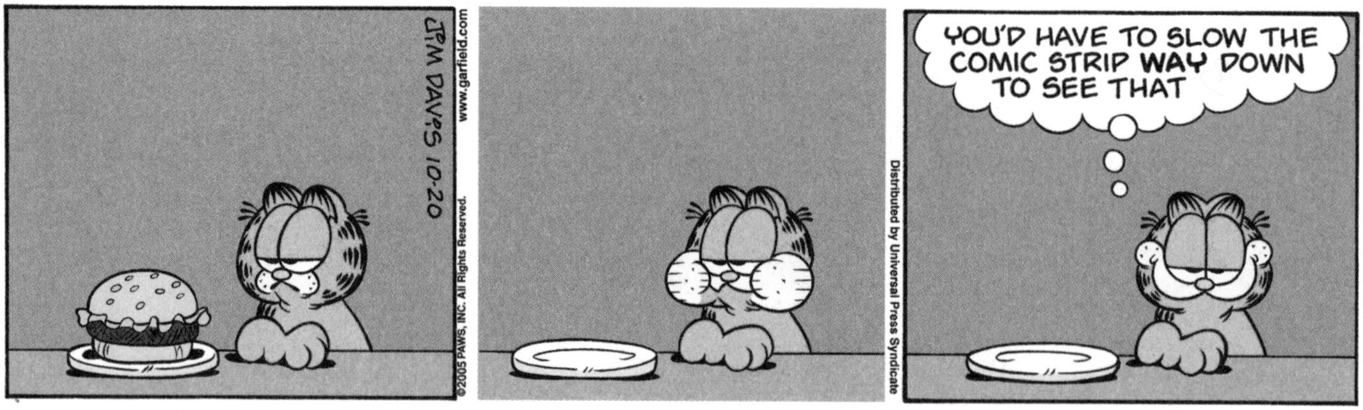
JIM DAVIS 10-20
www.garfield.com
©2005 PAWS, INC. All Rights Reserved.
Distributed by Universal Press Syndicate
YOU'D HAVE TO SLOW THE COMIC STRIP WAY DOWN TO SEE THAT

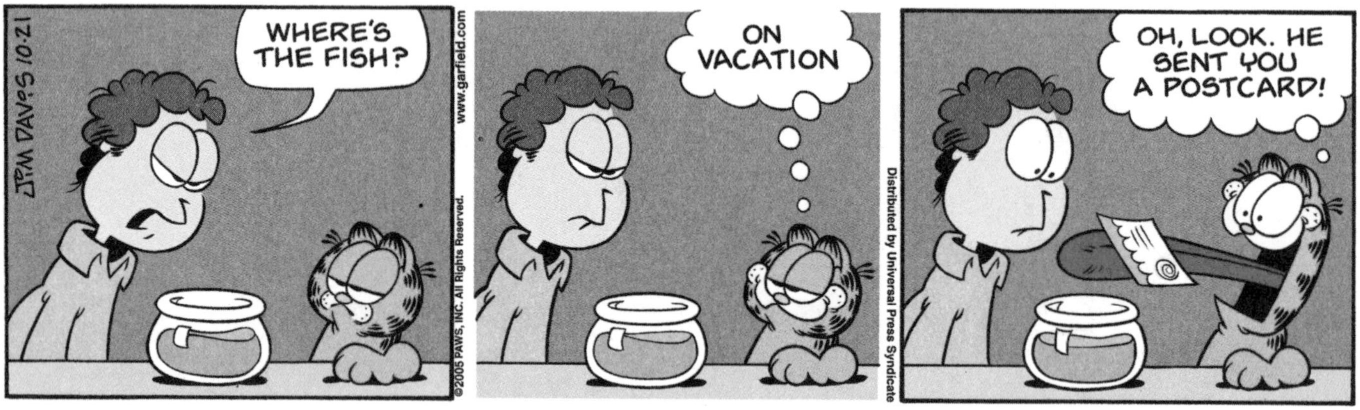
JIM DAVIS 10-21
WHERE'S THE FISH?
www.garfield.com
©2005 PAWS, INC. All Rights Reserved.
ON VACATION
Distributed by Universal Press Syndicate
OH, LOOK. HE SENT YOU A POSTCARD!

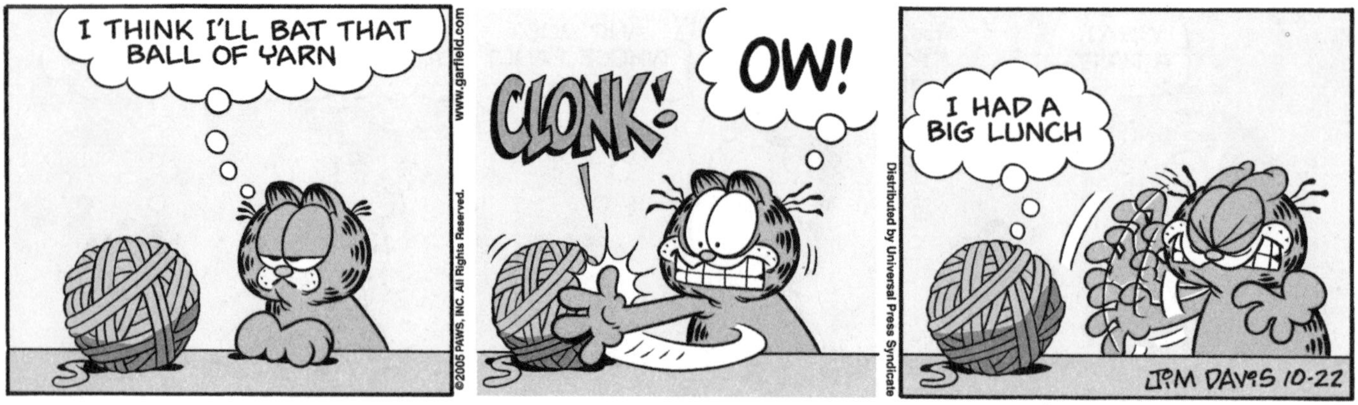
I THINK I'LL BAT THAT BALL OF YARN
www.garfield.com
©2005 PAWS, INC. All Rights Reserved.
CLONK!
OW!
Distributed by Universal Press Syndicate
I HAD A BIG LUNCH
JIM DAVIS 10-22

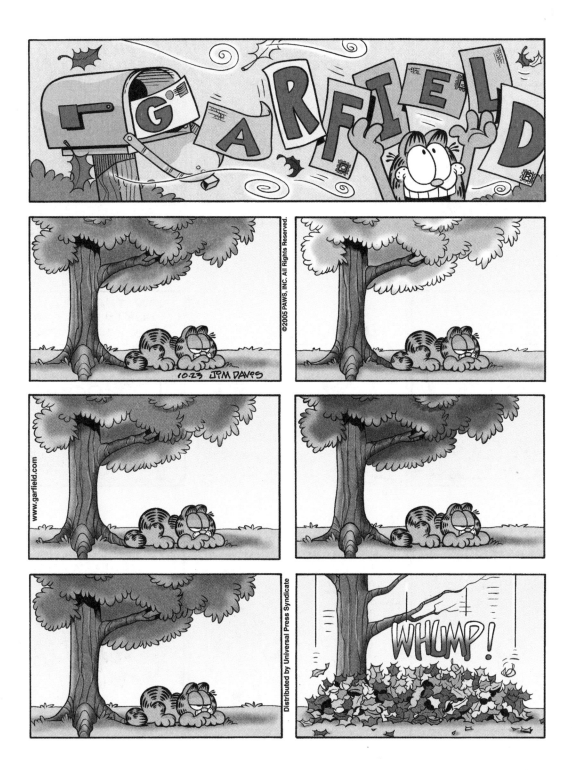

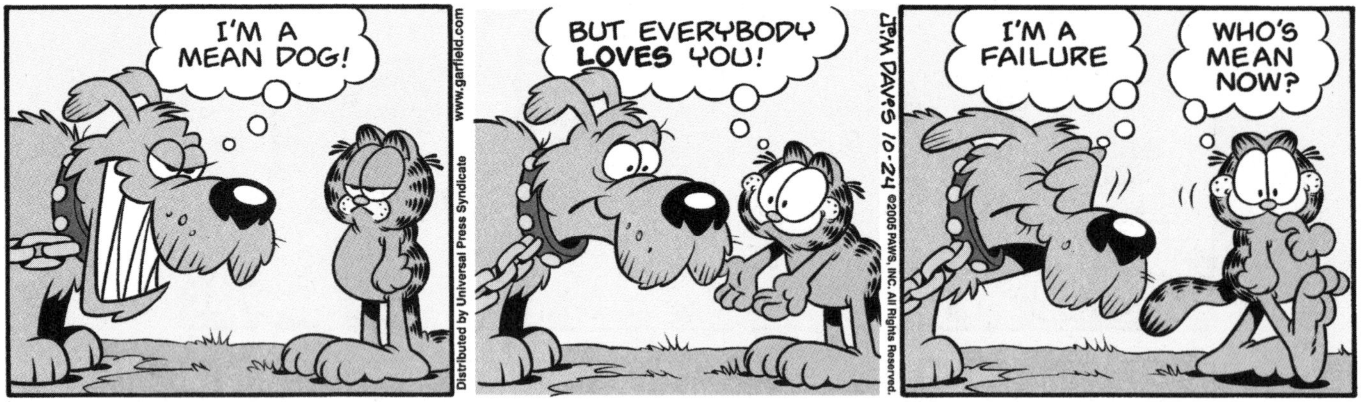
I'M A MEAN DOG!
www.garfield.com
Distributed by Universal Press Syndicate
BUT EVERYBODY LOVES YOU!
JIM DAVIS 10-24
©2005 PAWS, INC. All Rights Reserved.
I'M A FAILURE
WHO'S MEAN NOW?

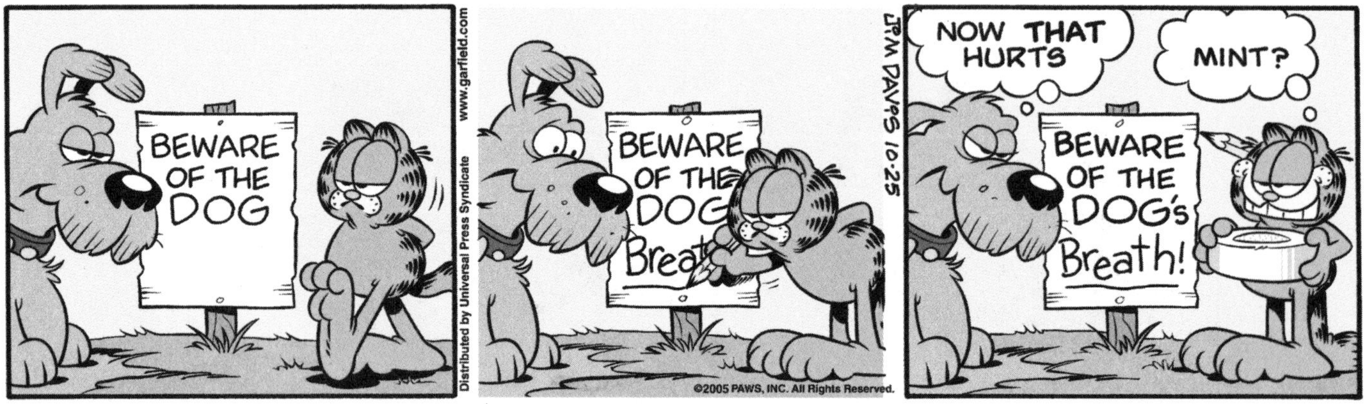
BEWARE OF THE DOG
www.garfield.com
Distributed by Universal Press Syndicate
BEWARE OF THE DOG Breat
©2005 PAWS, INC. All Rights Reserved.
JIM DAVIS 10-25
NOW THAT HURTS
MINT?
BEWARE OF THE DOG's Breath!

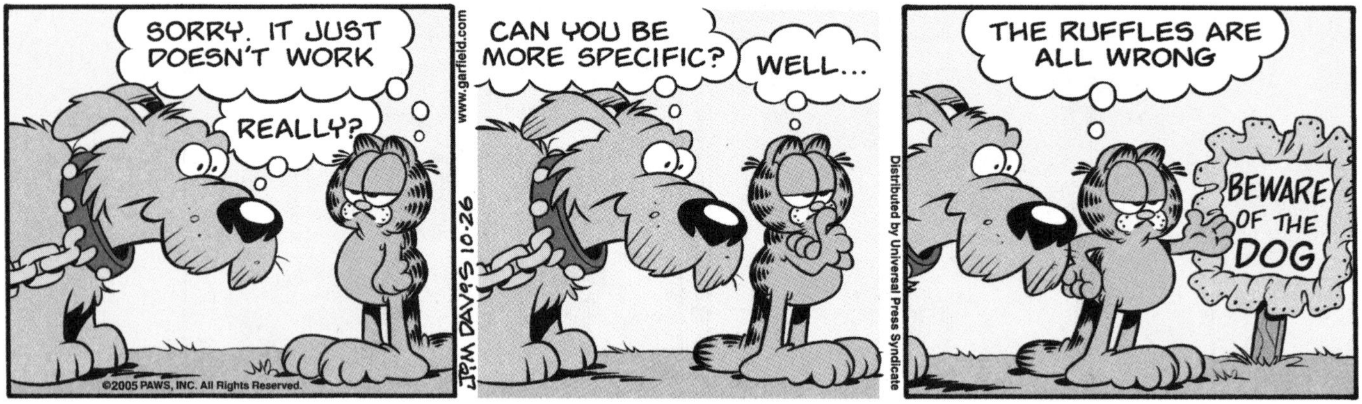
SORRY. IT JUST DOESN'T WORK
REALLY?
©2005 PAWS, INC. All Rights Reserved.
www.garfield.com
JIM DAVIS 10-26
CAN YOU BE MORE SPECIFIC?
WELL...
Distributed by Universal Press Syndicate
THE RUFFLES ARE ALL WRONG
BEWARE OF THE DOG

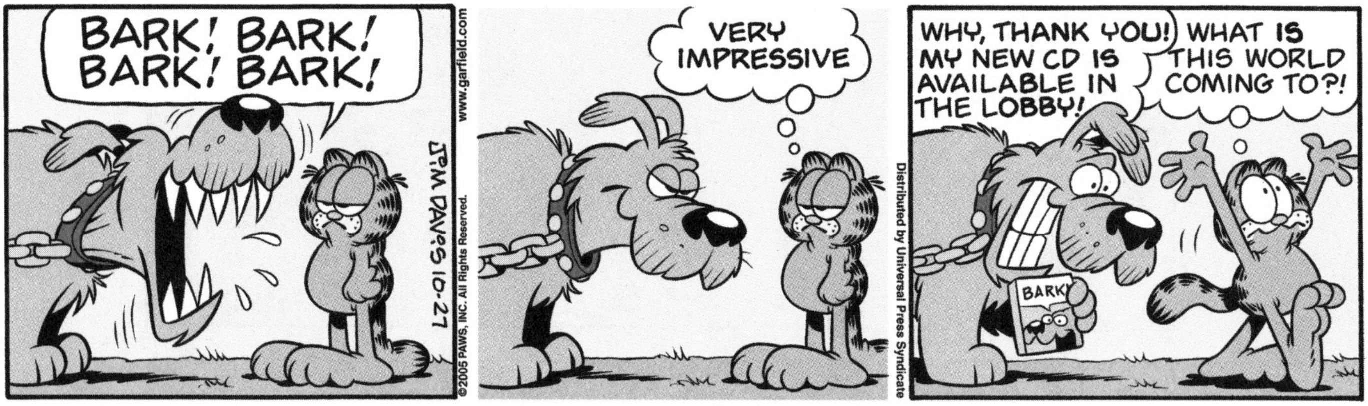
BARK! BARK! BARK! BARK!
JIM DAVIS 10-27
©2005 PAWS, INC. All Rights Reserved.
www.garfield.com
VERY IMPRESSIVE
Distributed by Universal Press Syndicate
WHY, THANK YOU! MY NEW CD IS AVAILABLE IN THE LOBBY!
WHAT IS THIS WORLD COMING TO?!
BARK

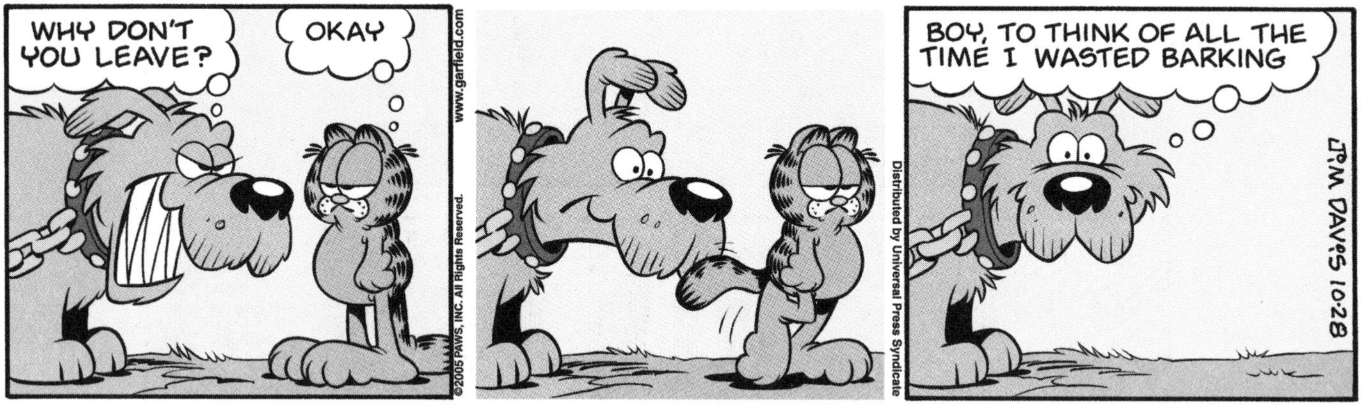
WHY DON'T YOU LEAVE?
OKAY
©2005 PAWS, INC. All Rights Reserved.
www.garfield.com
Distributed by Universal Press Syndicate
BOY, TO THINK OF ALL THE TIME I WASTED BARKING
JIM DAVIS 10-28

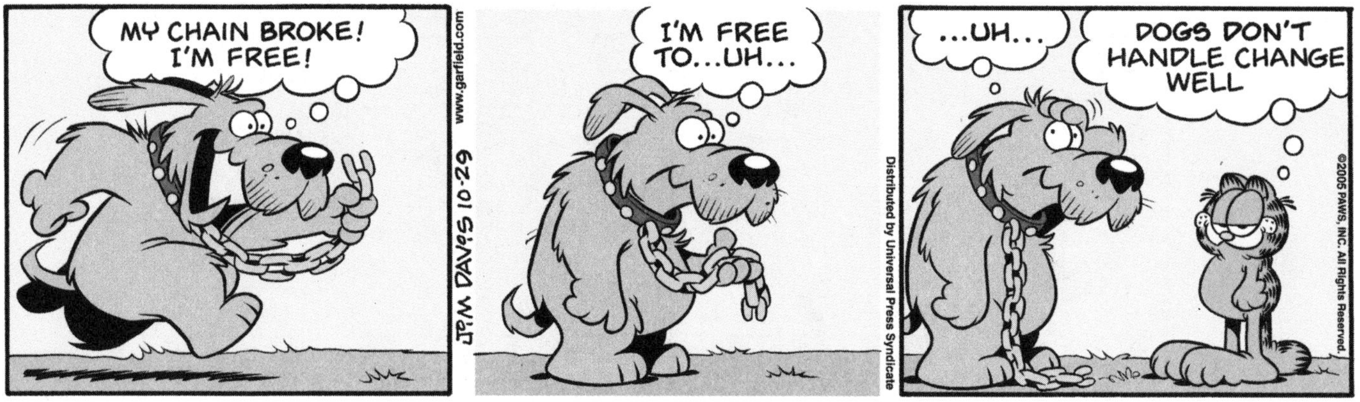
MY CHAIN BROKE! I'M FREE!
JIM DAVIS 10-29
www.garfield.com
I'M FREE TO...UH...
Distributed by Universal Press Syndicate
...UH...
DOGS DON'T HANDLE CHANGE WELL
©2005 PAWS, INC. All Rights Reserved.

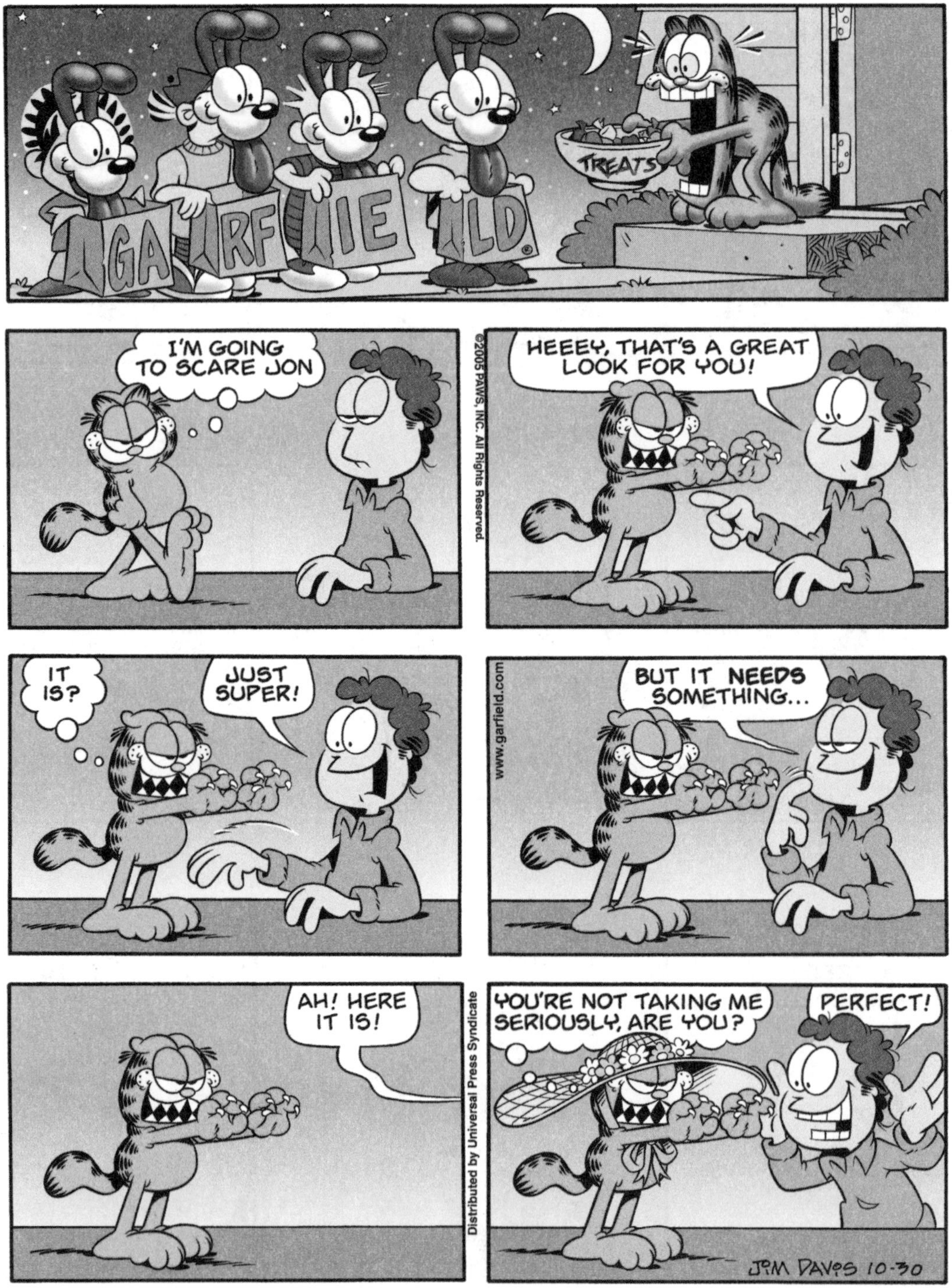
GA
RF
IE
LD
TREATS
I'M GOING TO SCARE JON
©2005 PAWS, INC. All Rights Reserved.
HEEEY, THAT'S A GREAT LOOK FOR YOU!
IT IS?
JUST SUPER!
www.garfield.com
BUT IT NEEDS SOMETHING...
AH! HERE IT IS!
Distributed by Universal Press Syndicate
YOU'RE NOT TAKING ME SERIOUSLY, ARE YOU?
PERFECT!
JIM DAVIS 10-30

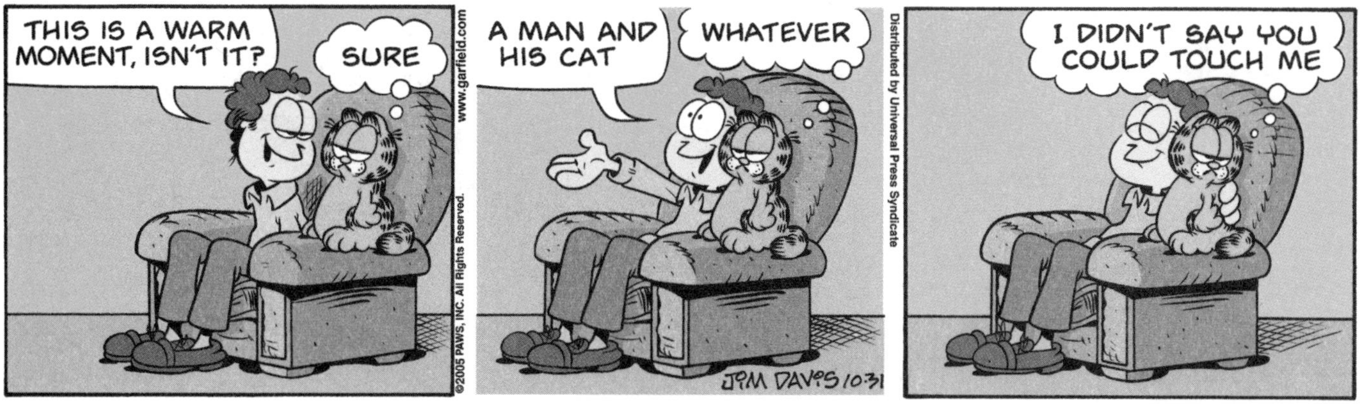
THIS IS A WARM MOMENT, ISN'T IT?
SURE
A MAN AND HIS CAT
WHATEVER
I DIDN'T SAY YOU COULD TOUCH ME
JIM DAVIS 10-31
©2005 PAWS, INC. All Rights Reserved. www.garfield.com
Distributed by Universal Press Syndicate

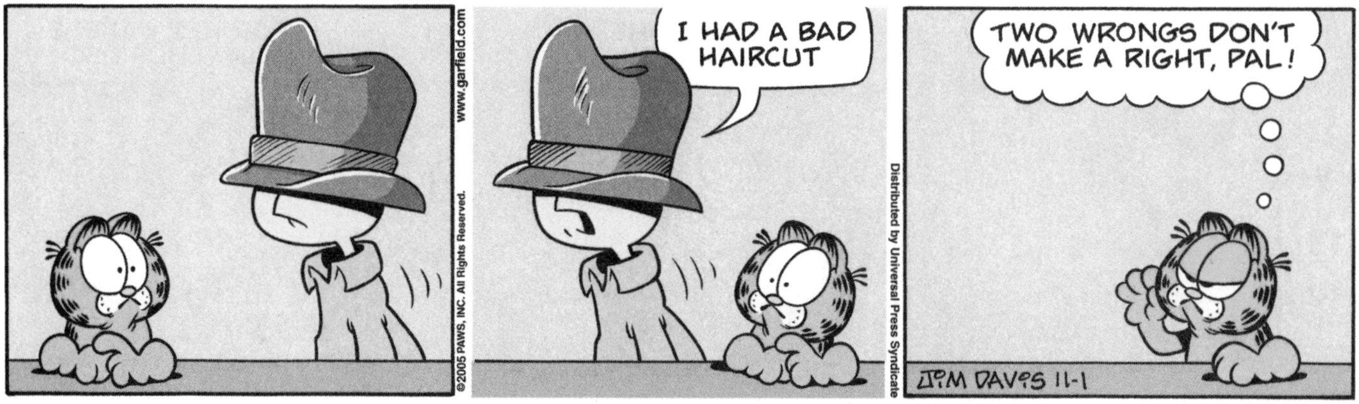
I HAD A BAD HAIRCUT
TWO WRONGS DON'T MAKE A RIGHT, PAL!
JIM DAVIS 11-1
©2005 PAWS, INC. All Rights Reserved. www.garfield.com
Distributed by Universal Press Syndicate

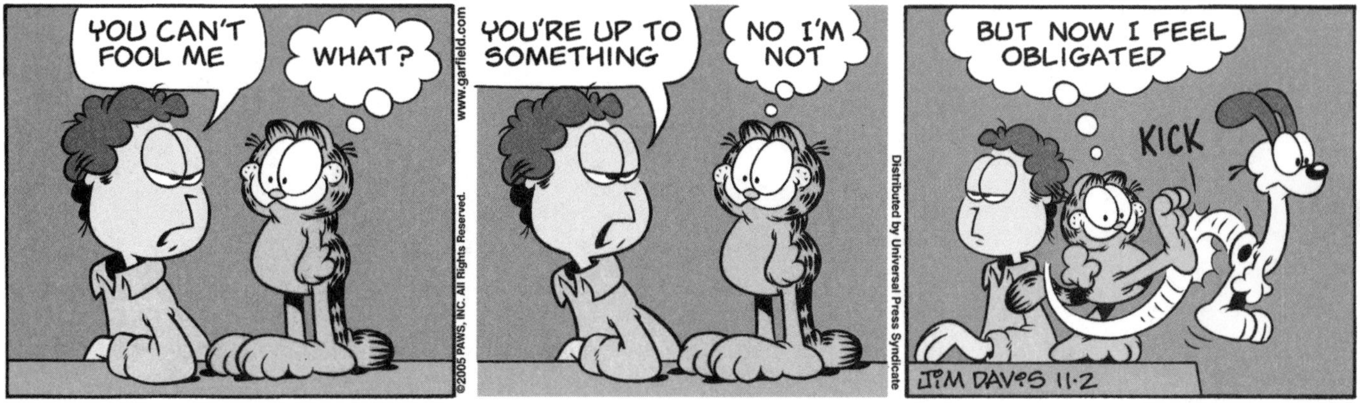
YOU CAN'T FOOL ME
WHAT?
YOU'RE UP TO SOMETHING
NO I'M NOT
BUT NOW I FEEL OBLIGATED
KICK
JIM DAVIS 11-2
©2005 PAWS, INC. All Rights Reserved. www.garfield.com
Distributed by Universal Press Syndicate

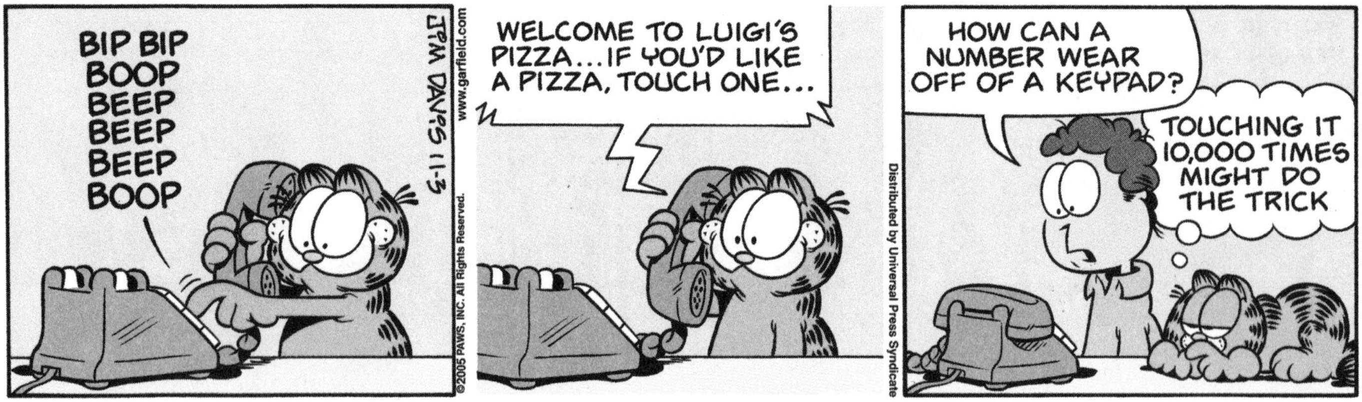
BIP BIP BOOP BEEP BEEP BEEP BOOP
JIM DAVIS 11-3
www.garfield.com
©2005 PAWS, INC. All Rights Reserved.
WELCOME TO LUIGI'S PIZZA... IF YOU'D LIKE A PIZZA, TOUCH ONE...
Distributed by Universal Press Syndicate
HOW CAN A NUMBER WEAR OFF OF A KEYPAD?
TOUCHING IT 10,000 TIMES MIGHT DO THE TRICK

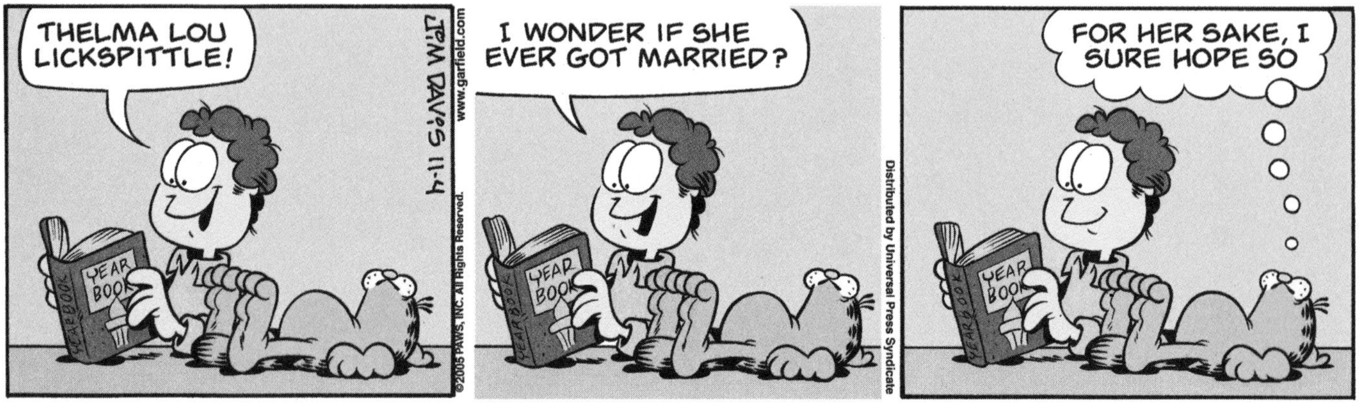
THELMA LOU LICKSPITTLE!
JIM DAVIS 11-4
www.garfield.com
©2005 PAWS, INC. All Rights Reserved.
YEAR BOOK
I WONDER IF SHE EVER GOT MARRIED?
Distributed by Universal Press Syndicate
FOR HER SAKE, I SURE HOPE SO

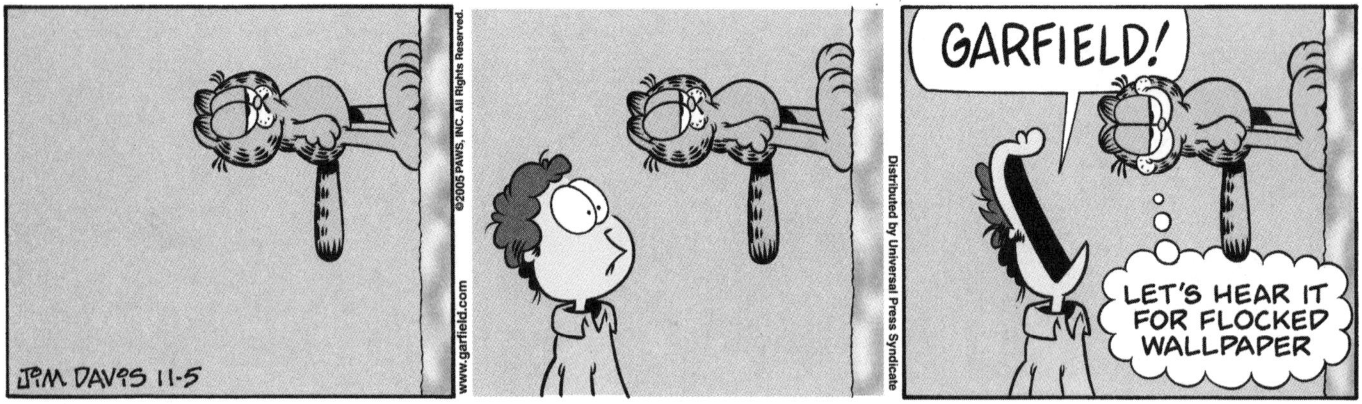
JIM DAVIS 11-5
www.garfield.com
©2005 PAWS, INC. All Rights Reserved.
Distributed by Universal Press Syndicate
GARFIELD!
LET'S HEAR IT FOR FLOCKED WALLPAPER

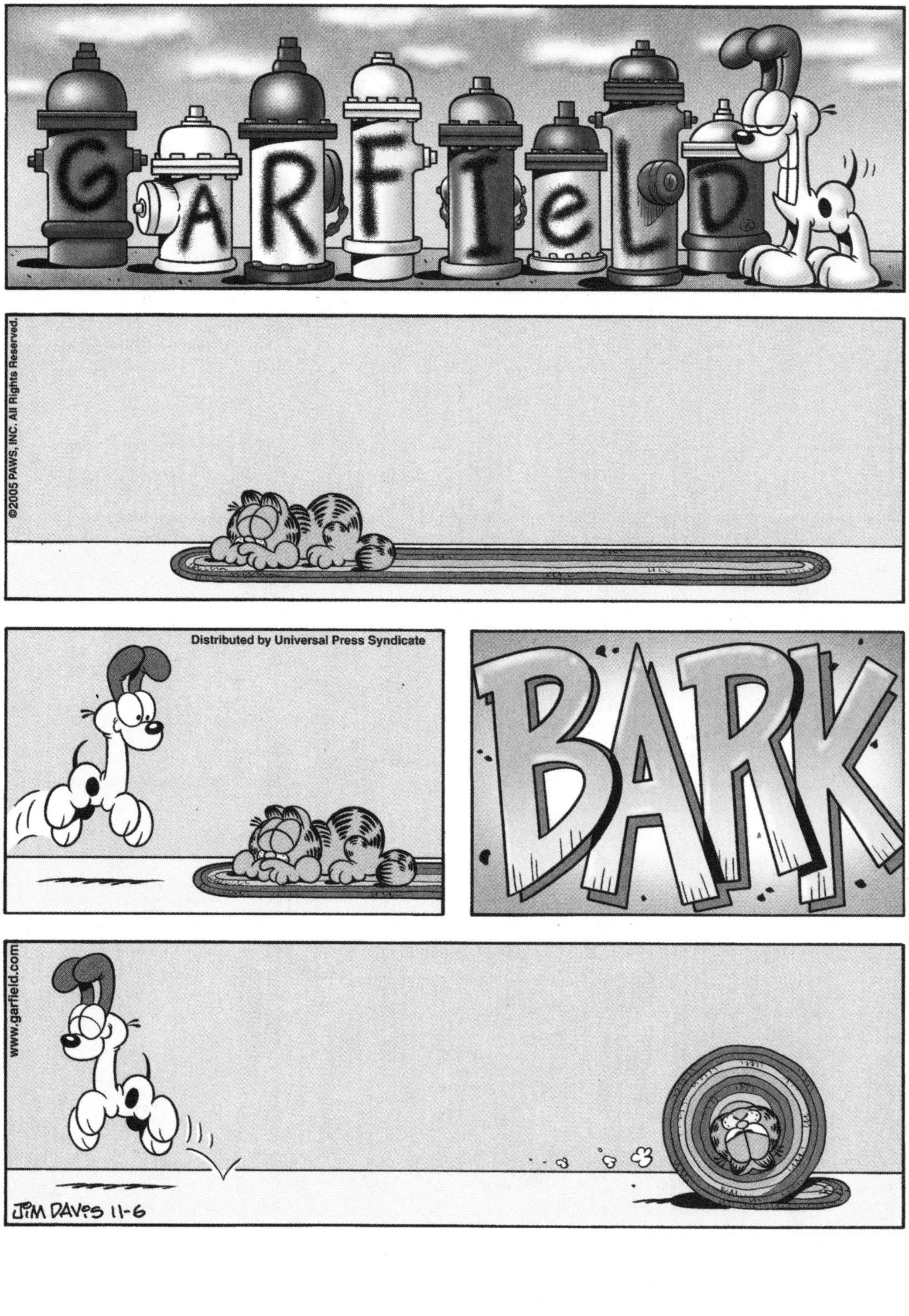
GARFIELD
©2005 PAWS, INC. All Rights Reserved.
Distributed by Universal Press Syndicate
BARK
www.garfield.com
JIM DAVIS 11-6

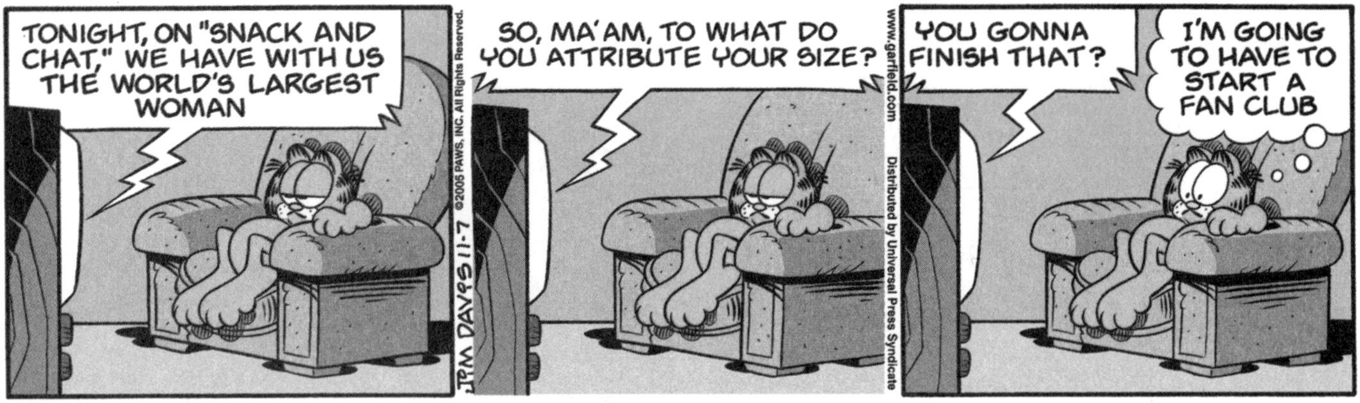
TONIGHT, ON "SNACK AND CHAT," WE HAVE WITH US THE WORLD'S LARGEST WOMAN
JIM DAVIS 11-7
©2005 PAWS, INC. All Rights Reserved.
SO, MA'AM, TO WHAT DO YOU ATTRIBUTE YOUR SIZE?
www.garfield.com
Distributed by Universal Press Syndicate
YOU GONNA FINISH THAT?
I'M GOING TO HAVE TO START A FAN CLUB

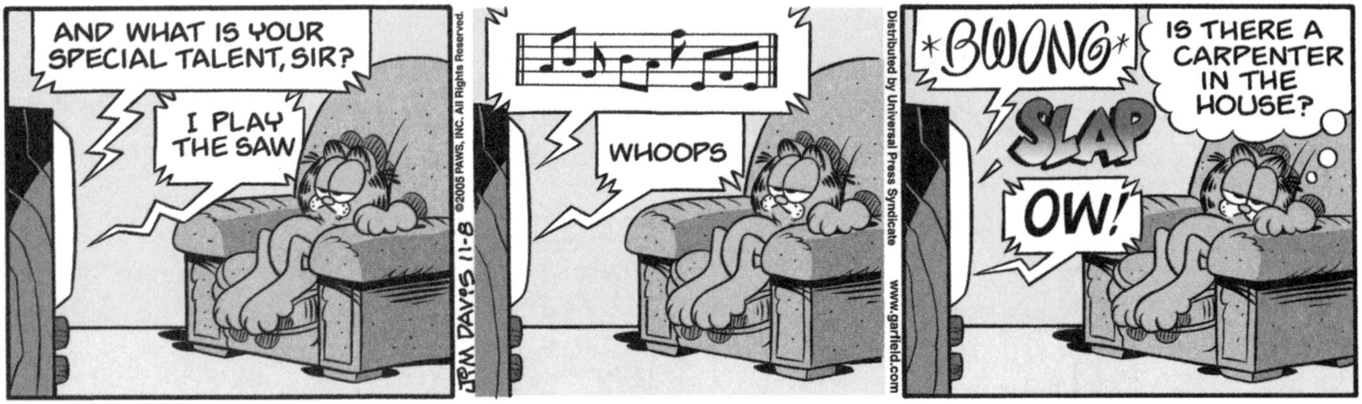
AND WHAT IS YOUR SPECIAL TALENT, SIR?
I PLAY THE SAW
JIM DAVIS 11-8
©2005 PAWS, INC. All Rights Reserved.
WHOOPS
Distributed by Universal Press Syndicate
www.garfield.com
BWONG
SLAP
OW!
IS THERE A CARPENTER IN THE HOUSE?

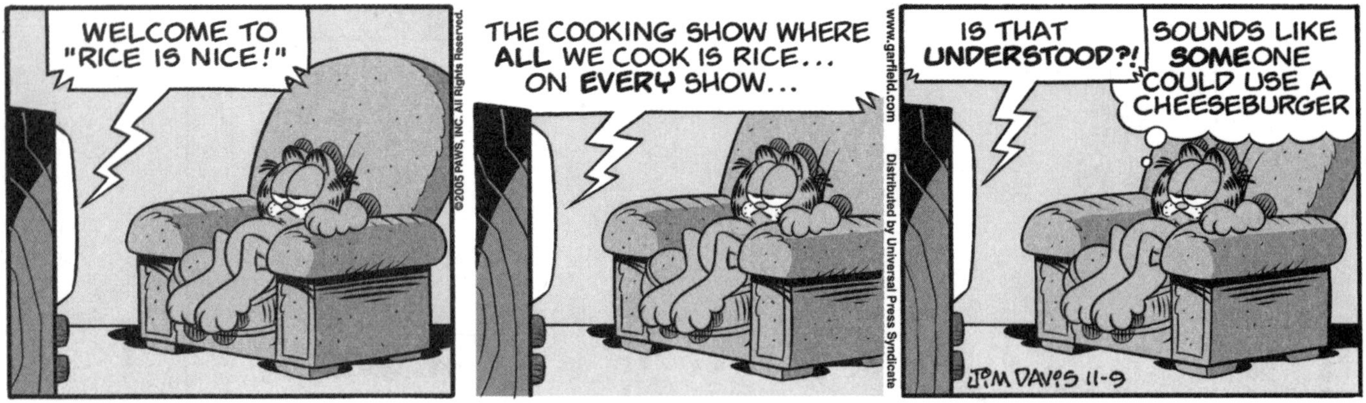
WELCOME TO "RICE IS NICE!"
©2005 PAWS, INC. All Rights Reserved.
THE COOKING SHOW WHERE ALL WE COOK IS RICE... ON EVERY SHOW...
www.garfield.com
Distributed by Universal Press Syndicate
IS THAT UNDERSTOOD?!
SOUNDS LIKE SOMEONE COULD USE A CHEESEBURGER
JIM DAVIS 11-9

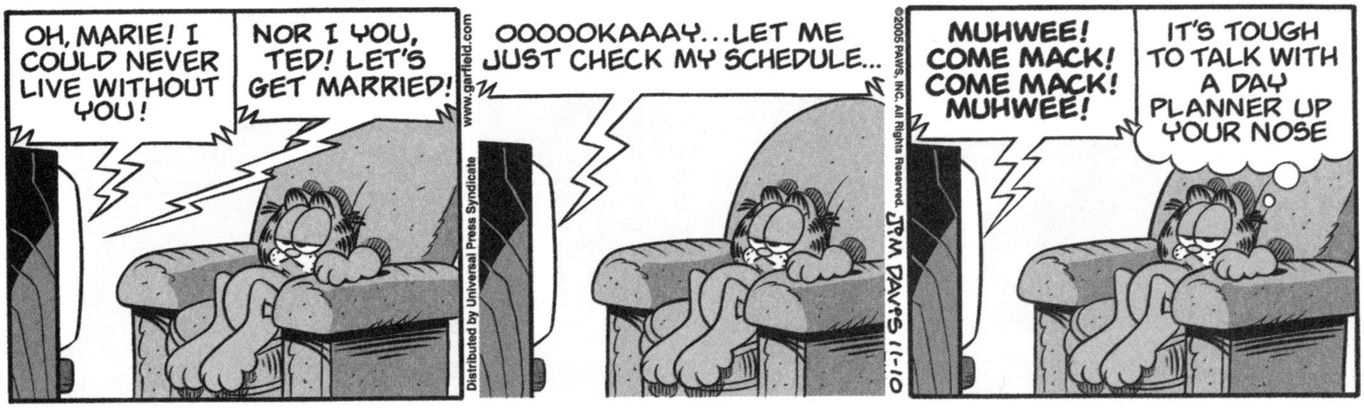
OH, MARIE! I COULD NEVER LIVE WITHOUT YOU!
NOR I YOU, TED! LET'S GET MARRIED!
OOOOOKAAAY...LET ME JUST CHECK MY SCHEDULE...
MUHWEE! COME MACK! COME MACK! MUHWEE!
IT'S TOUGH TO TALK WITH A DAY PLANNER UP YOUR NOSE
www.garfield.com
Distributed by Universal Press Syndicate
©2005 PAWS, INC. All Rights Reserved.

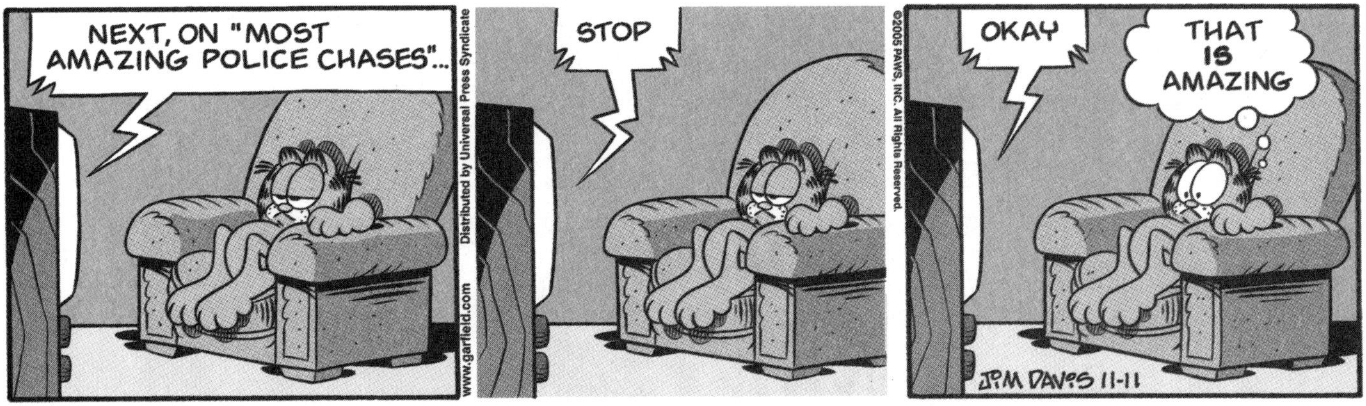
NEXT, ON "MOST AMAZING POLICE CHASES"...
STOP
OKAY
THAT IS AMAZING
www.garfield.com
Distributed by Universal Press Syndicate
©2005 PAWS, INC. All Rights Reserved.

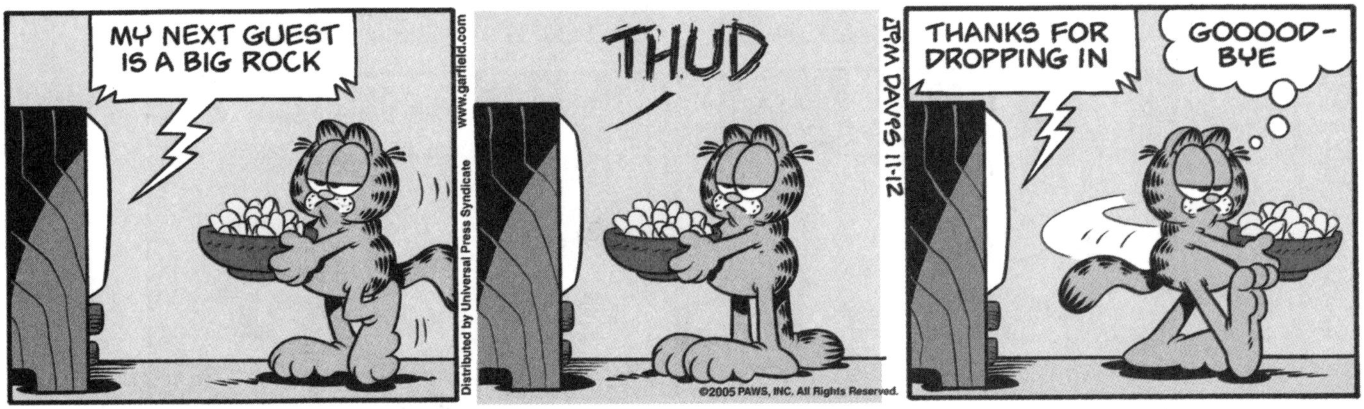
MY NEXT GUEST IS A BIG ROCK
THUD
THANKS FOR DROPPING IN
GOOOOD-BYE
www.garfield.com
Distributed by Universal Press Syndicate
©2005 PAWS, INC. All Rights Reserved.

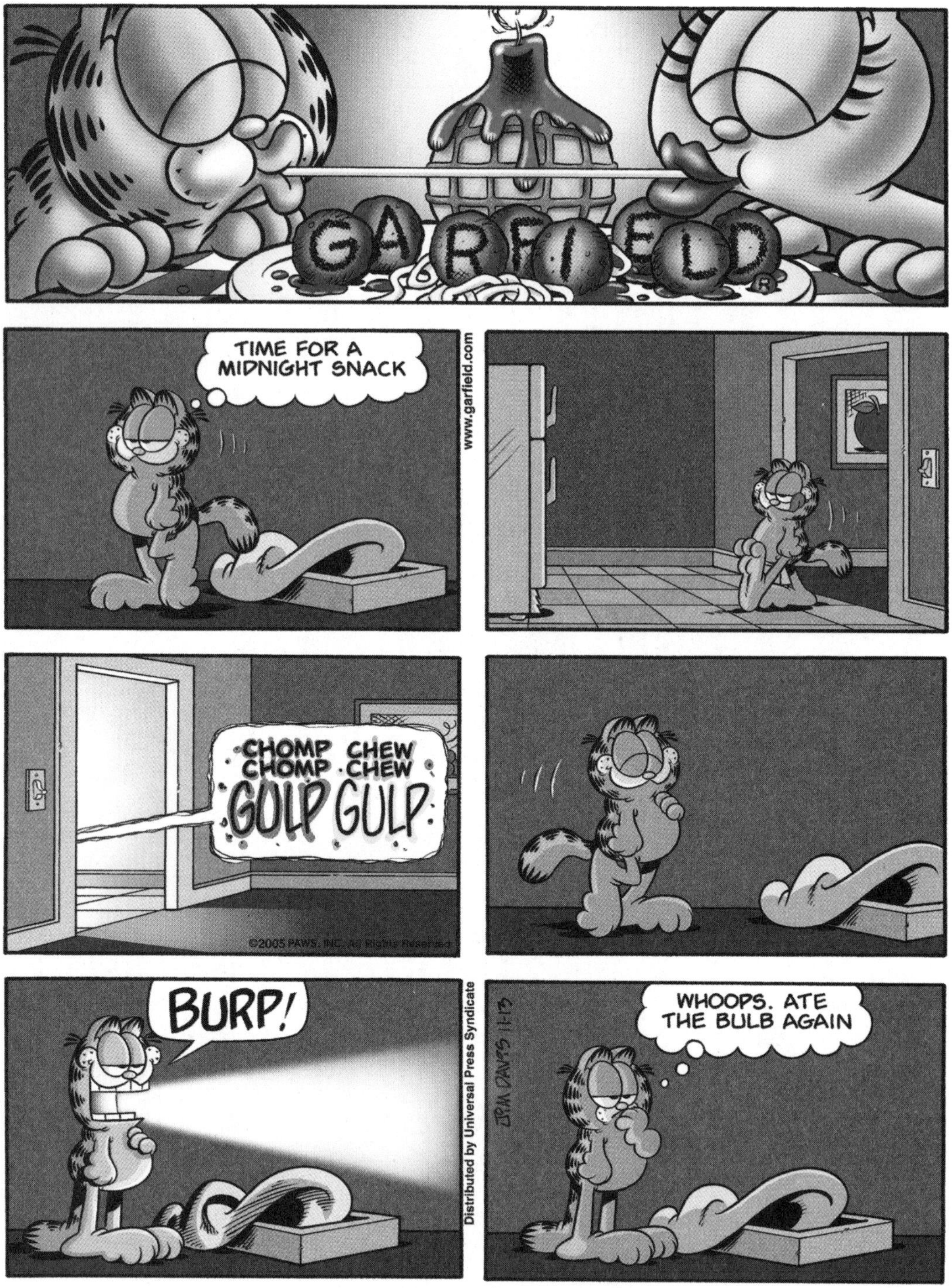
GARFIELD®
TIME FOR A MIDNIGHT SNACK
www.garfield.com
CHOMP CHEW CHOMP CHEW GOLP GULP
©2005 PAWS, INC. All Rights Reserved
BURP!
Distributed by Universal Press Syndicate
JPM DAVIS 11-13
WHOOPS. ATE THE BULB AGAIN

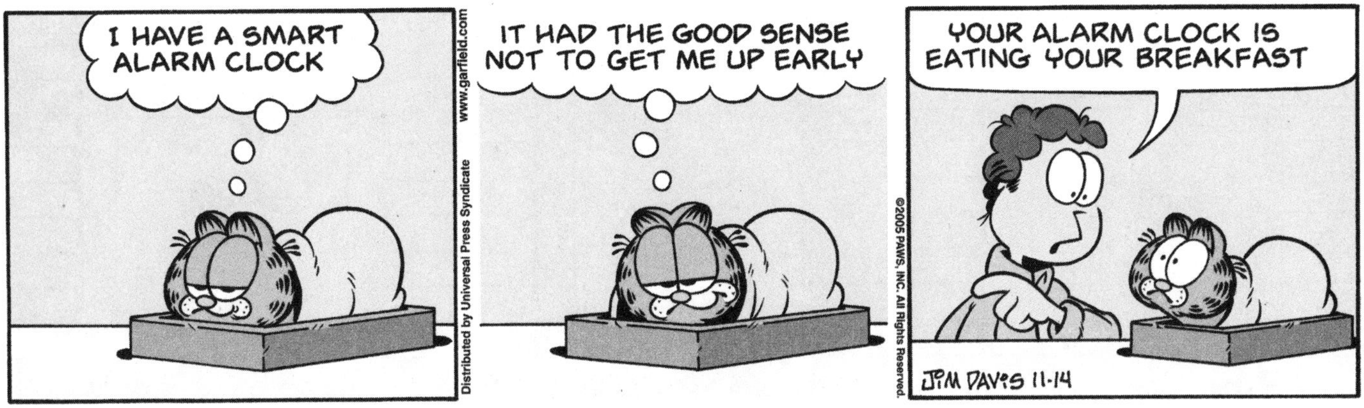
I HAVE A SMART ALARM CLOCK
www.garfield.com
Distributed by Universal Press Syndicate
IT HAD THE GOOD SENSE NOT TO GET ME UP EARLY
©2005 PAWS, INC. All Rights Reserved.
YOUR ALARM CLOCK IS EATING YOUR BREAKFAST
JIM DAVIS 11-14

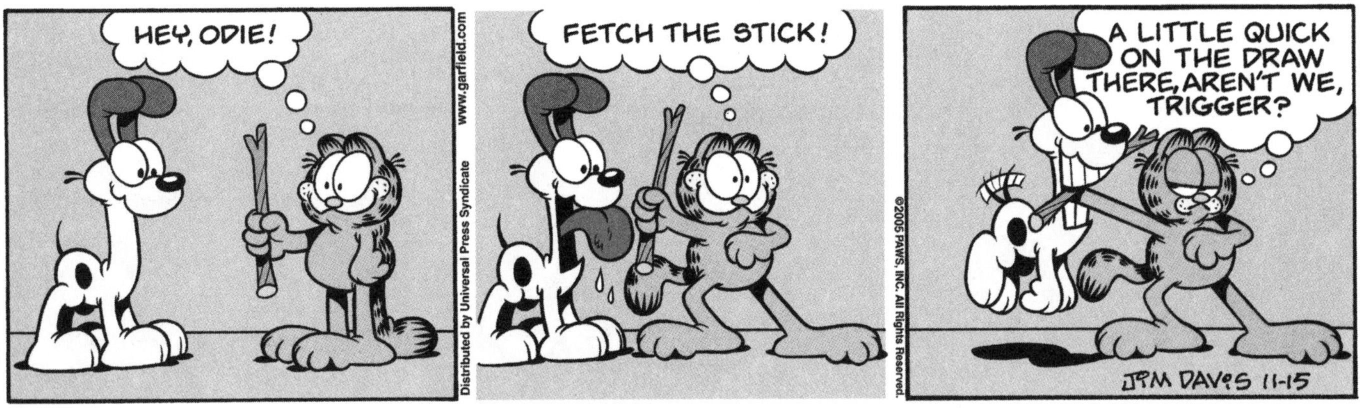
HEY, ODIE!
www.garfield.com
Distributed by Universal Press Syndicate
FETCH THE STICK!
©2005 PAWS, INC. All Rights Reserved.
A LITTLE QUICK ON THE DRAW THERE, AREN'T WE, TRIGGER?
JIM DAVIS 11-15

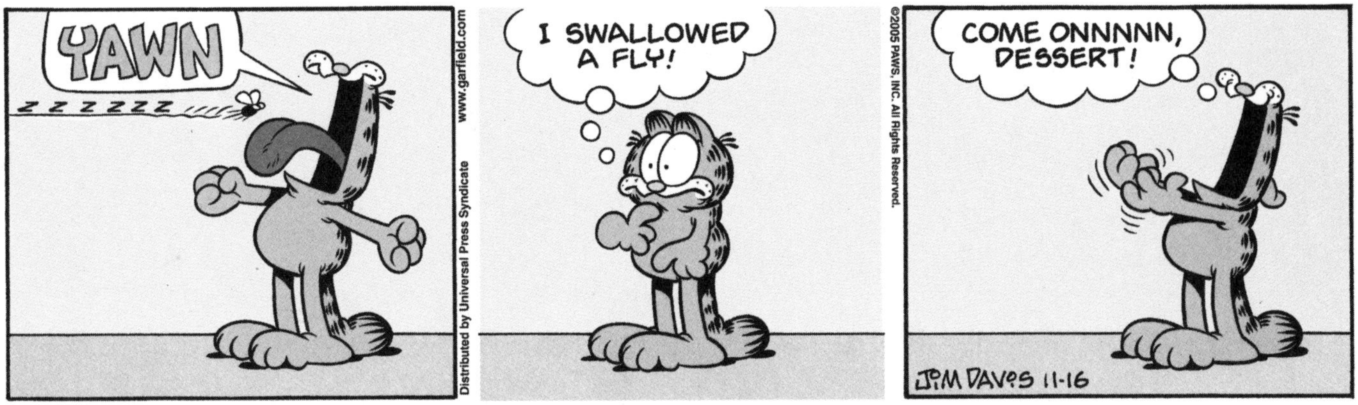
YAWN
Z Z Z Z Z Z
www.garfield.com
Distributed by Universal Press Syndicate
I SWALLOWED A FLY!
©2005 PAWS, INC. All Rights Reserved.
COME ONNNNN, DESSERT!
JIM DAVIS 11-16

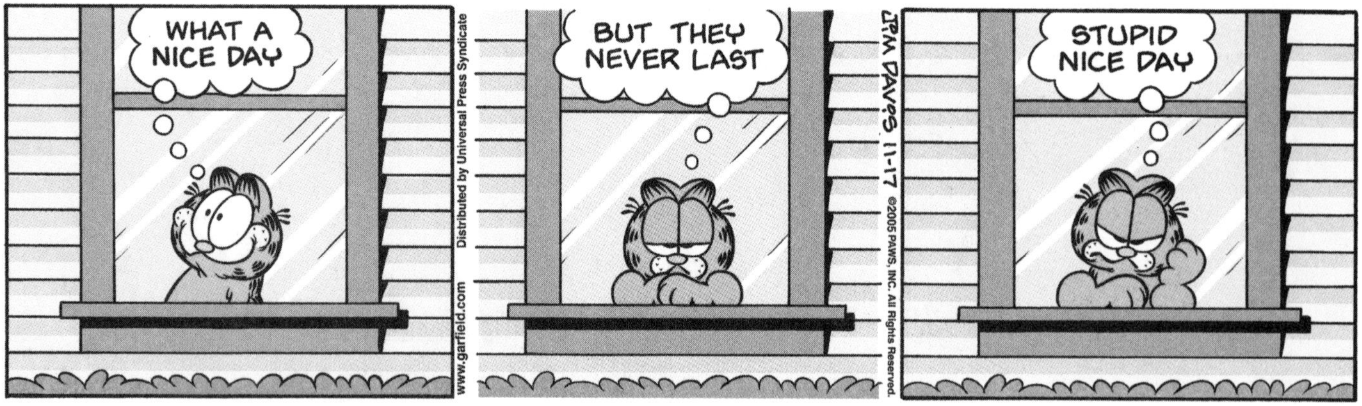
WHAT A NICE DAY
BUT THEY NEVER LAST
STUPID NICE DAY
JIM DAVIS 11-17
Distributed by Universal Press Syndicate
www.garfield.com
©2005 PAWS, INC. All Rights Reserved.

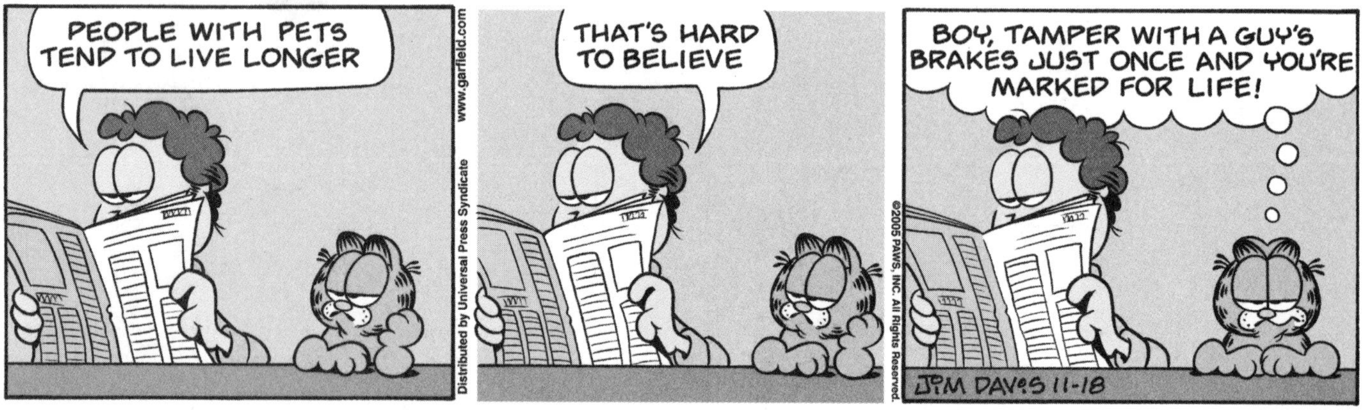
PEOPLE WITH PETS TEND TO LIVE LONGER
THAT'S HARD TO BELIEVE
BOY, TAMPER WITH A GUY'S BRAKES JUST ONCE AND YOU'RE MARKED FOR LIFE!
JIM DAVIS 11-18
Distributed by Universal Press Syndicate
www.garfield.com
©2005 PAWS, INC. All Rights Reserved.

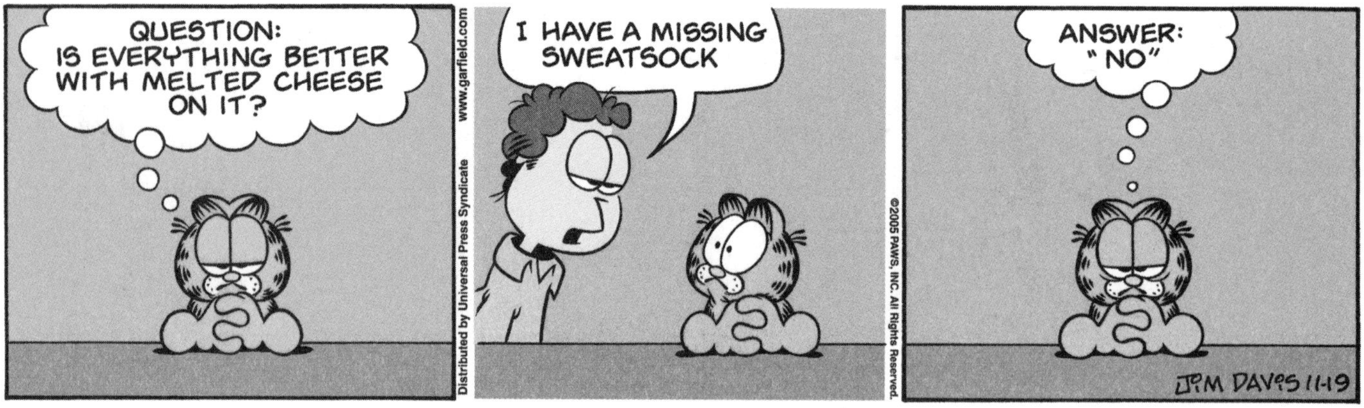
QUESTION: IS EVERYTHING BETTER WITH MELTED CHEESE ON IT?
I HAVE A MISSING SWEATSOCK
ANSWER: "NO"
JIM DAVIS 11-19
Distributed by Universal Press Syndicate
www.garfield.com
©2005 PAWS, INC. All Rights Reserved.

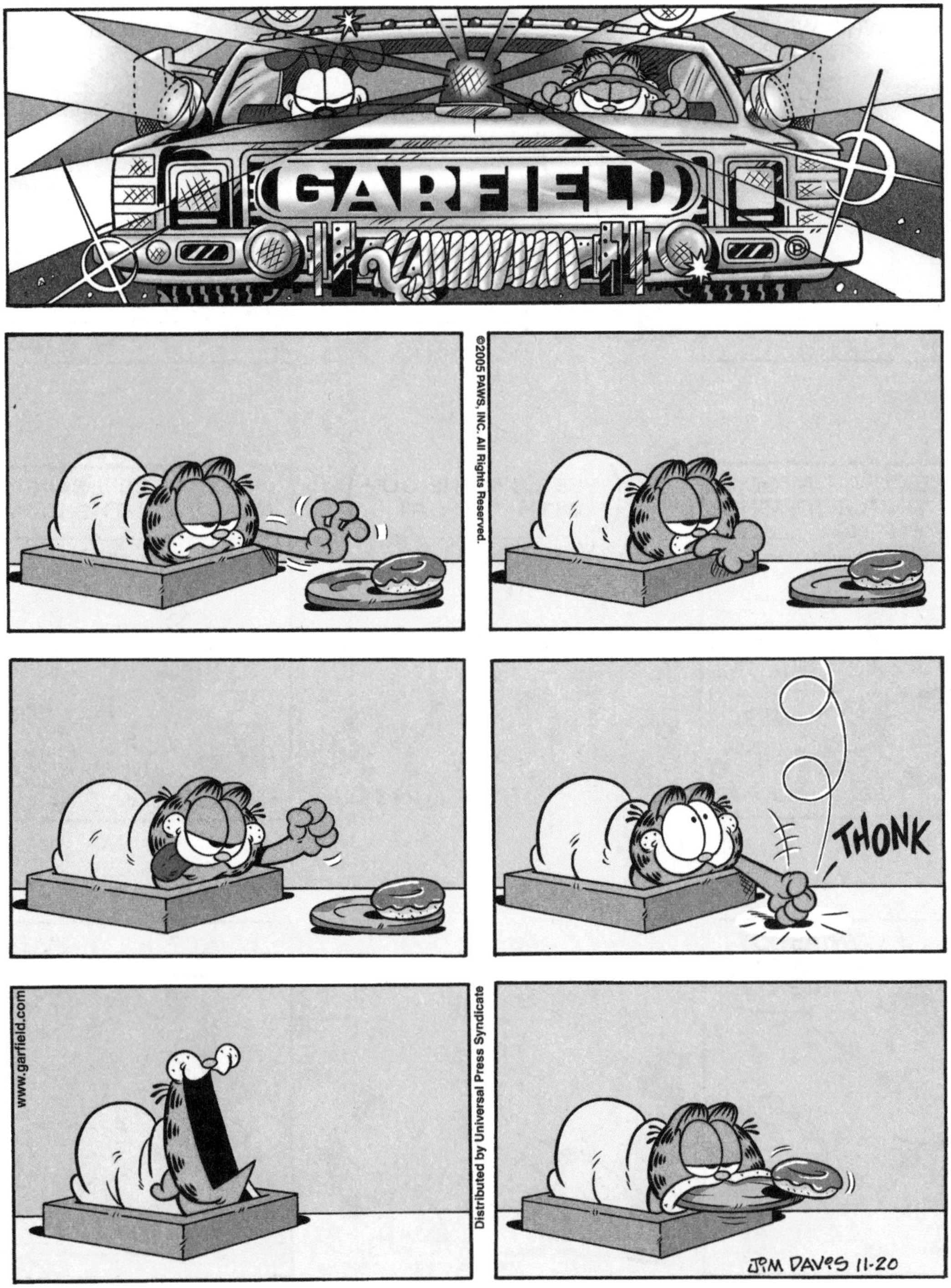

GARFIELD
©2005 PAWS, INC. All Rights Reserved.
THONK
www.garfield.com
Distributed by Universal Press Syndicate
JIM DAVIS 11-20

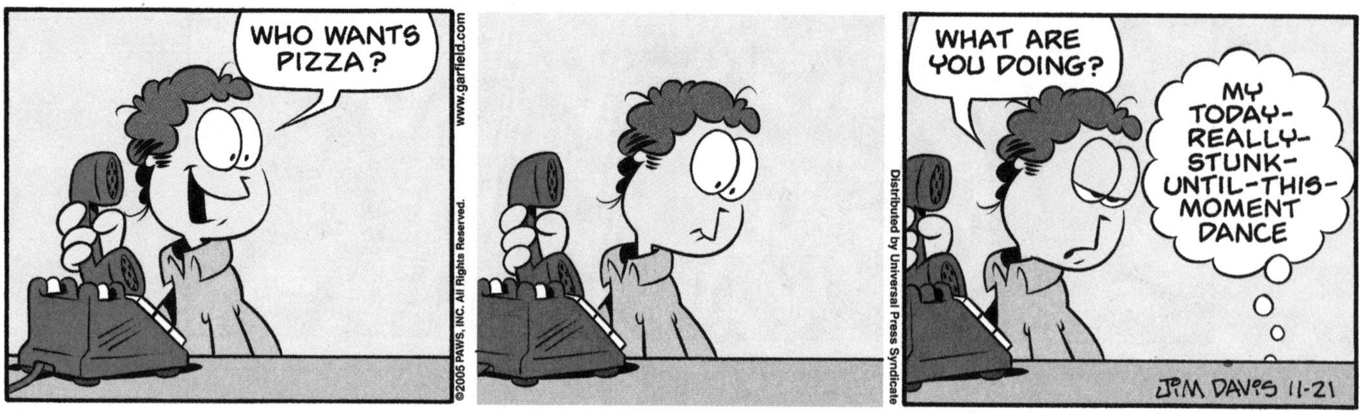
WHO WANTS PIZZA?
WHAT ARE YOU DOING?
MY TODAY-REALLY-STUNK-UNTIL-THIS-MOMENT DANCE
JIM DAVIS 11-21
©2005 PAWS, INC. All Rights Reserved. www.garfield.com
Distributed by Universal Press Syndicate

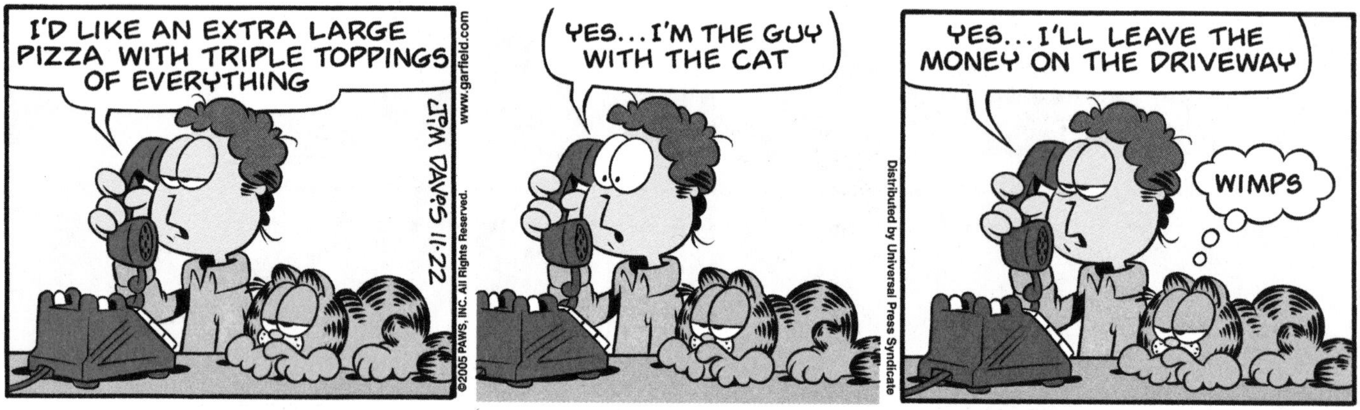
I'D LIKE AN EXTRA LARGE PIZZA WITH TRIPLE TOPPINGS OF EVERYTHING
YES... I'M THE GUY WITH THE CAT
YES... I'LL LEAVE THE MONEY ON THE DRIVEWAY
WIMPS
JIM DAVIS 11-22
©2005 PAWS, INC. All Rights Reserved. www.garfield.com
Distributed by Universal Press Syndicate

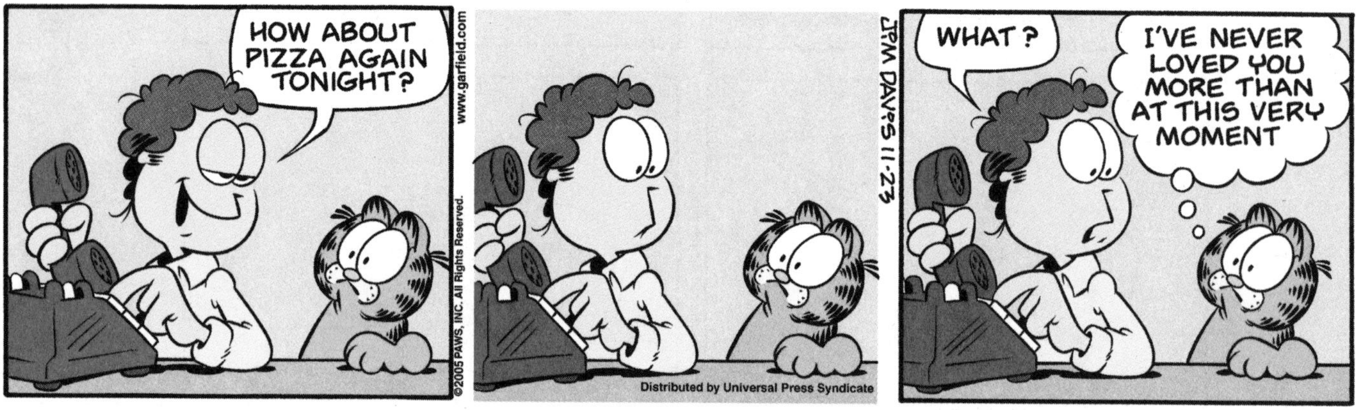
HOW ABOUT PIZZA AGAIN TONIGHT?
WHAT?
I'VE NEVER LOVED YOU MORE THAN AT THIS VERY MOMENT
JIM DAVIS 11-23
©2005 PAWS, INC. All Rights Reserved. www.garfield.com
Distributed by Universal Press Syndicate

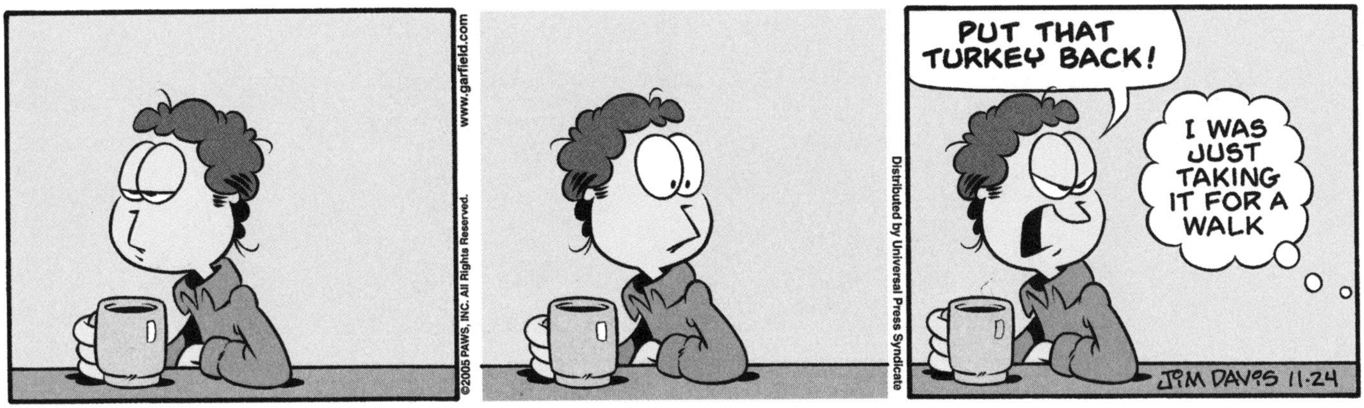
©2005 PAWS, INC. All Rights Reserved. www.garfield.com
Distributed by Universal Press Syndicate
PUT THAT TURKEY BACK!
I WAS JUST TAKING IT FOR A WALK
JIM DAVIS 11-24

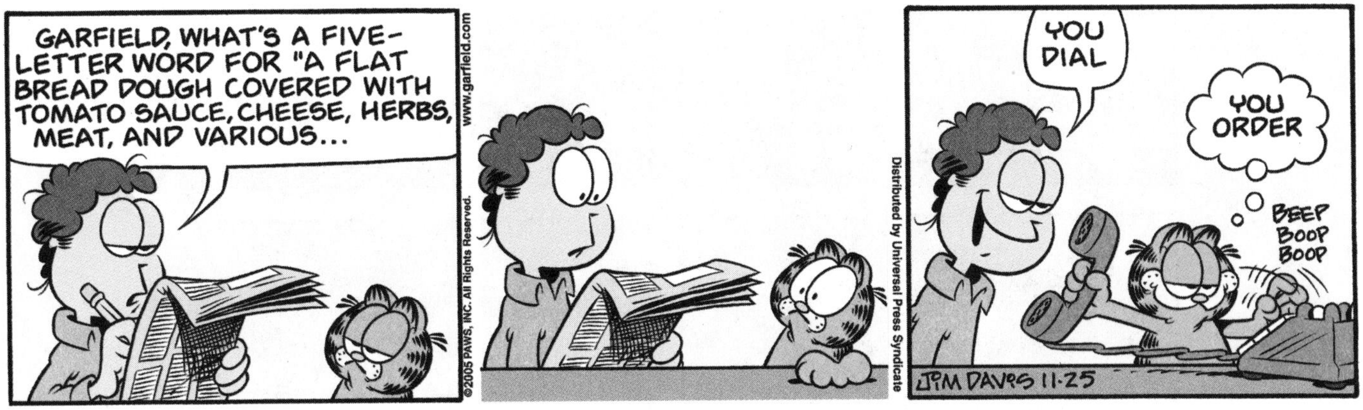
GARFIELD, WHAT'S A FIVE-LETTER WORD FOR "A FLAT BREAD DOUGH COVERED WITH TOMATO SAUCE, CHEESE, HERBS, MEAT, AND VARIOUS...
©2005 PAWS, INC. All Rights Reserved. www.garfield.com
Distributed by Universal Press Syndicate
YOU DIAL
YOU ORDER
BEEP BOOP BOOP
JIM DAVIS 11-25

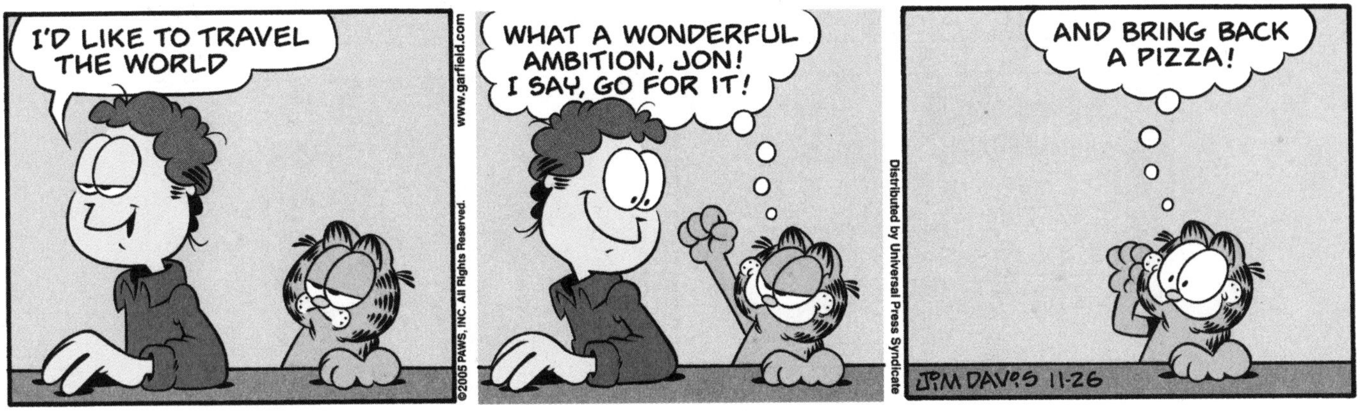
I'D LIKE TO TRAVEL THE WORLD
©2005 PAWS, INC. All Rights Reserved. www.garfield.com
WHAT A WONDERFUL AMBITION, JON! I SAY, GO FOR IT!
Distributed by Universal Press Syndicate
AND BRING BACK A PIZZA!
JIM DAVIS 11-26

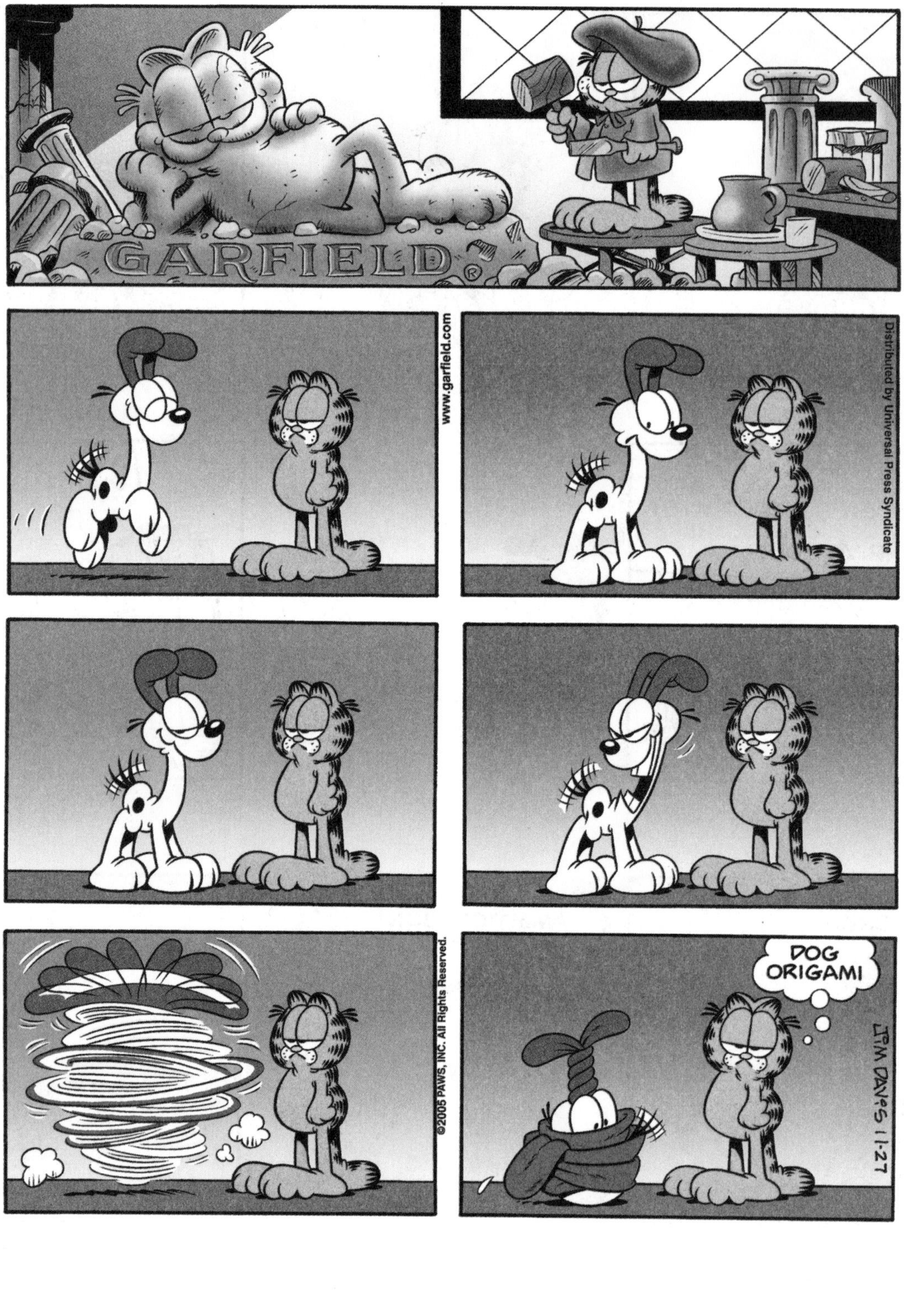
GARFIELD®
www.garfield.com
Distributed by Universal Press Syndicate
©2005 PAWS, INC. All Rights Reserved.
DOG ORIGAMI
JIM DAVIS 11-27

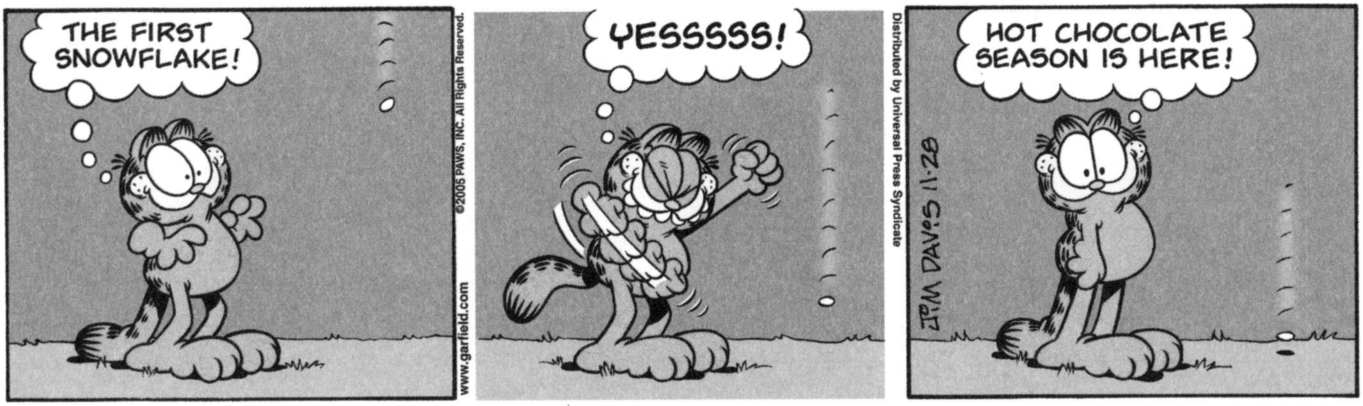
THE FIRST SNOWFLAKE!
YESSSSS!
HOT CHOCOLATE SEASON IS HERE!
JPM DAVPS 11·28
©2005 PAWS, INC. All Rights Reserved.
www.garfield.com
Distributed by Universal Press Syndicate

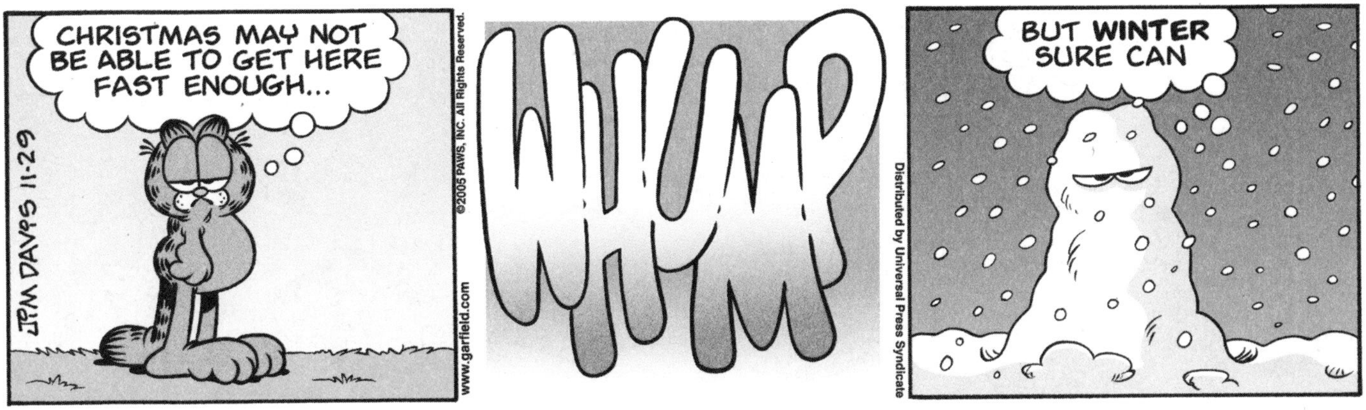
CHRISTMAS MAY NOT BE ABLE TO GET HERE FAST ENOUGH...
JPM DAVPS 11·29
WHUMP
BUT WINTER SURE CAN
©2005 PAWS, INC. All Rights Reserved.
www.garfield.com
Distributed by Universal Press Syndicate

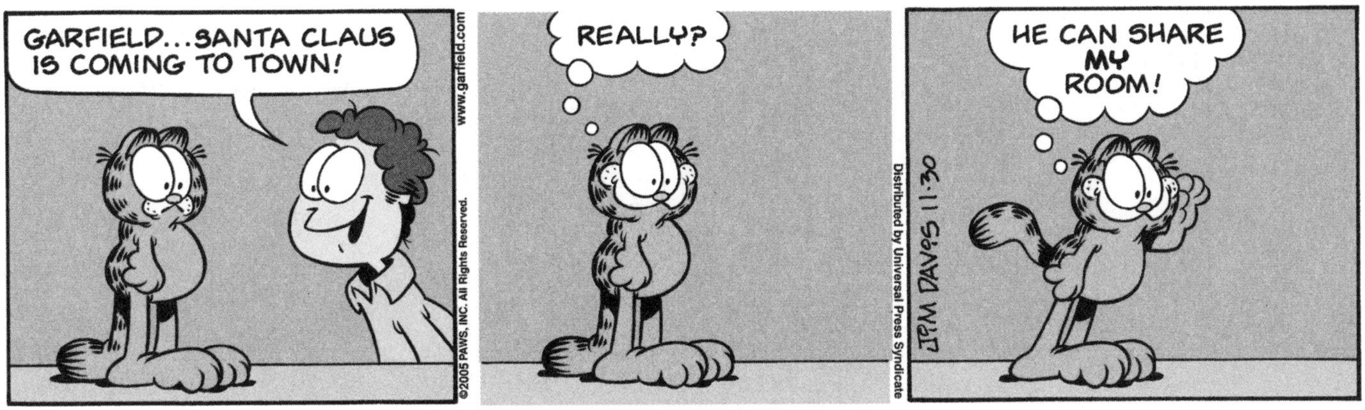
GARFIELD...SANTA CLAUS IS COMING TO TOWN!
REALLY?
HE CAN SHARE MY ROOM!
JPM DAVPS 11·30
©2005 PAWS, INC. All Rights Reserved.
www.garfield.com
Distributed by Universal Press Syndicate

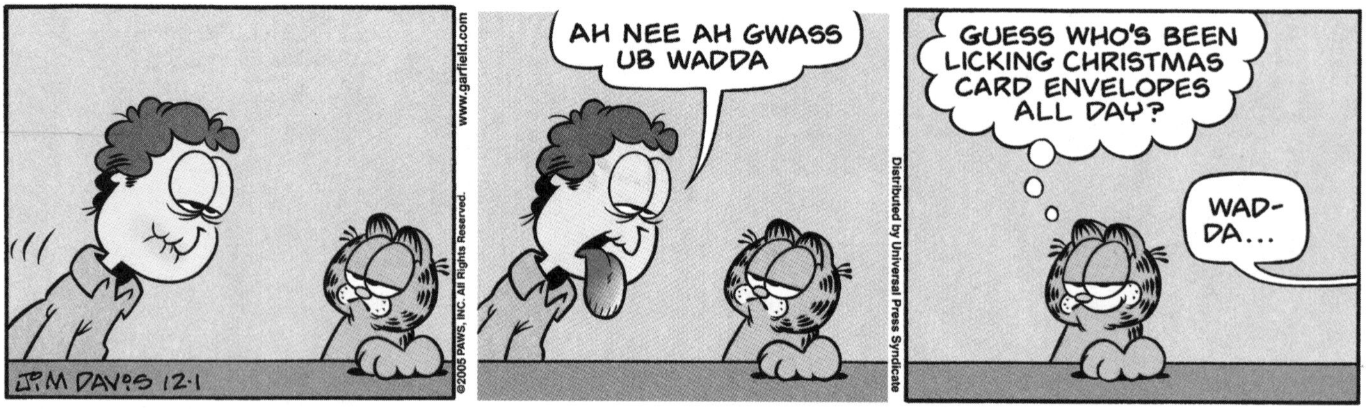
JIM DAVIS 12-1
AH NEE AH GWASS UB WADDA
GUESS WHO'S BEEN LICKING CHRISTMAS CARD ENVELOPES ALL DAY?
WAD-DA...
www.garfield.com
©2005 PAWS, INC. All Rights Reserved.
Distributed by Universal Press Syndicate

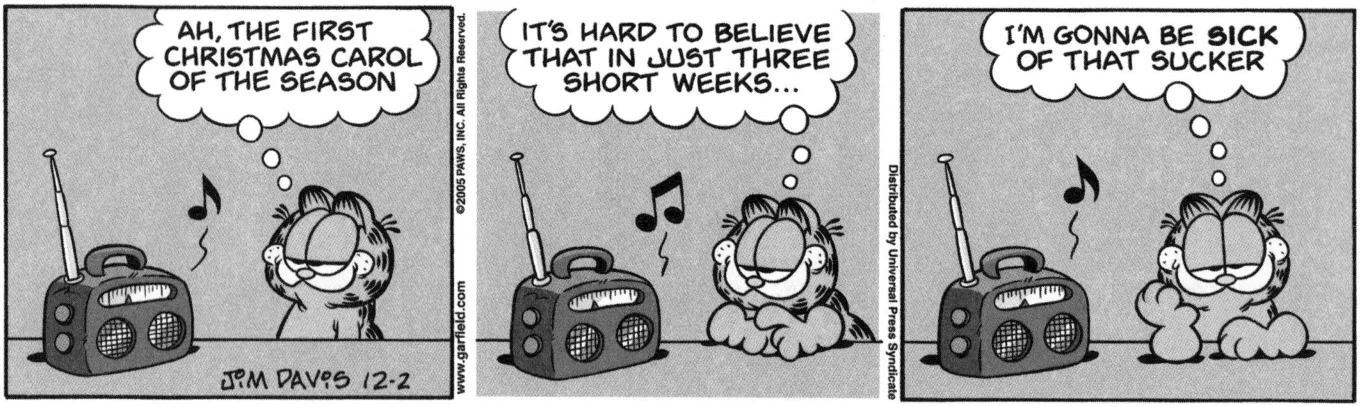
AH, THE FIRST CHRISTMAS CAROL OF THE SEASON
JIM DAVIS 12-2
IT'S HARD TO BELIEVE THAT IN JUST THREE SHORT WEEKS...
I'M GONNA BE SICK OF THAT SUCKER
©2005 PAWS, INC. All Rights Reserved.
www.garfield.com
Distributed by Universal Press Syndicate

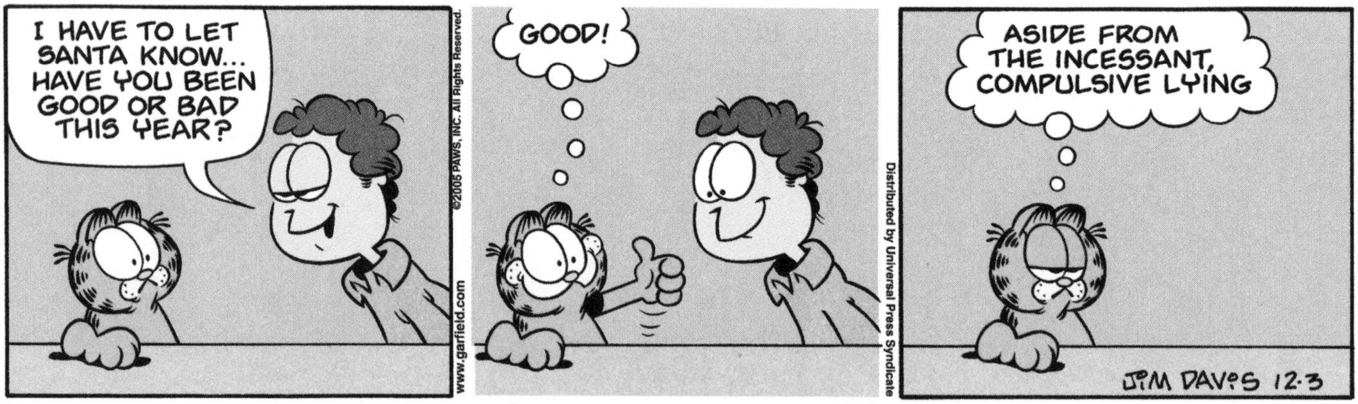
I HAVE TO LET SANTA KNOW... HAVE YOU BEEN GOOD OR BAD THIS YEAR?
GOOD!
ASIDE FROM THE INCESSANT, COMPULSIVE LYING
JIM DAVIS 12-3
©2005 PAWS, INC. All Rights Reserved.
www.garfield.com
Distributed by Universal Press Syndicate

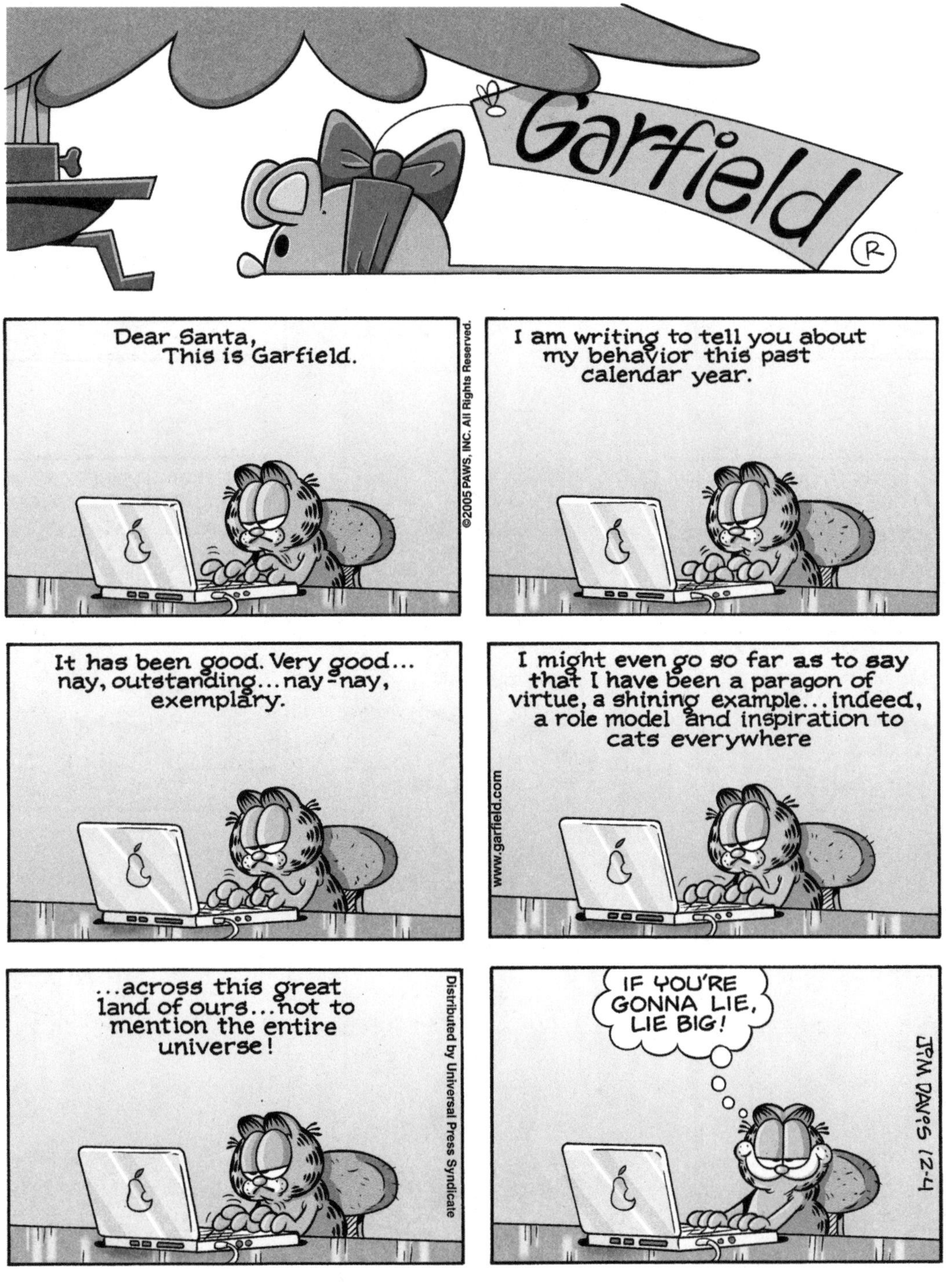
Garfield
Dear Santa,
This is Garfield.
©2005 PAWS, INC. All Rights Reserved.
I am writing to tell you about my behavior this past calendar year.
It has been good. Very good... nay, outstanding... nay-nay, exemplary.
www.garfield.com
I might even go so far as to say that I have been a paragon of virtue, a shining example... indeed, a role model and inspiration to cats everywhere
...across this great land of ours... not to mention the entire universe!
Distributed by Universal Press Syndicate
IF YOU'RE GONNA LIE, LIE BIG!
JIM DAVIS 12-4

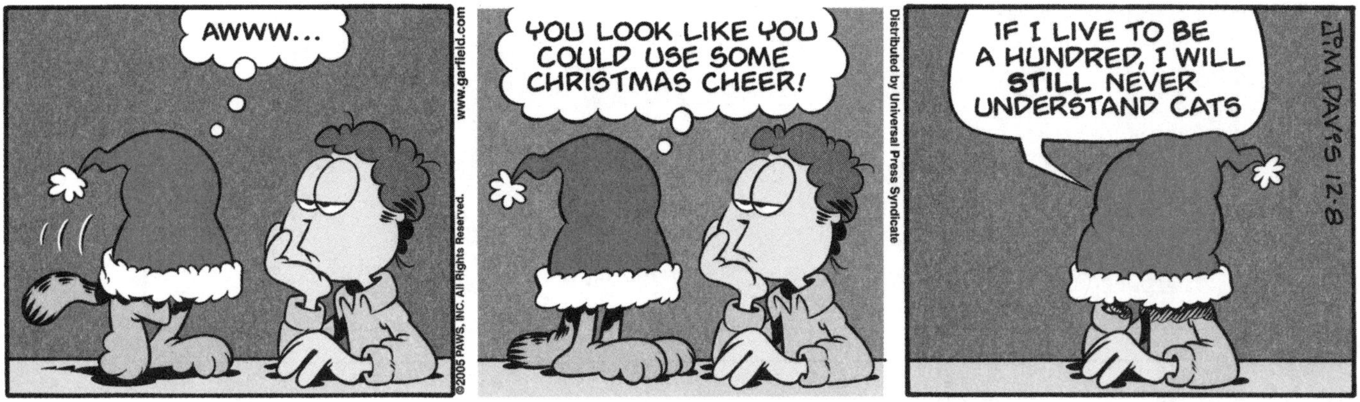
AWWW...
YOU LOOK LIKE YOU COULD USE SOME CHRISTMAS CHEER!
IF I LIVE TO BE A HUNDRED, I WILL STILL NEVER UNDERSTAND CATS
JIM DAVIS 12-8
©2005 PAWS, INC. All Rights Reserved. www.garfield.com
Distributed by Universal Press Syndicate

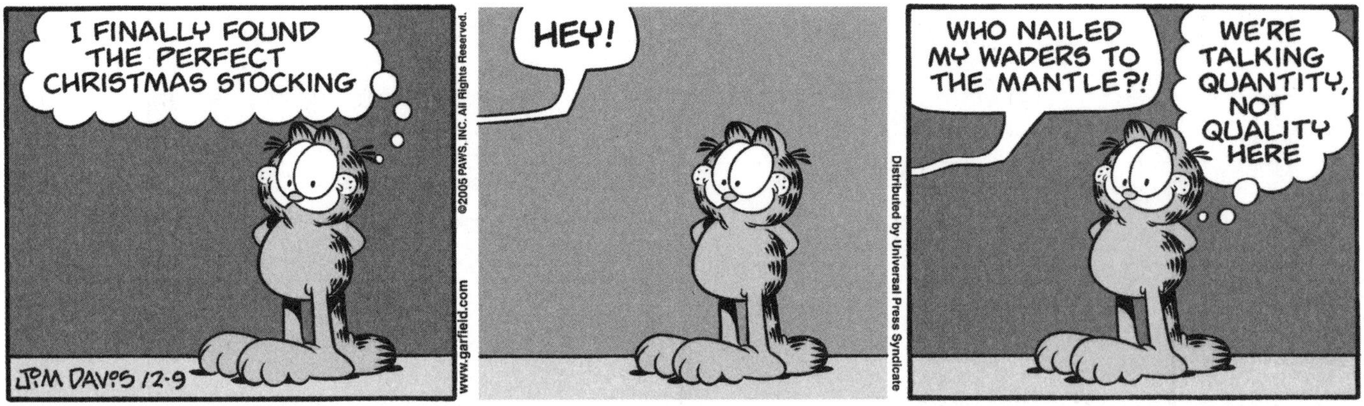
I FINALLY FOUND THE PERFECT CHRISTMAS STOCKING
JIM DAVIS 12-9
HEY!
WHO NAILED MY WADERS TO THE MANTLE?!
WE'RE TALKING QUANTITY, NOT QUALITY HERE
©2005 PAWS, INC. All Rights Reserved. www.garfield.com
Distributed by Universal Press Syndicate

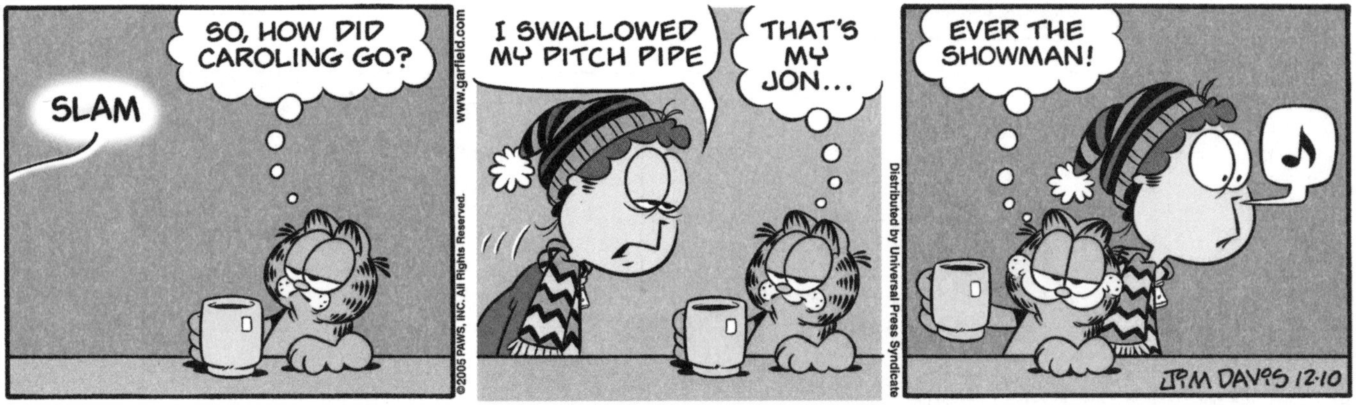
SLAM
SO, HOW DID CAROLING GO?
I SWALLOWED MY PITCH PIPE
THAT'S MY JON...
EVER THE SHOWMAN!
JIM DAVIS 12-10
©2005 PAWS, INC. All Rights Reserved. www.garfield.com
Distributed by Universal Press Syndicate

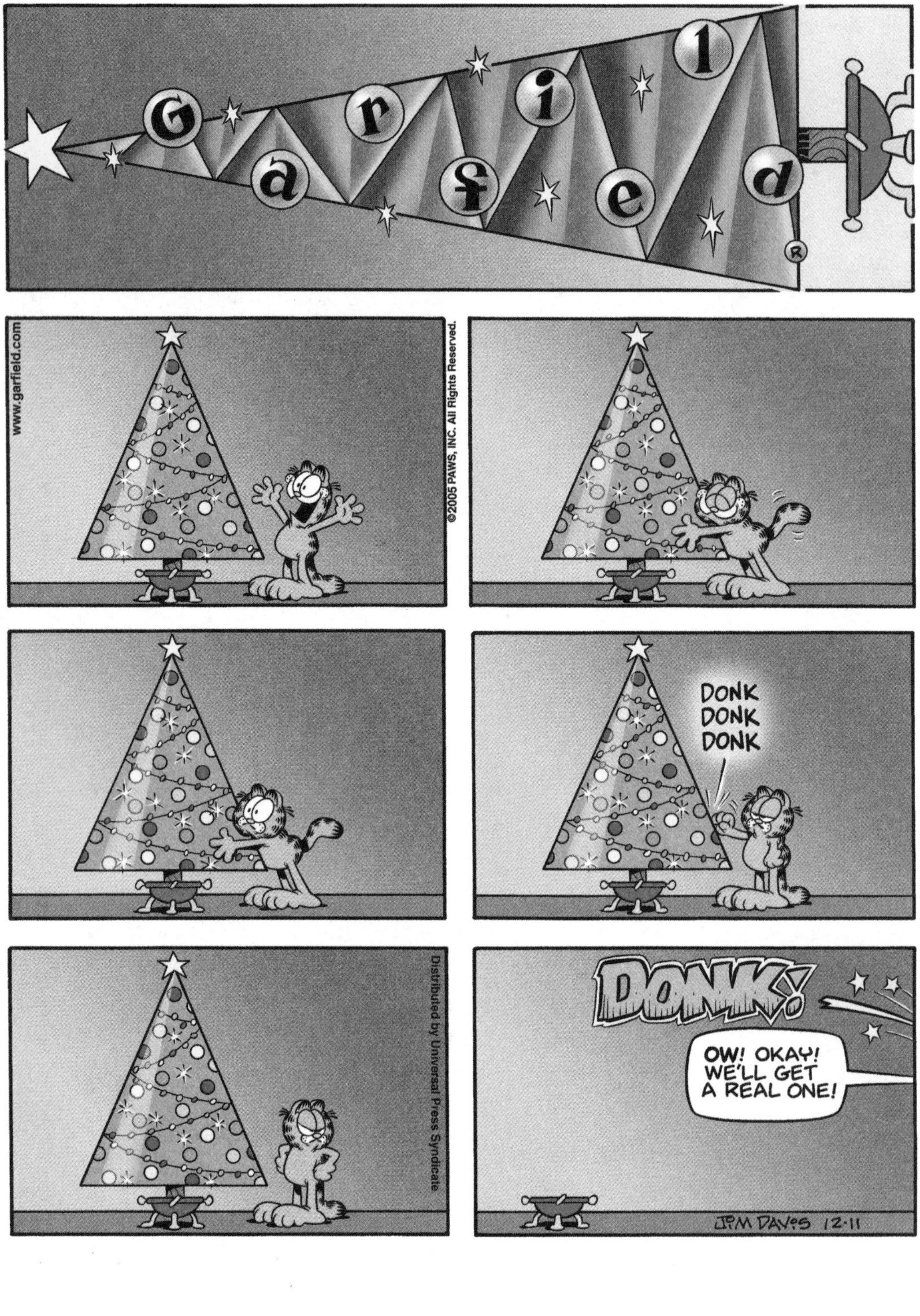
Garfield
www.garfield.com
©2005 PAWS, INC. All Rights Reserved.
DONK
DONK
DONK
Distributed by Universal Press Syndicate
DONK!
OW! OKAY! WE'LL GET A REAL ONE!
JIM DAVIS 12-11

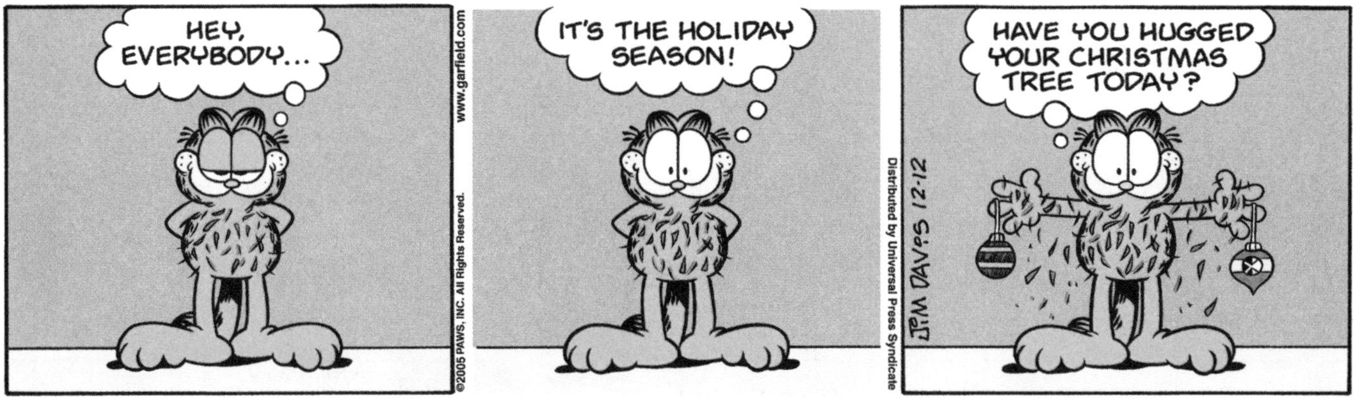
HEY, EVERYBODY...
©2005 PAWS, INC. All Rights Reserved.
www.garfield.com
IT'S THE HOLIDAY SEASON!
Distributed by Universal Press Syndicate
JPM DAVIS 12-12
HAVE YOU HUGGED YOUR CHRISTMAS TREE TODAY?

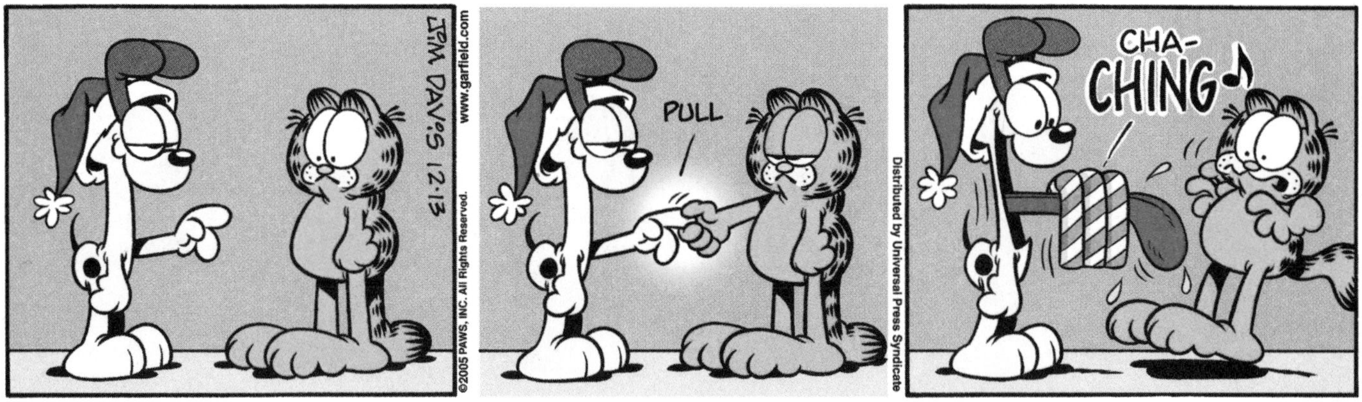
JPM DAVIS 12-13
©2005 PAWS, INC. All Rights Reserved.
www.garfield.com
PULL
Distributed by Universal Press Syndicate
CHA-CHING

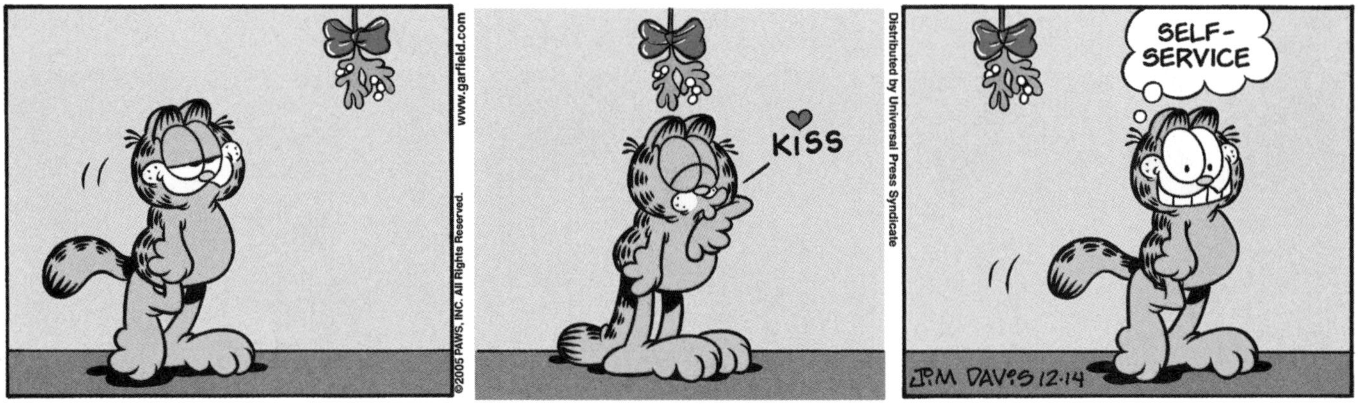
©2005 PAWS, INC. All Rights Reserved.
www.garfield.com
KISS
Distributed by Universal Press Syndicate
SELF-SERVICE
JPM DAVIS 12-14

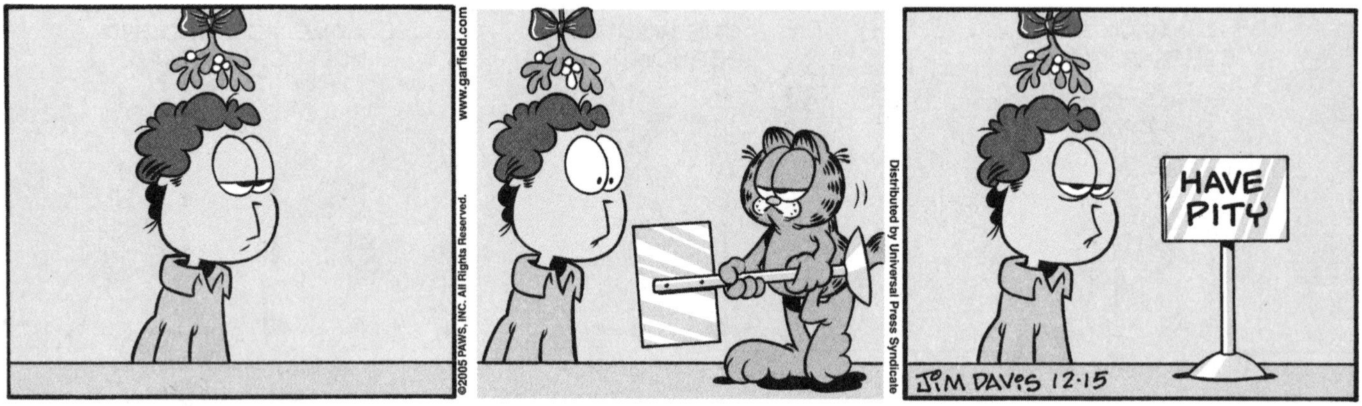
©2005 PAWS, INC. All Rights Reserved.
www.garfield.com
Distributed by Universal Press Syndicate
HAVE PITY
JIM DAVIS 12-15

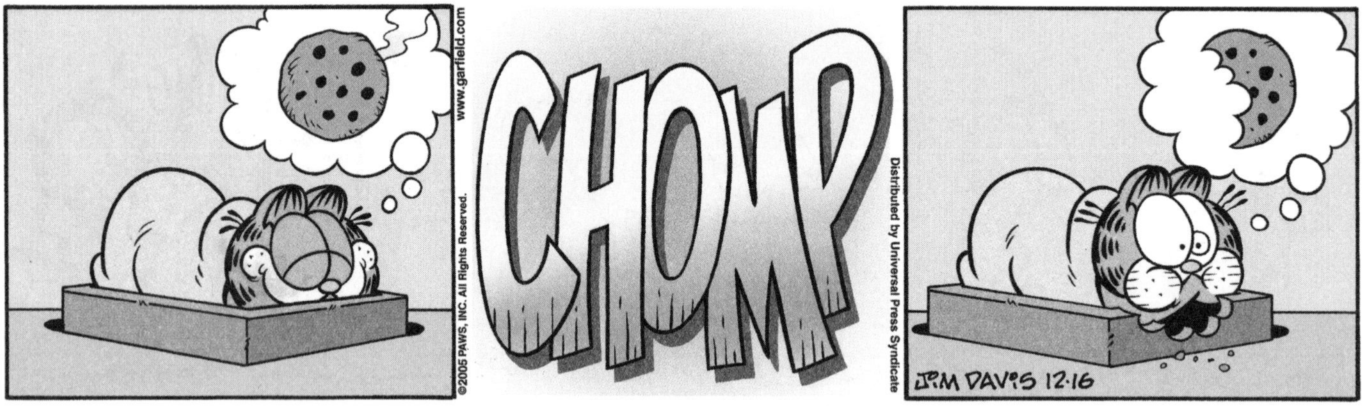
©2005 PAWS, INC. All Rights Reserved.
www.garfield.com
CHOMP
Distributed by Universal Press Syndicate
JIM DAVIS 12-16

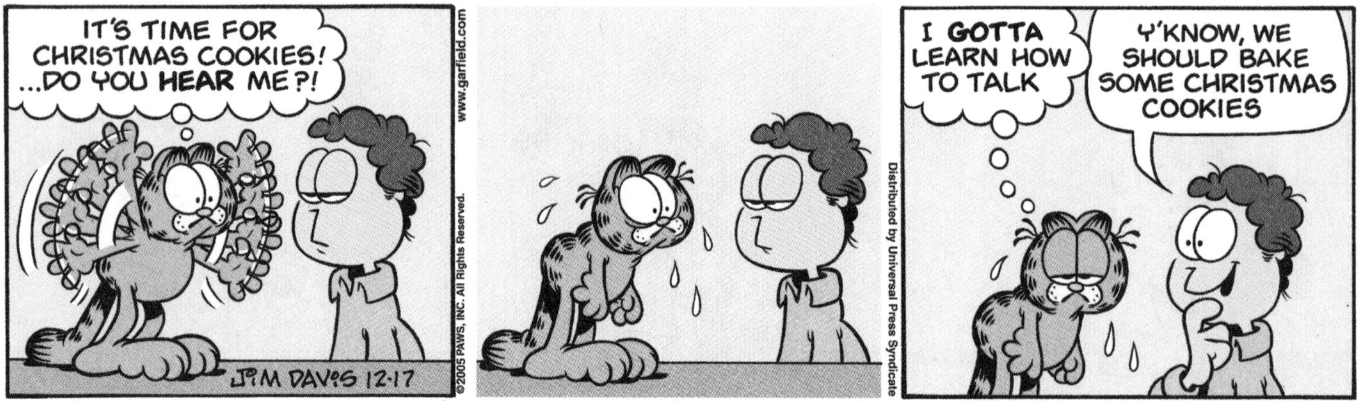
IT'S TIME FOR CHRISTMAS COOKIES! ...DO YOU **HEAR** ME?!
JIM DAVIS 12-17
©2005 PAWS, INC. All Rights Reserved.
www.garfield.com
Distributed by Universal Press Syndicate
I **GOTTA** LEARN HOW TO TALK
Y'KNOW, WE SHOULD BAKE SOME CHRISTMAS COOKIES

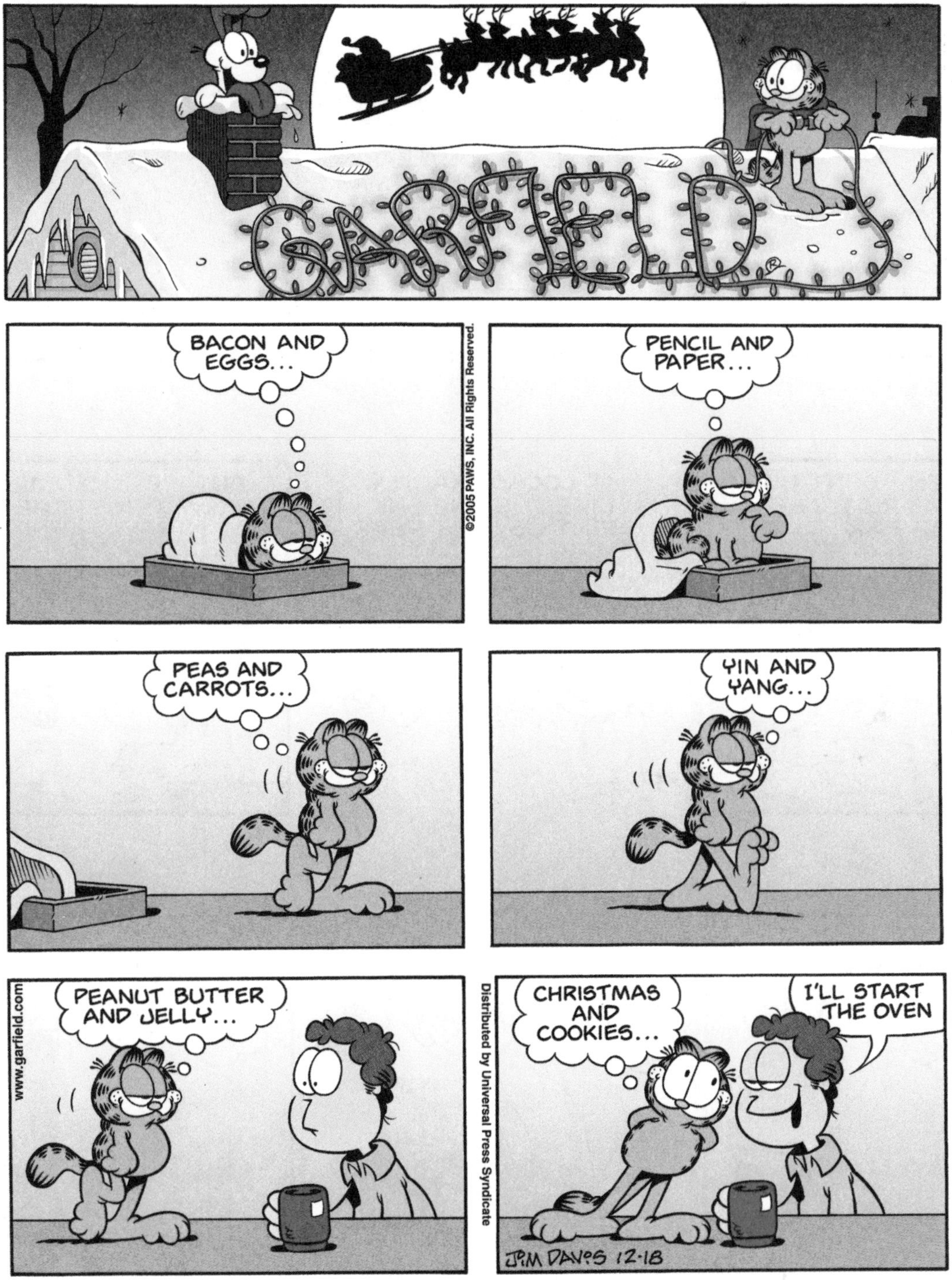
GARFIELD®
BACON AND EGGS...
©2005 PAWS, INC. All Rights Reserved.
PENCIL AND PAPER...
PEAS AND CARROTS...
YIN AND YANG...
www.garfield.com
PEANUT BUTTER AND JELLY...
Distributed by Universal Press Syndicate
CHRISTMAS AND COOKIES...
I'LL START THE OVEN
JPM DAVPS 12·18

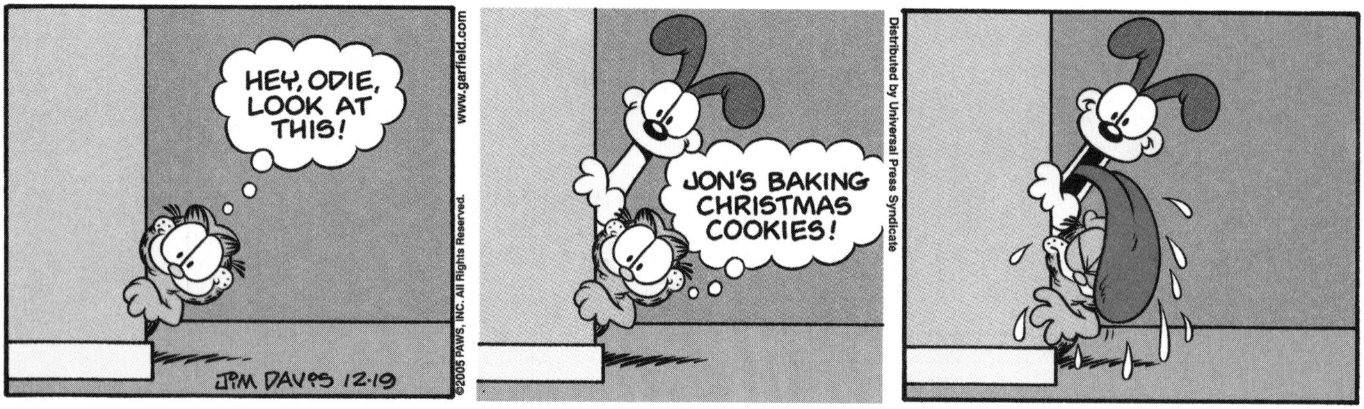
HEY, ODIE, LOOK AT THIS!
JIM DAVIS 12-19
©2005 PAWS, INC. All Rights Reserved.
www.garfield.com
JON'S BAKING CHRISTMAS COOKIES!
Distributed by Universal Press Syndicate

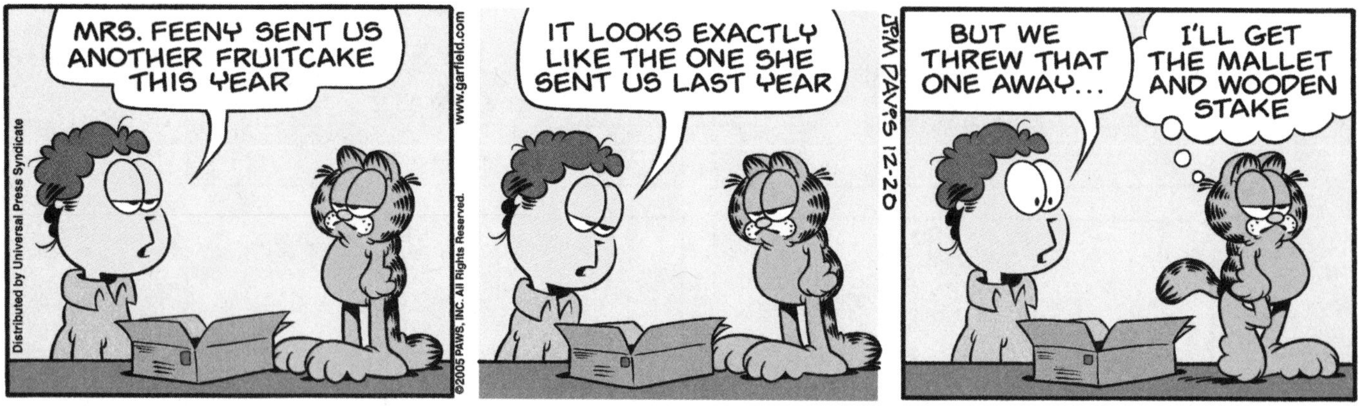
Distributed by Universal Press Syndicate
MRS. FEENY SENT US ANOTHER FRUITCAKE THIS YEAR
©2005 PAWS, INC. All Rights Reserved.
www.garfield.com
IT LOOKS EXACTLY LIKE THE ONE SHE SENT US LAST YEAR
JIM DAVIS 12-20
BUT WE THREW THAT ONE AWAY...
I'LL GET THE MALLET AND WOODEN STAKE

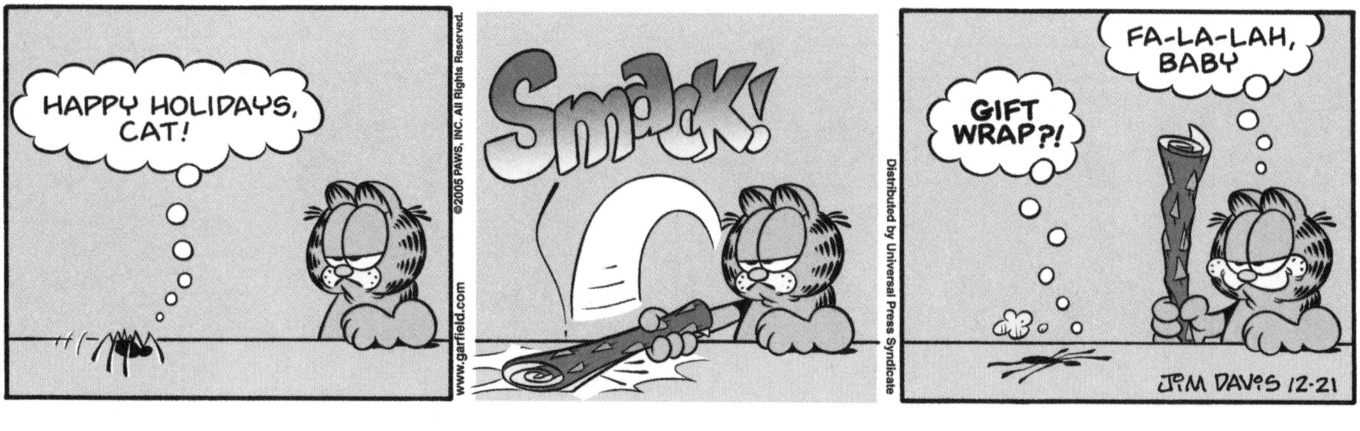
HAPPY HOLIDAYS, CAT!
©2005 PAWS, INC. All Rights Reserved.
www.garfield.com
SMACK!
Distributed by Universal Press Syndicate
GIFT WRAP?!
FA-LA-LAH, BABY
JIM DAVIS 12-21

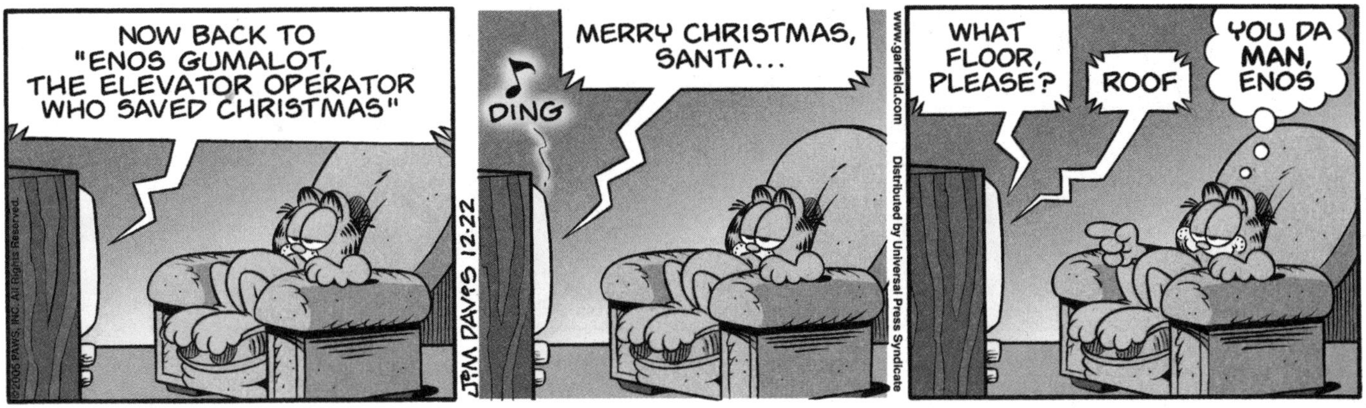
NOW BACK TO "ENOS GUMALOT, THE ELEVATOR OPERATOR WHO SAVED CHRISTMAS"
©2005 PAWS, INC. All Rights Reserved.
JIM DAVIS 12-22
DING
MERRY CHRISTMAS, SANTA...
www.garfield.com
Distributed by Universal Press Syndicate
WHAT FLOOR, PLEASE?
ROOF
YOU DA MAN, ENOS

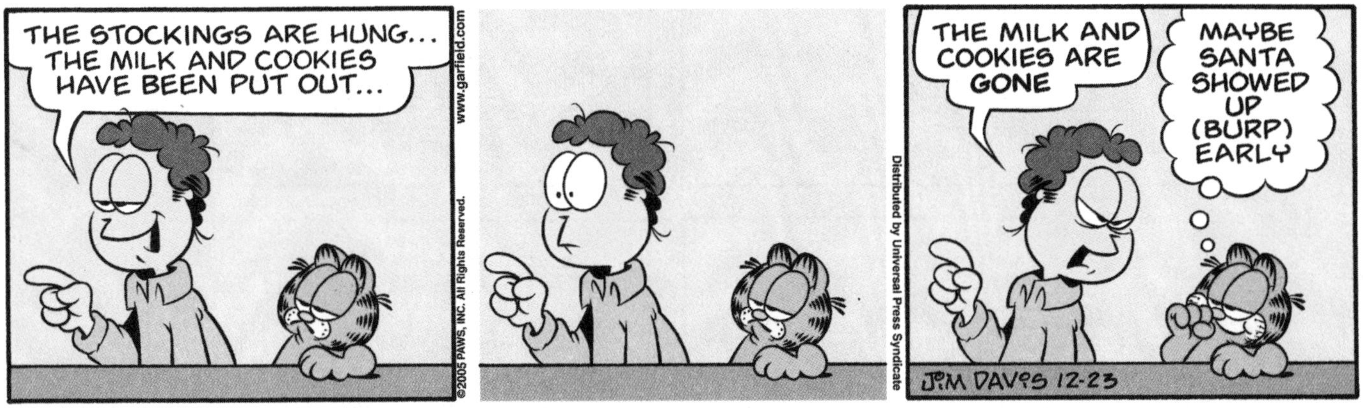
THE STOCKINGS ARE HUNG... THE MILK AND COOKIES HAVE BEEN PUT OUT...
www.garfield.com
©2005 PAWS, INC. All Rights Reserved.
Distributed by Universal Press Syndicate
THE MILK AND COOKIES ARE GONE
MAYBE SANTA SHOWED UP (BURP) EARLY
JIM DAVIS 12-23

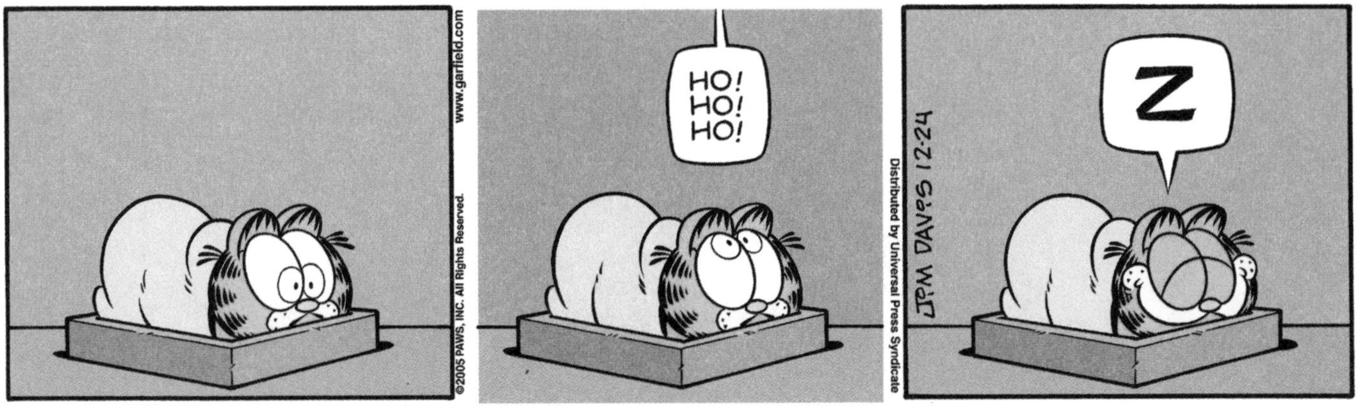
www.garfield.com
©2005 PAWS, INC. All Rights Reserved.
HO! HO! HO!
JIM DAVIS 12-24
Distributed by Universal Press Syndicate
Z

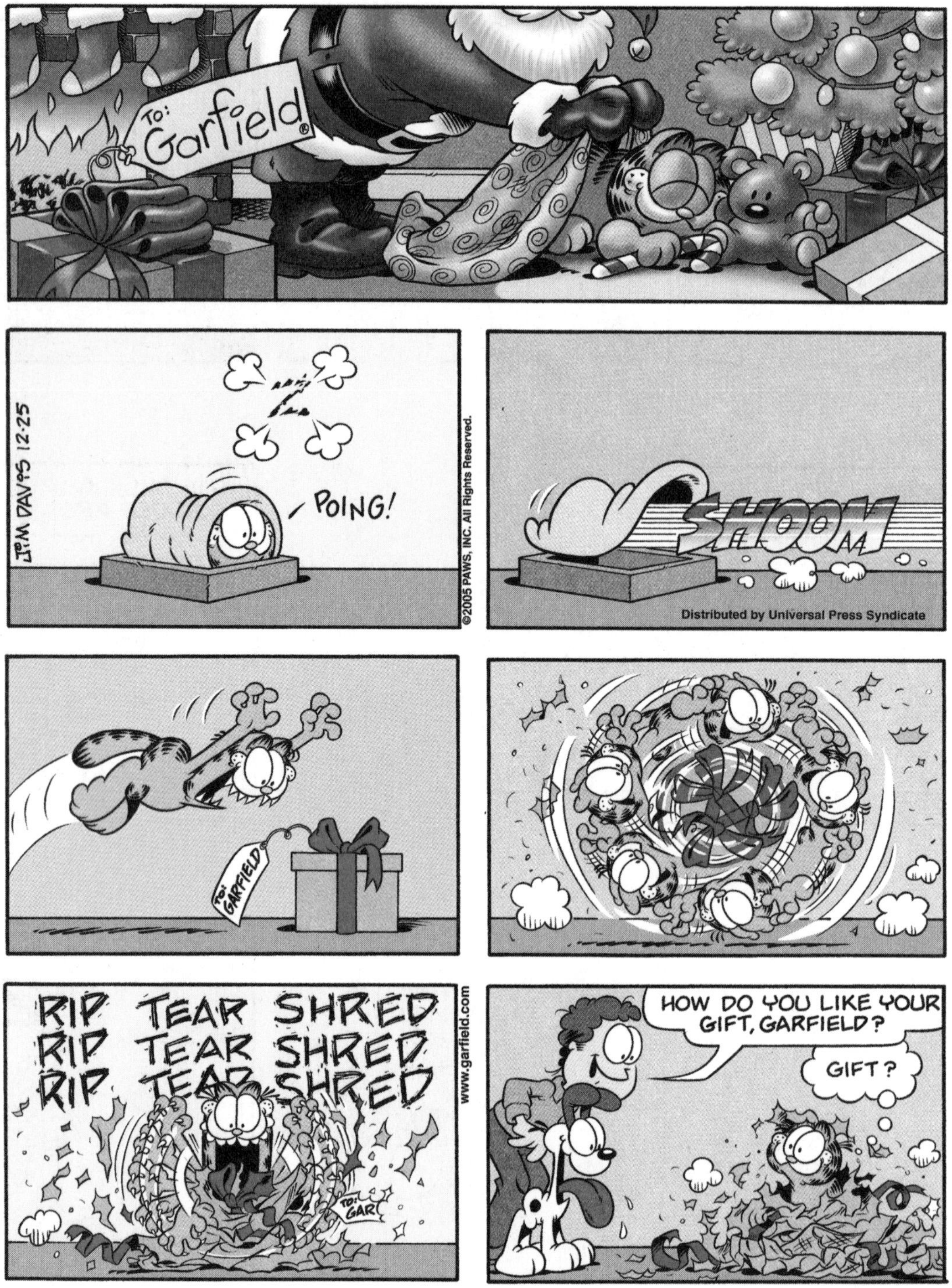
To: Garfield®
JIM DAVIS 12·25
POING!
©2005 PAWS, INC. All Rights Reserved.
SHOOM
Distributed by Universal Press Syndicate
TO: GARFIELD
RIP TEAR SHRED
RIP TEAR SHRED
RIP TEAR SHRED
www.garfield.com
TO: GAR
HOW DO YOU LIKE YOUR GIFT, GARFIELD?
GIFT?

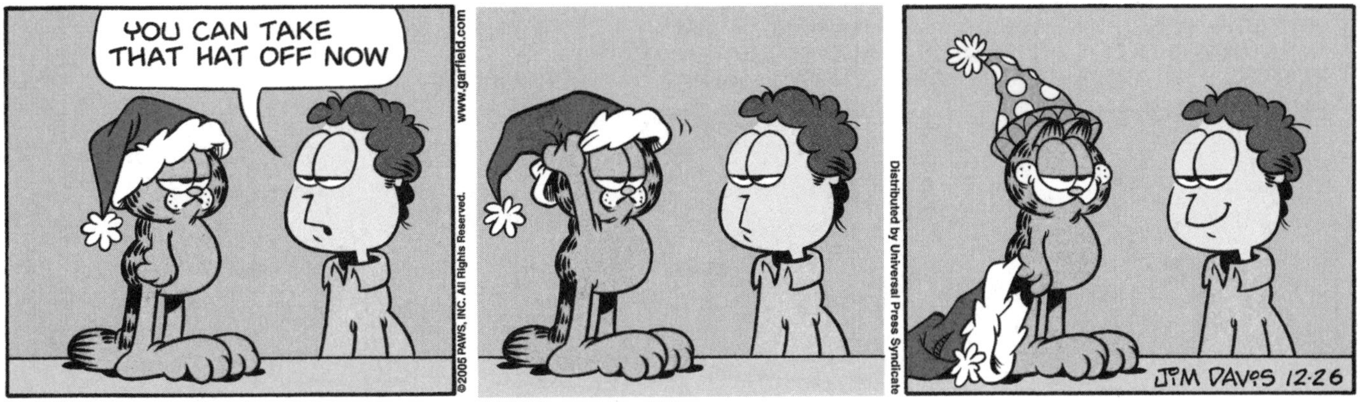
YOU CAN TAKE THAT HAT OFF NOW
©2005 PAWS, INC. All Rights Reserved.
www.garfield.com
Distributed by Universal Press Syndicate
JIM DAVIS 12-26

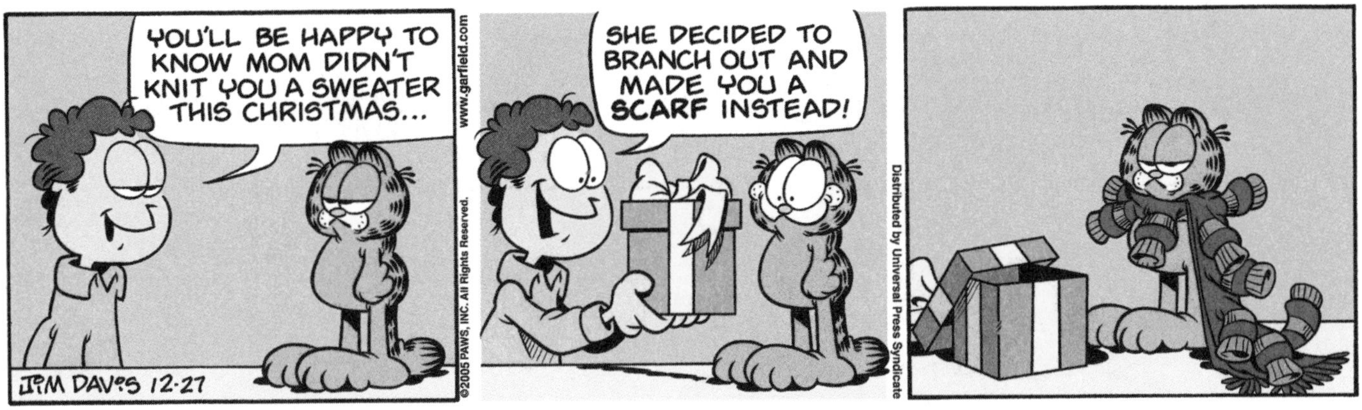
YOU'LL BE HAPPY TO KNOW MOM DIDN'T KNIT YOU A SWEATER THIS CHRISTMAS...
JIM DAVIS 12-27
©2005 PAWS, INC. All Rights Reserved.
www.garfield.com
SHE DECIDED TO BRANCH OUT AND MADE YOU A **SCARF** INSTEAD!
Distributed by Universal Press Syndicate

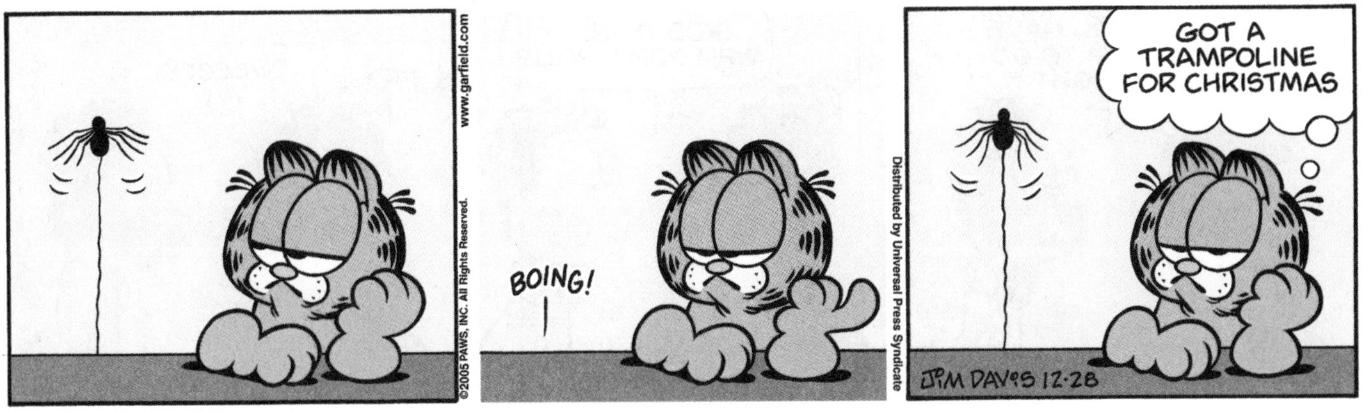
©2005 PAWS, INC. All Rights Reserved.
www.garfield.com
BOING!
Distributed by Universal Press Syndicate
GOT A TRAMPOLINE FOR CHRISTMAS
JIM DAVIS 12-28

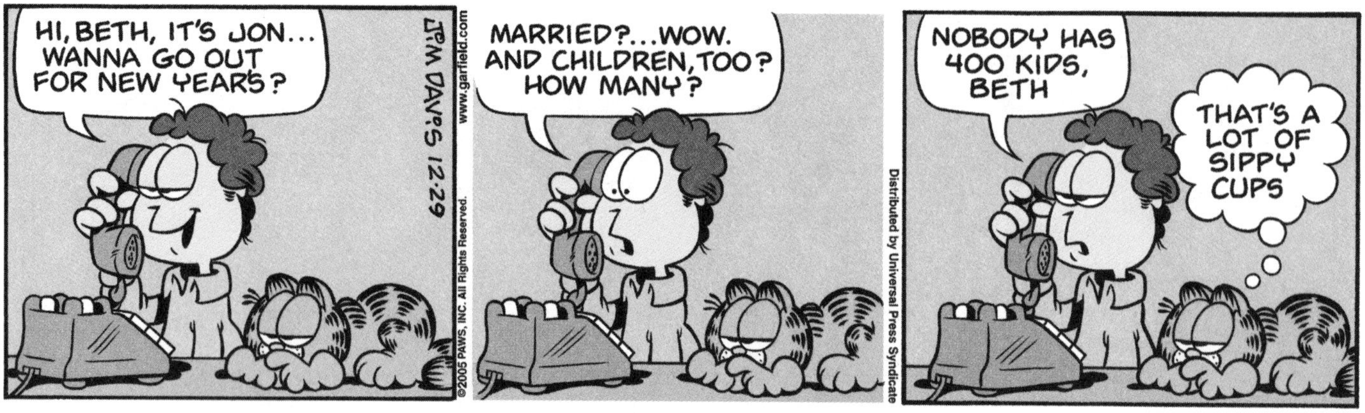
HI, BETH, IT'S JON... WANNA GO OUT FOR NEW YEAR'S?
JIM DAVIS 12·29
www.garfield.com
©2005 PAWS, INC. All Rights Reserved.
MARRIED?...WOW. AND CHILDREN, TOO? HOW MANY?
Distributed by Universal Press Syndicate
NOBODY HAS 400 KIDS, BETH
THAT'S A LOT OF SIPPY CUPS

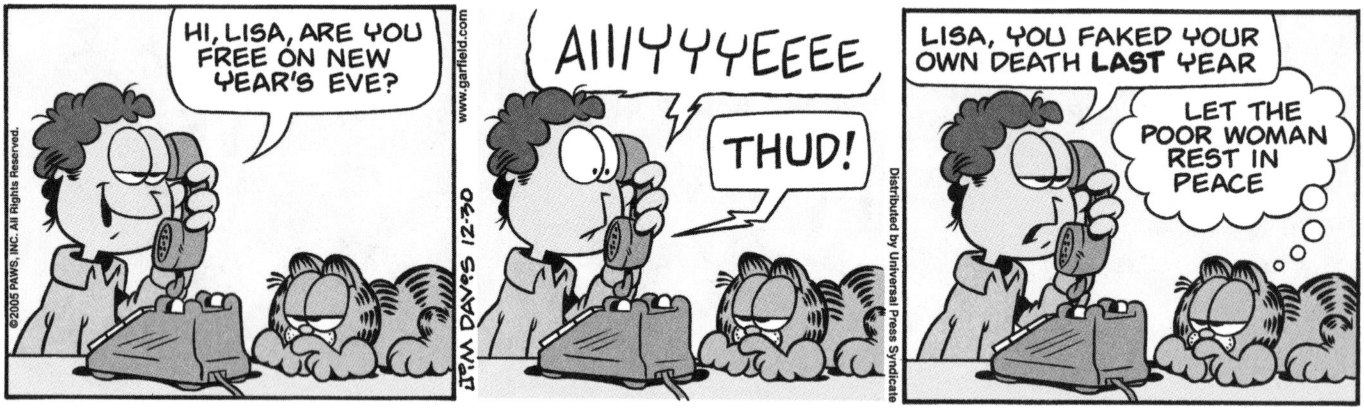
HI, LISA, ARE YOU FREE ON NEW YEAR'S EVE?
©2005 PAWS, INC. All Rights Reserved.
www.garfield.com
JIM DAVIS 12·30
AIIIYYYEEEE
THUD!
Distributed by Universal Press Syndicate
LISA, YOU FAKED YOUR OWN DEATH **LAST** YEAR
LET THE POOR WOMAN REST IN PEACE

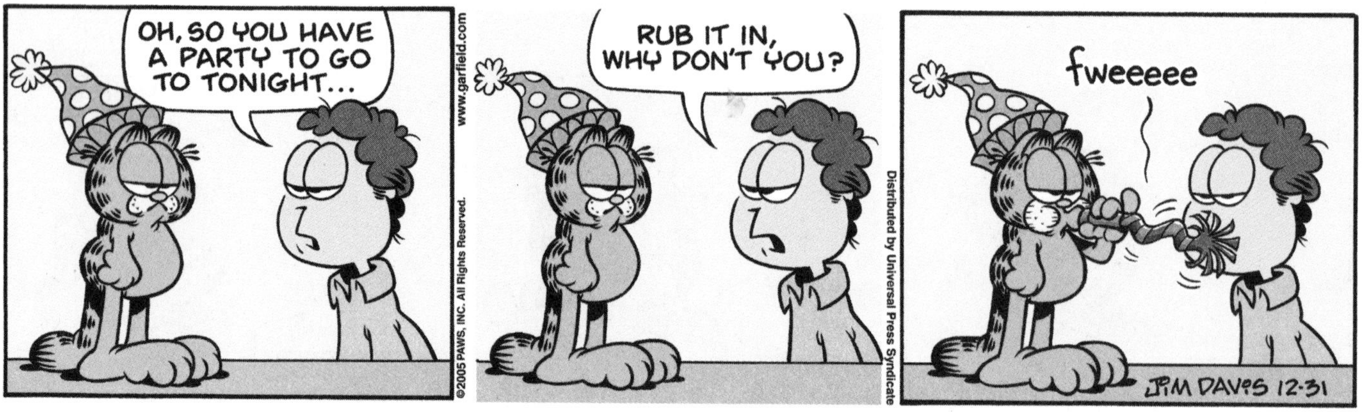
OH, SO YOU HAVE A PARTY TO GO TO TONIGHT...
www.garfield.com
©2005 PAWS, INC. All Rights Reserved.
RUB IT IN, WHY DON'T YOU?
Distributed by Universal Press Syndicate
fweeeee
JIM DAVIS 12·31

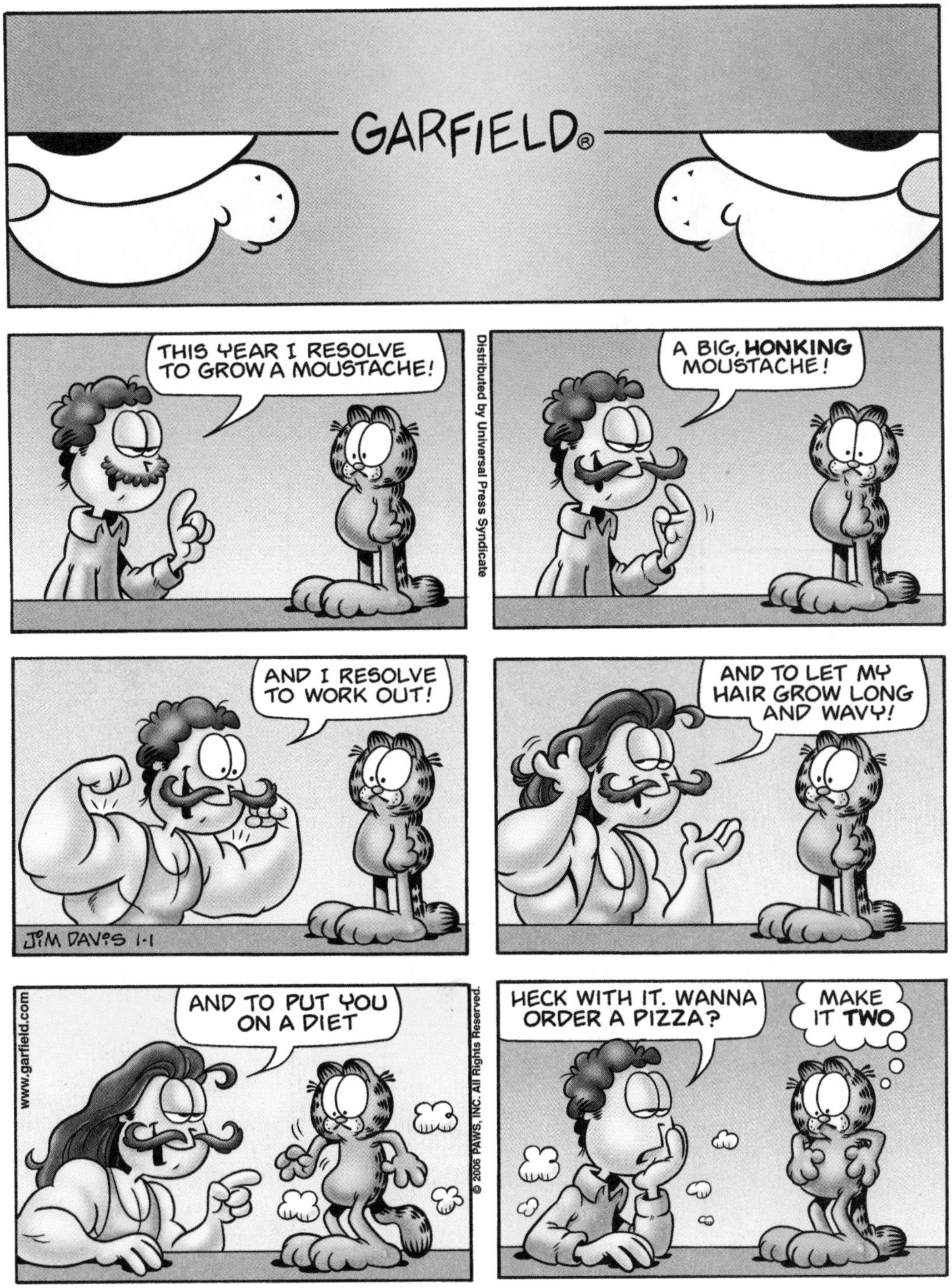
GARFIELD®
THIS YEAR I RESOLVE TO GROW A MOUSTACHE!
Distributed by Universal Press Syndicate
A BIG, **HONKING** MOUSTACHE!
AND I RESOLVE TO WORK OUT!
JIM DAVIS 1-1
AND TO LET MY HAIR GROW LONG AND WAVY!
www.garfield.com
AND TO PUT YOU ON A DIET
© 2006 PAWS, INC. All Rights Reserved.
HECK WITH IT. WANNA ORDER A PIZZA?
MAKE IT **TWO**

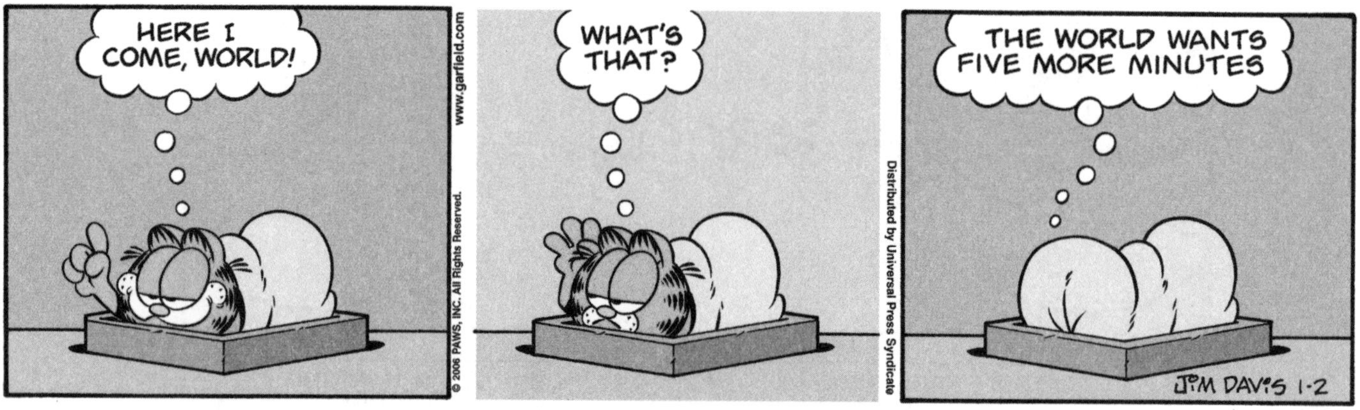
HERE I COME, WORLD!
WHAT'S THAT?
THE WORLD WANTS FIVE MORE MINUTES
© 2006 PAWS, INC. All Rights Reserved. www.garfield.com
Distributed by Universal Press Syndicate
JIM DAVIS 1-2

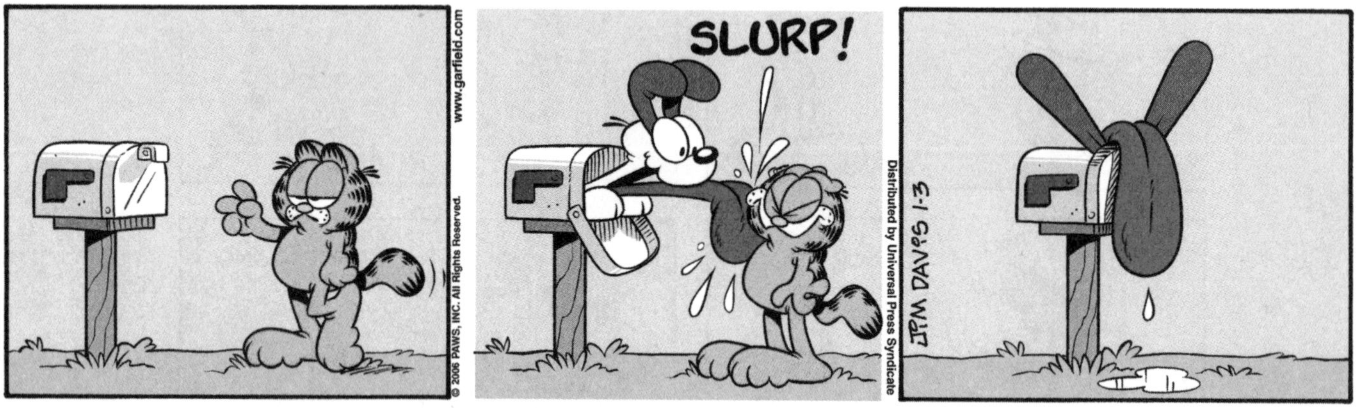
SLURP!
© 2006 PAWS, INC. All Rights Reserved. www.garfield.com
Distributed by Universal Press Syndicate
JIM DAVIS 1-3

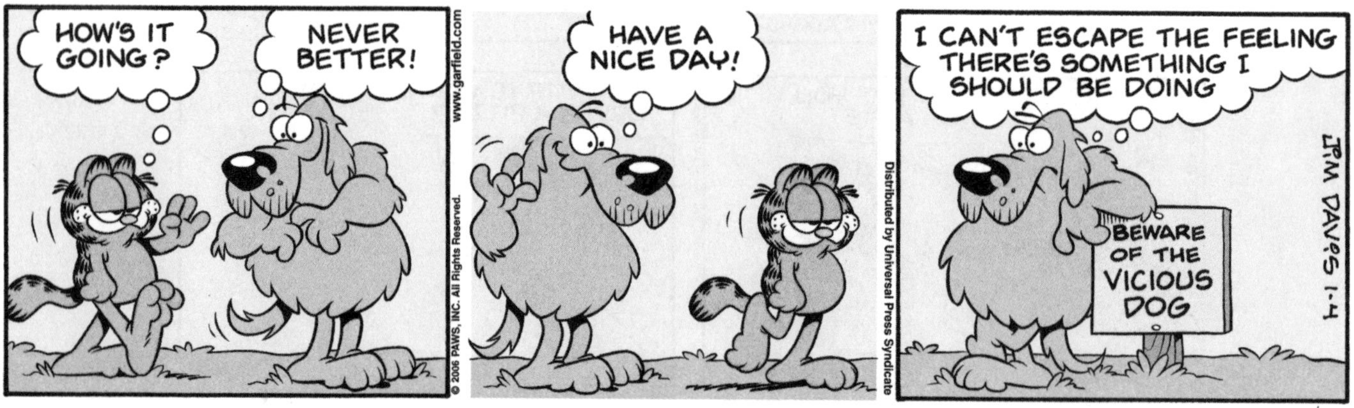
HOW'S IT GOING?
NEVER BETTER!
HAVE A NICE DAY!
I CAN'T ESCAPE THE FEELING THERE'S SOMETHING I SHOULD BE DOING
BEWARE OF THE VICIOUS DOG
© 2006 PAWS, INC. All Rights Reserved. www.garfield.com
Distributed by Universal Press Syndicate
JIM DAVIS 1-4

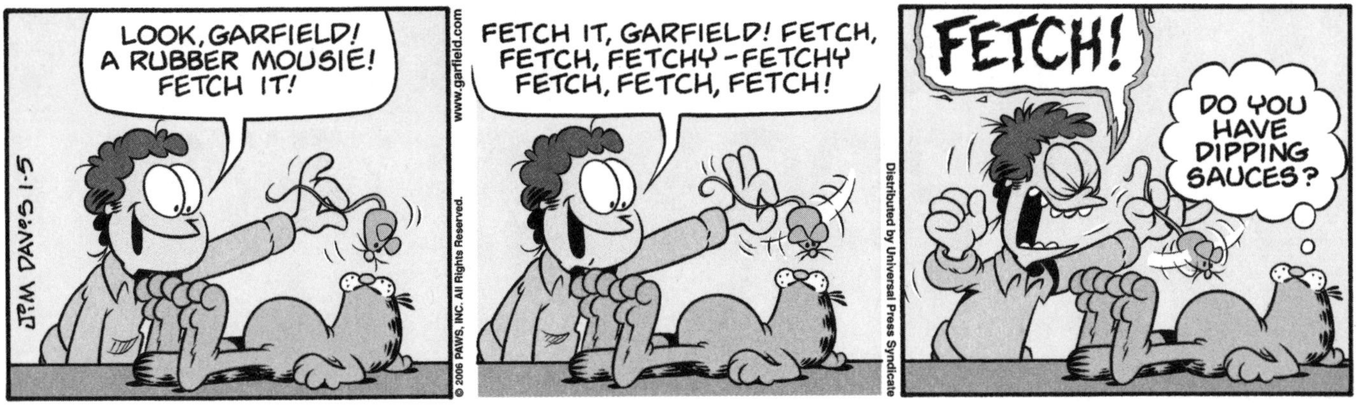
LOOK, GARFIELD! A RUBBER MOUSIE! FETCH IT!
JIM DAVIS 1·5
© 2006 PAWS, INC. All Rights Reserved. www.garfield.com
FETCH IT, GARFIELD! FETCH, FETCH, FETCHY-FETCHY FETCH, FETCH, FETCH!
Distributed by Universal Press Syndicate
FETCH!
DO YOU HAVE DIPPING SAUCES?

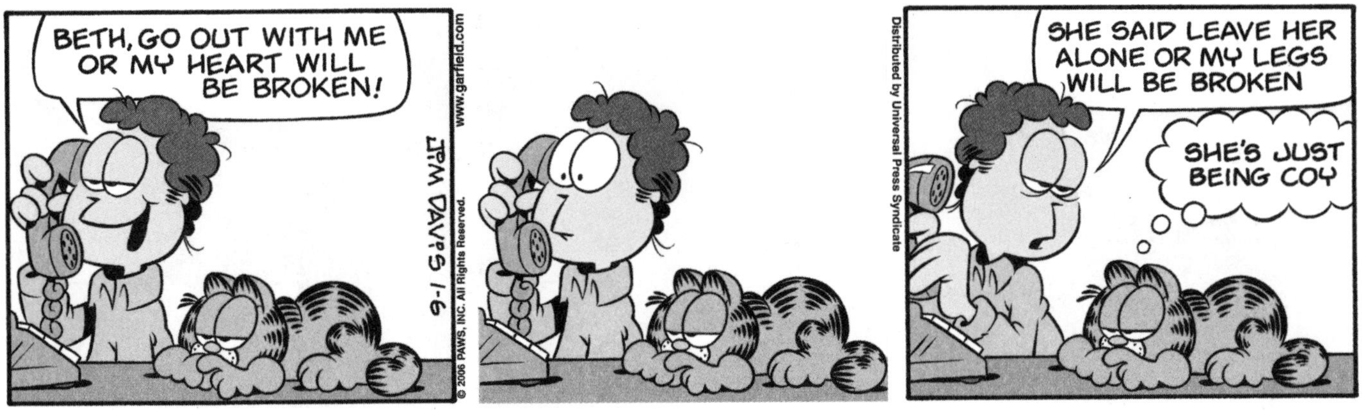
BETH, GO OUT WITH ME OR MY HEART WILL BE BROKEN!
JIM DAVIS 1-6
© 2006 PAWS, INC. All Rights Reserved. www.garfield.com
Distributed by Universal Press Syndicate
SHE SAID LEAVE HER ALONE OR MY LEGS WILL BE BROKEN
SHE'S JUST BEING COY

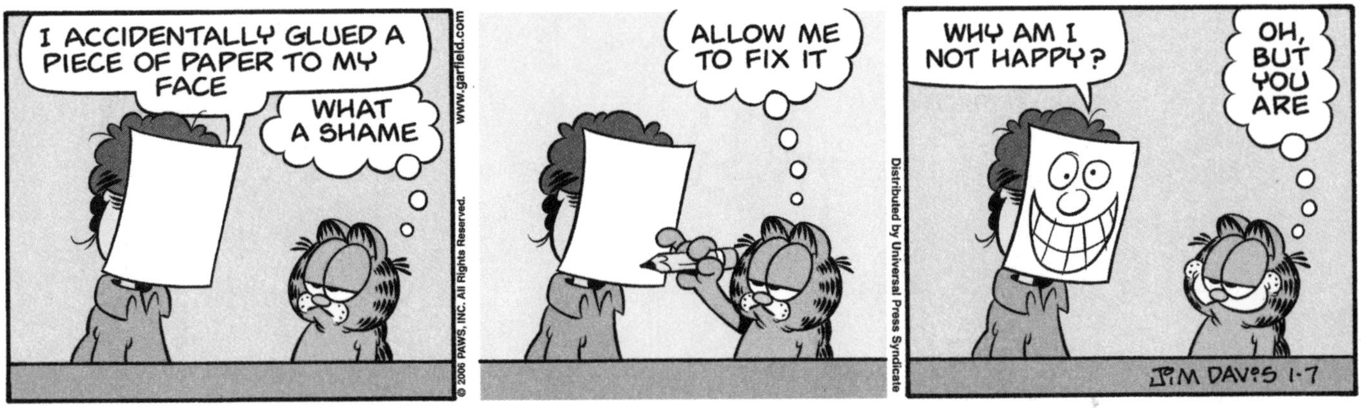
I ACCIDENTALLY GLUED A PIECE OF PAPER TO MY FACE
WHAT A SHAME
© 2006 PAWS, INC. All Rights Reserved. www.garfield.com
ALLOW ME TO FIX IT
Distributed by Universal Press Syndicate
WHY AM I NOT HAPPY?
OH, BUT YOU ARE
JIM DAVIS 1·7

A SECOND HELPING OF FOODIE FUN

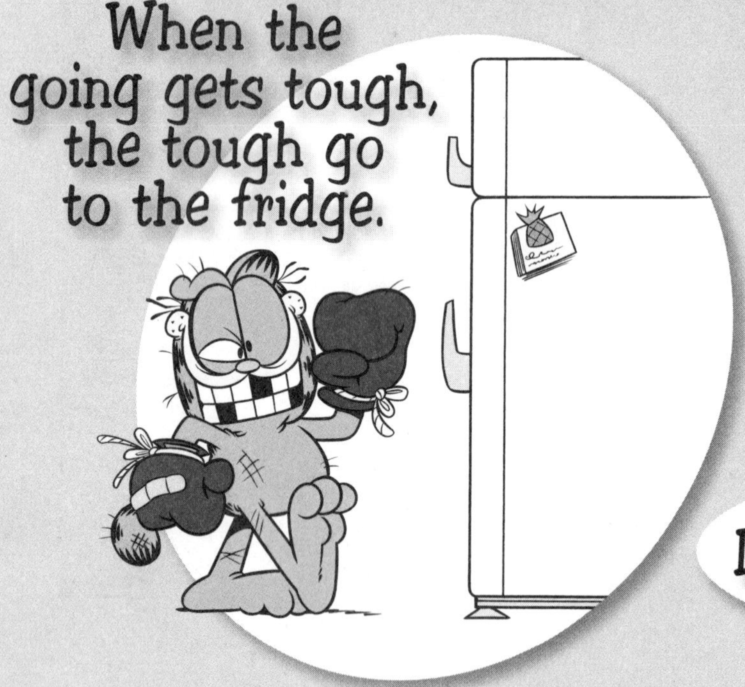
When the going gets tough, the tough go to the fridge.

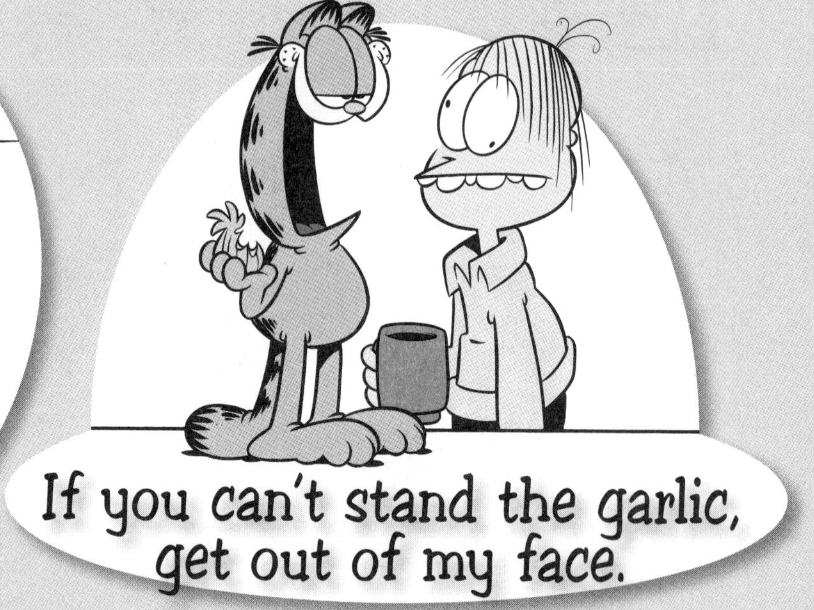
If you can't stand the garlic, get out of my face.

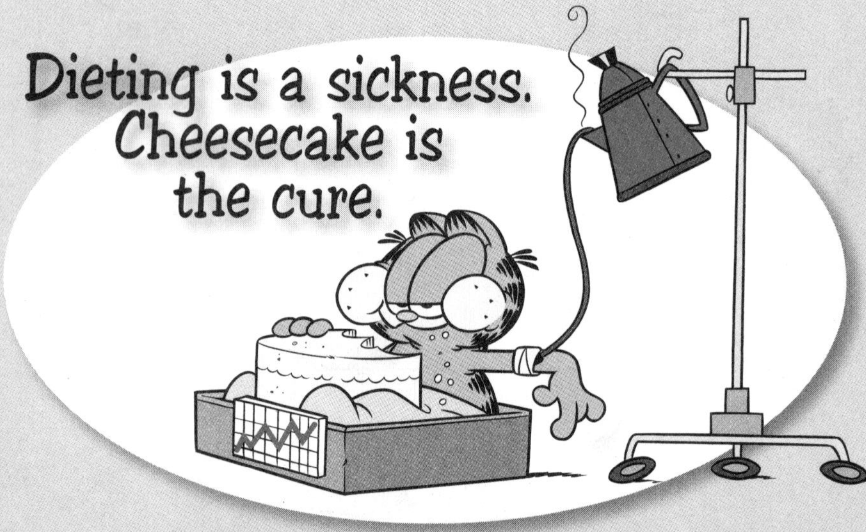
Dieting is a sickness. Cheesecake is the cure.

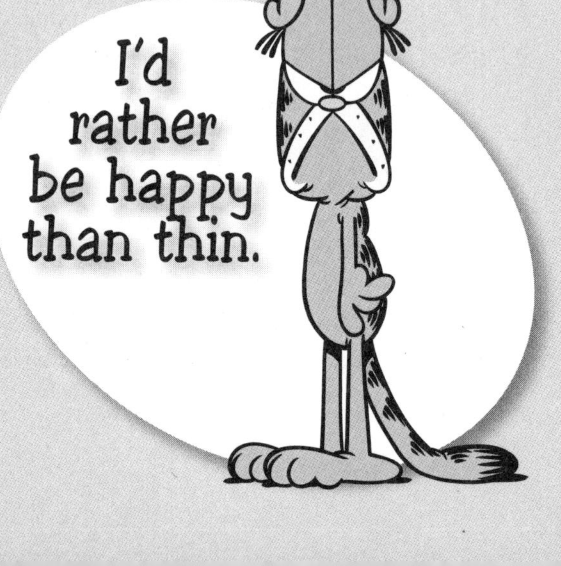
I'd rather be happy than thin.

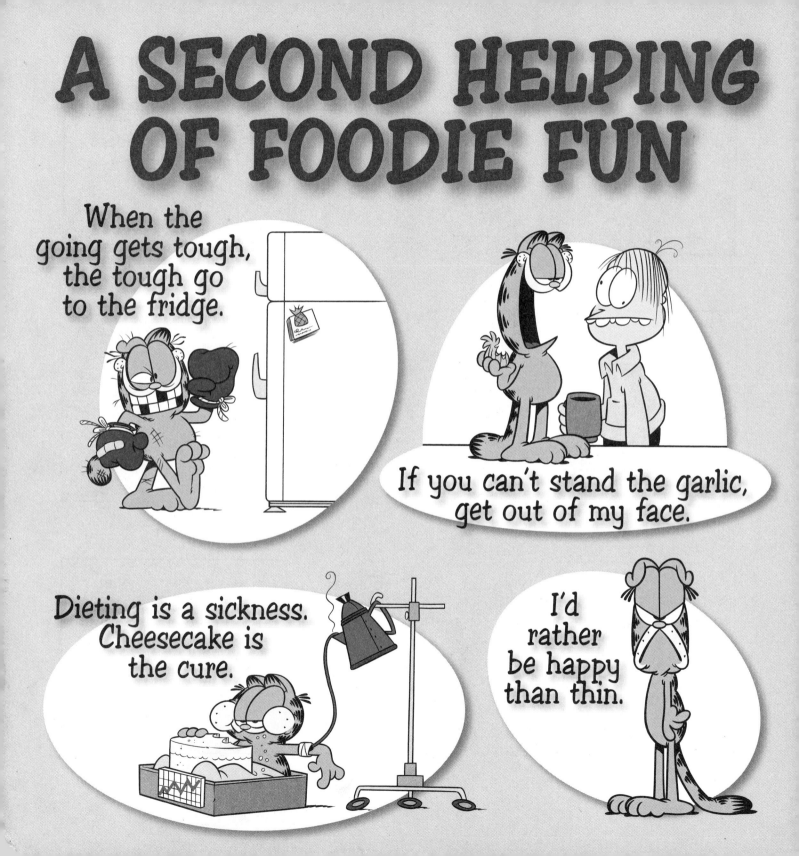

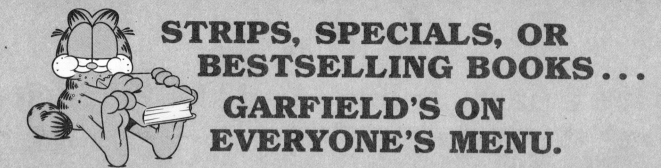

STRIPS, SPECIALS, OR BESTSELLING BOOKS . . . GARFIELD'S ON EVERYONE'S MENU.

Don't miss even one episode in the Tubby Tabby's hilarious series!

- GARFIELD AT LARGE ....(#1) 978-0-345-44382-3
- GARFIELD GAINS WEIGHT ....(#2) 978-0-345-44975-7
- GARFIELD BIGGER THAN LIFE ....(#3) 978-0-345-45027-2
- GARFIELD WEIGHS IN ....(#4) 978-0-345-45205-4
- GARFIELD TAKES THE CAKE ....(#5) 978-0-345-44978-8
- GARFIELD EATS HIS HEART OUT ....(#6) 978-0-345-46459-0
- GARFIELD SITS AROUND THE HOUSE...(#7) 978-0-345-46463-7
- GARFIELD TIPS THE SCALES ....(#8) 978-0-345-46909-0
- GARFIELD LOSES HIS FEET ....(#9) 978-0-345-46467-5
- GARFIELD MAKES IT BIG....................(#10) 978-0-345-46468-2
- GARFIELD ROLLS ON ....(#11) 978-0-345-47561-9
- GARFIELD OUT TO LUNCH..................(#12) 978-0-345-47562-6
- GARFIELD FOOD FOR THOUGHT ......(#13) 978-0-345-47563-3
- GARFIELD SWALLOWS HIS PRIDE....(#14) 978-0-345-91386-9
- GARFIELD WORLDWIDE ....(#15) 978-0-345-91754-6
- GARFIELD ROUNDS OUT.....................(#16) 978-0-345-49169-5
- GARFIELD CHEWS THE FAT................(#17) 978-0-345-49170-1
- GARFIELD GOES TO WAIST ....(#18) 978-0-345-36430-2
- GARFIELD HANGS OUT........................(#19) 978-0-345-36835-5
- GARFIELD TAKES UP SPACE ....(#20) 978-0-345-37029-7
- GARFIELD SAYS A MOUTHFUL ....(#21) 978-0-345-37368-7
- GARFIELD BY THE POUND..................(#22) 978-0-345-37579-7
- GARFIELD KEEPS HIS CHINS UP ....(#23) 978-0-345-37959-7
- GARFIELD TAKES HIS LICKS..............(#24) 978-0-345-38170-5
- GARFIELD HITS THE BIG TIME ....(#25) 978-0-345-38332-7
- GARFIELD PULLS HIS WEIGHT...........(#26) 978-0-345-38666-3
- GARFIELD DISHES IT OUT..................(#27) 978-0-345-39287-9
- GARFIELD LIFE IN THE FAT LANE .....(#28) 978-0-345-39776-8
- GARFIELD TONS OF FUN ....(#29) 978-0-345-40386-5
- GARFIELD BIGGER AND BETTER......(#30) 978-0-345-40770-2
- GARFIELD HAMS IT UP ....(#31) 978-0-345-41241-6
- GARFIELD THINKS BIG.......................(#32) 978-0-345-41671-1
- GARFIELD THROWS HIS WEIGHT AROUND ....(#33) 978-0-345-42749-6
- GARFIELD LIFE TO THE FULLEST .....(#34) 978-0-345-43239-1
- GARFIELD FEEDS THE KITTY ....(#35) 978-0-345-43673-3
- GARFIELD HOGS THE SPOTLIGHT ...(#36) 978-0-345-43922-2
- GARFIELD BEEFS UP ....(#37) 978-0-345-44109-6
- GARFIELD GETS COOKIN'.................(#38) 978-0-345-44582-7
- GARFIELD EATS CROW ....(#39) 978-0-345-45201-6
- GARFIELD SURVIVAL OF THE FATTEST....................................(#40) 978-0-345-46458-3
- GARFIELD OLDER AND WIDER..........(#41) 978-0-345-46462-0
- GARFIELD PIGS OUT ....(#42) 978-0-345-46466-8
- GARFIELD BLOTS OUT THE SUN ......(#43) 978-0-345-46615-0
- GARFIELD GOES BANANAS ....(#44) 978-0-345-91346-3
- GARFIELD LARGE & IN CHARGE.......(#45) 978-0-345-49172-5
- GARFIELD SPILLS THE BEANS ....(#46) 978-0-345-49177-0

DVD TIE-INS

- GARFIELD AS HIMSELF.................................978-0-345-47805-4
- GARFIELD HOLIDAY CELEBRATIONS.........978-0-345-47930-3
- GARFIELD TRAVEL ADVENTURES 978-0-345-48087-3

AND DON'T MISS...

- GARFIELD AT 25: IN DOG YEARS I'D BE DEAD 978-0-345-45204-7
- GARFIELD'S JOKE ZONE/INSULTS..............978-0-345-46263-3
- GARFIELD FAT CAT 3-PACK/ VOL. 1 978-0-345-46455-2
- GARFIELD FAT CAT 3-PACK/ VOL. 2 978-0-345-46465-1
- GARFIELD FAT CAT 3-PACK/ VOL. 3 978-0-345-48088-0
- GARFIELD FAT CAT 3-PACK/ VOL. 4 978-0-345-49171-8
- GARFIELD FAT CAT 3-PACK/ VOL. 13 978-0-345-46460-6
- SEASON'S EATINGS: A VERY MERRY GARFIELD CHRISTMAS 978-0-345-47560-2
- GARFIELD'S GUIDE TO EVERYTHING 978-0-345-46461-3
- ODIE UNLEASHED! 978-0-345-46464-4
- GARFIELD'S BOOK OF CAT NAMES............978-0-345-48516-8
- THE GARFIELD JOURNAL.............................978-0-345-46469-9
- LIGHTS, CAMERA, HAIRBALLS!: GARFIELD AT THE MOVIES 978-0-345-49134-3
- 30 YEARS OF LAUGHS AND LASAGNA 978-0-345-50379-4
- GARFIELD MINUS GARFIELD.......................978-0-345-51387-8

New larger, full-color format! (titles #1–#17)